Praise for

NUCLEAR TERRORISM

THE ULTIMATE PREVENTABLE CATASTROPHE

"[Allison presents] a compelling message: We are courting colossal disaster, and we need to take action now."

—*The Washington Post Book World*

"Allison walks us through the problem, inducing an increasing sense of looming terror with facts, not inflammatory language. His cold-blooded presentation of the case, in fact, makes it even more terrifying in its promise. The book is an absolute 'must' read."

—*Pittsburgh Post-Gazette*

"*Nuclear Terrorism* succeeds at its chief task: making one superbly literate in the frightening realities of its subject."

—*The Philadelphia Inquirer*

"Graham Allison is eminently qualified to ring the alarm bells. . . . His book offers a concrete plan of action . . . utterly persuasive."

—*San Francisco Chronicle*

"Mr. Allison is one of the country's preeminent academic experts on national security. . . . His prognostication needs to be taken seriously."

—*The Washington Times*

"*Nuclear Terrorism* is full immersion in the darkest waters of your post-9/11 consciousness." —*New York Press*

NUCLEAR
TERRORISM

A HOLT PAPERBACK

HENRY HOLT AND COMPANY

NEW YORK

NUCLEAR TERRORISM

THE ULTIMATE
PREVENTABLE
CATASTROPHE

GRAHAM ALLISON

Holt Paperbacks
Henry Holt and Company, LLC
Publishers since 1866
175 Fifth Avenue
New York, New York 10010
www.henryholt.com

Library of Congress Cataloging-in-Publication Data

Allison, Graham T.
    Nuclear terrorism : the ultimate preventable catastrophe /
Graham Allison.—1st ed.
        p.   cm.
    Includes index.
    ISBN-13: 978-0-8050-7852-7
    ISBN-10: 0-8050-7852-5
    1. Nuclear terrorism—United States—Prevention.   I. Title.
HV6432.A45   2004
363.32—dc22

Henry Holt books are available for special promotions and premiums.
For details contact: Director, Special Markets.

Originally published in hardcover in 2004 by Times Books
First Holt Paperbacks Edition 2005

Designed by Jo Anne Metsch

Printed in the United States of America

To Sam Nunn, Dick Lugar, David Hamburg,
and Andrew Marshall

Pioneers in Prevention

CONTENTS

INTRODUCTION

Since the advent of the Nuclear Age, everything has
changed save our modes of thinking and we thus drift
toward unparalleled catastrophe.

ALBERT EINSTEIN

ON OCTOBER 11, 2001, a month to the day after the terrorist assault on
the World Trade Center and the Pentagon, President George W.
Bush faced an even more terrifying prospect. At that morning's
Presidential Daily Intelligence Briefing, George Tenet, the director
of central intelligence, informed the president that a CIA agent
code-named Dragonfire had reported that Al Qaeda terrorists possessed a ten-kiloton nuclear bomb, evidently stolen from the Russian arsenal. According to Dragonfire, this nuclear weapon was now
on American soil, in New York City.[1]

The CIA had no independent confirmation of this report, but
neither did it have any basis on which to dismiss it. Did Russia's
arsenal include a large number of ten-kiloton weapons? Yes. Could
the Russian government account for all the nuclear weapons the
Soviet Union had built during the Cold War? No. Could Al Qaeda
have acquired one or more of these weapons? Yes. Could it have
smuggled a nuclear weapon through American border controls into

New York City without anyone's knowledge? Yes. In a moment of gallows humor, someone quipped that the terrorists could have wrapped the bomb in one of the bales of marijuana that are routinely smuggled into cities like New York.

In the hours that followed, national security adviser Condoleezza Rice analyzed what strategists call the "problem from hell." Unlike the Cold War, when the United States and the Soviet Union knew that an attack against the other would elicit a retaliatory strike or greater measure, Al Qaeda—with no return address—had no such fear of reprisal. Even if the president were prepared to negotiate, Al Qaeda had no phone number to call.

Clearly no decision could be taken without much more information about the threat and those behind it. But how could Rice engage a wider circle of experts and analysts without the White House's suspicions leaking to the press? A CNN flash that the White House had information about an Al Qaeda nuclear weapon in Manhattan would create chaos. New Yorkers would flee the city in terror, and residents of other metropolitan areas would panic. The stock market, which was just then stabilizing from the shock of 9/11, could collapse.

Concerned that Al Qaeda could have smuggled a nuclear weapon into Washington as well, the president ordered Vice President Dick Cheney to leave the capital for an "undisclosed location," where he would remain for many weeks to follow. This was standard procedure to ensure "continuity of government" in case of a decapitation strike against the U.S. political leadership. Several hundred federal employees from more than a dozen government agencies joined the vice president at this secret site, the core of an alternative government that would seek to cope in the aftermath of a nuclear explosion that destroyed Washington. The president also immediately dispatched NEST specialists (Nuclear Emergency Support Teams of scientists and engineers) to New York to search for the weapon. But no one in the city was informed of the threat, not even Mayor Rudolph Giuliani.

Six months earlier the CIA's Counterterrorism Center had picked up chatter in Al Qaeda channels about an "American Hiroshima."[2] The CIA knew that Osama bin Laden's fascination with nuclear weapons went back at least to 1992, when he attempted to buy highly enriched uranium from South Africa.[3] Al Qaeda operatives were alleged to have negotiated with Chechen separatists in Russia to buy a nuclear warhead, which the Chechen warlord Shamil Basayev claimed to have acquired from Russian arsenals.[4] The CIA's special task force on Al Qaeda had noted the terrorist group's emphasis on thorough planning, intensive training, and repetition of successful tactics. The task force also highlighted Al Qaeda's strong preference for symbolic targets and spectacular attacks.

As the CIA's analysts examined Dragonfire's report and compared it with other bits of information, they noted that the attack on the World Trade Center in September had set the bar higher for future terrorist spectaculars. Psychologically, a nuclear attack would stagger the world's imagination as dramatically as 9/11 did. Considering where Al Qaeda might detonate such a bomb, they noted that New York was, in the jargon of national security experts, "target rich." Among hundreds of potential targets, what could be more compelling than Times Square, the most famous address in the self-proclaimed capital of the world?

Amid this sea of unknowns, analysts could definitively answer at least one question. They knew what kind of devastation a nuclear explosion would cause. If Al Qaeda was to rent a van to carry the ten-kiloton Russian weapon into the heart of Times Square and detonate it adjacent to the Morgan Stanley headquarters at 1585 Broadway, Times Square would vanish in the twinkling of an eye. The blast would generate temperatures reaching into the tens of millions of degrees Fahrenheit. The resulting fireball and blast wave would destroy instantaneously the theater district, the New York Times building, Grand Central Terminal, and every other structure within a third of a mile of the point of detonation. The ensuing firestorm would engulf Rockefeller Center, Carnegie Hall, the Empire State Building, and Madison Square Garden, leaving a landscape resembling the World Trade Center site. From the United Nations headquarters on the East River and the Lincoln Tunnel under the Hudson River, to the Metropolitan Museum in the eighties and the Flatiron Building in the twenties, structures would remind one of the Alfred P. Murrah Federal Office Building following the Oklahoma City bombing.

On a normal workday, more than half a million people crowd the area within a half-mile radius of Times Square. A noon detonation in midtown Manhattan could kill them all. Hundreds of thousands of others would die from collapsing buildings, fire, and fallout in the ensuing hours. The electromagnetic pulse generated by the blast would fry cell phones, radios, and other electronic communications. Hospitals, doctors, and emergency services would be overwhelmed by the wounded. Firefighters would be battling an uncontrolled ring of fires for many days thereafter.

The threat of nuclear terrorism, moreover, is not limited to New York City. While New York is widely seen as the most likely target, it is clear that Al Qaeda is not only capable of, but also interested in, mounting attacks on other American cities, where people may be less prepared. Imagine the consequences of a ten-kiloton weapon exploding in San Francisco, Houston, Washington, Chicago, Los Angeles, or any other city Americans call home. From the epicenter of the blast to a distance of approximately a third of a mile, every structure and individual would vanish in a vaporous haze. A second circle of destruction, extending three-quarters of a mile from ground zero, would leave buildings looking like the Murrah building in Oklahoma City. A third circle, reaching out one and one-half miles, would be ravaged by fires and radiation.

In San Francisco, if the bomb was detonated in Union Square, everything to the Museum of Modern Art would vaporize; everything from the Transamerica building to Nob Hill would be sites of massive destruction; everything within the perimeter of Coit Tower and the San Francisco–Oakland Bay Bridge would go up in flames.

In Houston, an explosion in Chinatown would instantly destroy both Minute Maid Park (home of the Houston Astros) and the Toyota Center (home of the Rockets and the Aeros). From the curves of the Buffalo Bayou to the edge of Sam Houston Park, buildings would be shattered shells; landmarks as far away from downtown as the University of Houston would be engulfed by fire.

In Washington, a bomb going off at the Smithsonian Institution would destroy everything from the White House to the lawn of the Capitol building; everything from the Supreme Court to the FDR Memorial would be left in rubble; uncontrollable fires would reach all the way out to the Pentagon.

An explosion at the Sears Tower in Chicago would cause everything from the Navy Pier to the Eisenhower Expressway (I-90) to disappear; the United Center and all of Grant Park would be destroyed; the firestorm would approach both Comiskey Park and Wrigley Field.

In Los Angeles, a bomb exploded at the intersection of Hollywood Boulevard and Highland Avenue would vaporize the historic Mann's Chinese Theater and the Hollywood Walk of Fame; the Pantages Theater (the former home of the Academy Awards) would crumble; the blast's outer circle would erase the sign in the Hollywood Hills.

In my own hometown, Charlotte, North Carolina, a nuclear detonation at the Square would vaporize the Bank of America building, the First Union Center, and all of downtown; only the skeletal remains of the Federal Reserve building and Federal Courthouse would be left standing; and Ericsson Stadium (home to the Carolina Panthers) would be burned to cinders.°

In a cover story in the *New York Times Magazine* in May 2002, Bill Keller interviewed Eugene Habiger, the retired four-star general

°To visualize these consequences in the city of their choice, readers can visit www.nuclearterror.org, where concentric circles of destruction are mapped for a portfolio of plausible nuclear terrorist attacks.

who had overseen strategic nuclear weapons until 1998 and had run nuclear antiterror programs for the Department of Energy until 2001. Summarizing his decade of daily experience dealing with threats, Habiger offered a categorical conclusion about nuclear terrorism: "it is not a matter of if; it's a matter of *when.*"

"That," Keller noted drily, "may explain why he now lives in San Antonio."[5]

THE SECOND SHOE

In the end, the Dragonfire report turned out to be a false alarm. But in the weeks and months following 9/11, the American national security community focused on what was called the question of the "second shoe." No one believed that the attacks on the World Trade Center and the Pentagon were an isolated occurrence. The next question had to be when, and where, the second shoe would drop and what form it would take. From the inner circle of presidential advisers to a thick network of external consultants, the nation's best analysts examined an array of potential terrorist attacks, or "horribles." Earlier in the 1990s, when I served as an assistant secretary of defense, I prepared a highly classified memorandum, titled "A Hundred Horribles," that provoked some controversy. On that list, an attack by hijacked aircraft on trophy buildings fell in the lower half of potential terrorist attacks, ranked in terms of damage to America.

First place on everyone's list goes to an attack with a nuclear bomb on an American city. When Secretary of Homeland Security Tom Ridge is asked what he worries about when he wakes up at night, he answers in one word: "nuclear."[6] Only a nuclear explosion can kill hundreds of thousands of people instantly. But everyone's list also includes other associated forms of nuclear terror, like attacks on nuclear power plants and so-called dirty bombs.

The American Airlines flight that struck the North Tower of the

World Trade Center could just as readily have hit the Indian Point nuclear power plant, forty miles north of Times Square. The United Airlines flight that crashed in Pennsylvania on its way to the Capitol might instead have targeted Three Mile Island. The airplane that attacked the Pentagon could have targeted the North Anna power plant near Richmond, Virginia. At the Counterterrorism Center, analysts recalled that in November 1972, three Americans with pistols and hand grenades hijacked Southern Airways Flight 49. The pilot was ordered to fly to Oak Ridge, Tennessee, where the plane circled over a nuclear research reactor. When the hijackers' ransom demands received a lukewarm response, they forced the pilot to begin a steep descent on Oak Ridge, pulling up only when the airline said it would give the hijackers $2 million. That incident ended in Cuba with the imprisonment of the hijackers.[7]

The consequences of an attack on a nuclear plant would depend largely on where the plane hit. If the aircraft penetrated the containment dome, the attack could cause the reactor to melt down, releasing hundreds of millions of curies of radioactivity into the surrounding environment, hundreds of times that released by the Hiroshima and Nagasaki atomic bombs. We already know what such an incident would look like. In April 1986, an accidental explosion inside the Soviet nuclear reactor at Chernobyl (near Kiev, in what is now Ukraine) ignited a powerful fire that raged for ten days. The resulting radiation forced the evacuation and resettlement of over 350,000 people and caused an estimated $300 billion of economic damage, and is likely to lead ultimately to tens of thousands of excess cancer deaths among those exposed to the fallout.[8]

An even more vulnerable target at a nuclear plant is the building that houses the spent fuel rods, which are stored in pools of water to prevent the heat from their residual radioactivity from melting them. Designed to remain intact in case of an earthquake, these structures are open to the air in some instances and housed in only light-duty buildings in others, which means that a plane attacking from above might drain the pool, destroy backup safety systems, and ignite the fuel. The resulting fire would spew radioactivity into the environment in amounts that could reach three or four Chernobyls.

Further potential "second shoes" include dirty bombs, conventional explosives packed into radioactive material. While such bombs do not produce a nuclear explosion, they can disperse radiological material over a large area, causing widespread contamination. The consensus in the national security community has long been that a dirty bomb attack is inevitable, indeed long overdue. The integration of various forms of radioactive material in modern life, from X-rays in dentists' offices and hospitals to smoke detectors, has made control of such material impossible. Prior to 9/11, the U.S. government had no serious program even to account for and track the more dangerous materials. Thus newspapers carry almost weekly stories of theft of radioactive material, not only in Russia and the former Soviet Union but here at home as well.

The good news about dirty bombs is that they are weapons of mass disruption, not mass destruction. Potential radiation bombs cover a spectrum from a stick of dynamite in a shoe box containing weak radioactive material to aerosolized plutonium injected into the ventilation system of a skyscraper or an enclosed sports arena. While the former could create temporary panic, the latter could give lung cancer to everyone on an entire floor of a skyscraper. Experts at Los Alamos National Laboratory who studied this threat concluded that "a RDD [radiological dispersal device] attack somewhere in the world is overdue."[9] But as one national security official related, if a radiological dispersal device was the best shot Al Qaeda could now take, we should declare victory.[10]

THE SUM OF ALL FEARS

Polls taken in 2003 found that four out of every ten Americans say that they "often worry about the chances of a nuclear attack by terrorists."[11] Are these fears exaggerated? Not in the best judgment of those who have carefully examined the evidence. In 2000, two of the most respected and thoughtful Americans who had no previous responsibility in this arena, Howard Baker and Lloyd Cutler, conducted an official review of this issue. Baker, a Republican, is currently the U.S. ambassador to Japan, having served previously as President Ronald Reagan's chief of staff and as majority leader of the Senate. Cutler, a Democrat, has been counsel to the president in both the Carter and the Clinton administrations. The principal finding of the Report Card they presented to the Bush administration in January 2001 states bluntly: "The *most urgent unmet national security threat* to the United States today is the danger that weapons of mass destruction or weapons-usable material in Russia could be stolen, sold to terrorists or hostile nation-states and used against American troops abroad or citizens at home."[12] As Baker testified to the Senate Foreign Relations Committee: "It really boggles my mind that there could be 40,000 nuclear weapons, or maybe 80,000, in the former Soviet Union, poorly controlled and poorly stored, and that the world isn't in a near state of hysteria about the danger."[13]

The imminence of this threat becomes evident as one considers three points. First, thefts of weapons-usable material and attempts to steal nuclear weapons are not a hypothetical possibility, but a proven and recurring fact.[14] Thousands of weapons and tens of thousands of potential weapons (softball-size lumps of highly enriched uranium and plutonium) remain today in unsecured storage facilities in Russia, vulnerable to theft by determined criminals who could then sell them to terrorists. In the years since the collapse of the Soviet Union, there have been hundreds of confirmed cases of successful theft of nuclear materials in which the thieves were captured, sometimes in Russia, on other occasions in the Czech Republic, Germany, and elsewhere. Every month those who follow current events closely will learn of yet another occasion in which nuclear material was stolen or a theft attempted.

In 1997, Boris Yeltsin's assistant for national security affairs,

General Alexander Lebed, acknowledged that 84 of some 132 special KGB "suitcase" nuclear weapons were not accounted for in Russia. These weapons are miniature nuclear devices (0.1 to 1 kiloton), small enough to fit into a suitcase carried by a single individual. Under pressure from colleagues, Lebed later recanted his statement, retreating to the official Russian line that the Soviet Union had never made any such nuclear weapons; that it was inconceivable that Russia could have lost a nuclear weapon; and that, in any case, all such Russian weapons and nuclear materials were secure. But in the process, Lebed and his colleagues left more questions than answers. Contrary to the Russian government's claims, there can be no doubt about the fact that enough nuclear material to build more than twenty nuclear weapons was lost in the transition from the Soviet Union to Russia. Indeed, over one thousand pounds of highly enriched uranium (HEU) was purchased by the U.S. government, removed from an unprotected site in Almaty, Kazakhstan, and is now securely stored in Oak Ridge. But, as former CIA director John Deutch observed, "It's not so much what I know that worries me, as what I know that I don't know."[15]

Second, in the winter of 2002–2003, President Bush argued that "if the Iraqi regime is able to produce, buy, or steal an amount of uranium a little bigger than a softball, it could have a nuclear weapon in less than a year," a charge that served as part of his case for war with Iraq. What the president failed to mention is that with the same quantity of HEU, terrorist groups like Al Qaeda, Hezbollah, and Hamas could do the same thing. The only high hurdle to creating a nuclear bomb is access to fissionable material—an ingredient that is, fortunately, difficult and expensive to manufacture. But as John Foster, a leading American bomb maker and former director of the Lawrence Livermore National Laboratories, wrote a quarter century ago, "If the essential nuclear materials are at hand, it is possible to make an atomic bomb using information that is available in the open literature."[16]

Third, terrorists would not find it difficult to smuggle such a nuclear device into the United States. The nuclear material in question is smaller than a football. Even an assembled device, like a suitcase nuclear weapon, could be sent in a Federal Express package, shipped in a cargo container, or checked as airline baggage. Of the seven million cargo containers that arrive in U.S. ports each year, fewer than 5 percent are opened for inspection. As the chief executive of CSX Lines, one of the foremost container-shipping companies, noted, "If you can smuggle heroin in containers, you may be able to smuggle in a nuclear bomb."[17]

Unfortunately, the former Soviet Union is not the only potential source of nuclear weapons or fissile material from which a nuclear weapon could be fashioned. Pakistan has an arsenal of about fifty nuclear weapons and materials for making at least that many more. Given the extensive ties between Pakistani intelligence services and the Taliban, it is not unreasonable to envision Pakistan as the source of a ten-kiloton weapon in New York. Unfolding revelations about fissile material production lines in North Korea, Iran, and Libya lengthen the list for potential sources of the first nuclear terrorist's weapon.

After Tom Clancy published *The Sum of All Fears,* his 1991 bestseller about a stolen nuclear weapon being detonated at the Super Bowl, the author received comments from several knowledgeable insiders that left him uneasy. Thus the paperback edition of the book includes a remarkable afterword written, as Clancy confesses candidly, "to salve my conscience, *not* in my reasonable expectation that it matters a damn."

> All of the material in this novel relating to weapons technology and fabrication is readily available in any one of dozens of books. . . . I was first bemused, then stunned, as my research revealed just how easy such a project might be today. It is generally known that nuclear secrets are not as secure as we would like—in fact, the situation is worse than even well-informed people appreciate. What required billions of dollars in the 1940s is much less expensive

today. A modern personal computer has far more power and reliability than the first Eniac, and the "hydrocodes" which enable a
computer to test and validate a weapon's design are easily dupli-
cated. The exquisite machine tools used to fabricate parts can be
had for the asking. When I asked explicitly for specifications for
the very machines used at Oak Ridge and elsewhere, they arrived
Federal Express the next day. Some highly specialized items
designed specifically for bomb manufacture may now be found in
stereo speakers. The fact of the matter is that a sufficiently wealthy
individual could, over a period of from five to ten years, produce
a multistage thermonuclear device. Science is all in the public
domain, and allows few secrets.

Clancy wrote this afterword in 1992, which means his five- to
ten-year period has elapsed.

FOUR MILLION AMERICANS

Nine months after the attack on New York, Osama bin Laden's official
press spokesman, Suleiman Abu Gheith, made a chilling announcement on a now defunct Al Qaeda–associated Web site, www.alneda.
com. *"We have the right,"* Abu Gheith asserted, *"to kill 4 million
Americans—2 million of them children—and to exile twice as many
and wound and cripple hundreds of thousands."*

Four million Americans—an eerily specific and precise figure,
clearly not one pulled out of thin air. More troubling than Abu
Gheith's number is the logic, and even the bizarre coherence, of the
calculations that led Al Qaeda to this stark conclusion. In an
extended, three-part article, Abu Gheith explains "why we fight the
United States" and seeks to provide "the Islamic justification for Al
Qaeda's jihad against the U.S." The bottom line of the case he
makes for Al Qaeda members and affiliates around the world is four
million dead Americans.[18]

About the attacks on the World Trade Center, he proclaims, "What happened to America is something natural, an expected event for a country that uses terror, arrogant policy, and suppression against the nations and peoples, and imposes a single method, thought, and way of life, as if the people of the entire world are clerks in its government offices and employed by the commercial companies and institutions. Anyone who was surprised, did not understand the nature of man and the effects of oppression and tyranny on man's emotions and feelings." Echoing a phrase used by Palestinian militants to characterize Israel's tactics in the West Bank and Gaza, he says, "They thought that oppression begets surrender."

Why target the United States? His answer is clear: "America with the collaboration of the Jews is the leader of corruption and the breakdown of values, whether moral, ideological, political, or economic corruption. It disseminates abomination and licentiousness among the people via the cheap media and the vile curricula." In sum, "America is the reason for all oppression, injustice, licentiousness, or suppression that is the Muslim's lot. It stands behind all the disasters that were caused and are still being caused to the Muslims; it is immersed in the blood of Muslims and can not hide this."

Abu Gheith's indictment then itemizes deaths and injuries the United States and Israel have (in his view) caused Muslims:

- For fifty years in Palestine, the Jews—with the blessing and support of the Americans—carried out abominations of murder, suppression, abuse, and exile. The Jews exiled nearly 5 million Palestinians and killed nearly 260,000. They wounded nearly 180,000 and crippled nearly 160,000.
- As a result of the American bombings and siege of Iraq, more than 1.2 million Muslims were killed in the past decade. Due to the siege, over one million children are killed annually; that is 83,333 children on average per month, 2,777 children per day. (This refers to the sanctions and enforcement of UN resolutions *before* the American-led invasion in 2003.)

- In its war against the Taliban and Al Qaeda in Afghanistan, America killed 12,000 Afghan civilians and 350 Arab jihad fighters.
- In Somalia, America killed 13,000 Somalis.

How should honorable Muslims respond? he asks. Citing the Koran and other Islamic religious texts and traditions, he answers that "anyone who peruses these sources reaches a single conclusion: the sages have agreed that the reciprocal punishment to which the verses referred is not limited to a specific instance. It is a valid rule for punishments for infidels, for the licentious Muslims, and for the oppressors."

In conclusion, "according to the numbers in the previous section of the lives lost among Muslims because of the Americans, directly or indirectly," therefore, "we are still at the beginning of the way. The Americans have still not tasted from our hands what we have tasted from theirs. We have not reached parity with them." For Al Qaeda, "parity will require killing 4 million Americans." For, according to Abu Gheith, "America knows only the language of force. This is the only way to make it take its hands off the Muslims. America can be kept at bay by blood alone."

Nearly three thousand Americans died in the 9/11 attacks. It would take 1,400 similar assaults to reach that figure of 4 million. Or it could take just one, if Al Qaeda had access to the right nuclear weapon. Al Qaeda has made its intentions clear; the challenge to America is to prevent it from succeeding.

INEVITABLE OR PREVENTABLE?

The world's most successful investor is also a legendary odds maker in pricing insurance policies for unlikely but catastrophic events like earthquakes. Warren Buffett has described a nuclear terrorist attack as "the ultimate depressing thing. It will happen. It's inevitable.

I don't see any way that it won't happen."[19] Given the number of actors with serious intent, the accessibility of weapons or nuclear materials from which elementary weapons could be constructed, and the almost limitless ways in which terrorists could smuggle a weapon through American borders, a betting person would have to go with Buffett. In my own considered judgment, on the current path, a nuclear terrorist attack on America in the decade ahead is more likely than not.

And yet I am not a pessimist. The central but largely unrecognized truth is that nuclear terrorism is *preventable*. As a simple matter of physics, without fissile material, there can be no nuclear explosion. There is a vast, but not unlimited, amount of highly enriched uranium and weapons-grade plutonium in the world, and it is within our power to keep it secure. The United States does not lose gold from Fort Knox, nor Russia treasures from the Kremlin Armory. Thus all that the United States and its allies have to do to prevent nuclear terrorism is to prevent terrorists from acquiring a weapon or nuclear material. The "all" required calls for a substantial, sustained, but nonetheless finite undertaking that can be accomplished by a finite effort. It is a challenge to our will, our conviction, and our courage, not to our technical capacity.

Part 1 of this book provides an overview of the necessary who, what, where, when, and how of the nuclear terrorism threat to show the particulars of the challenge we face. Against that backdrop, part 2 sets out an ambitious but feasible agenda of actions that could prevent terrorists from ever being able to explode a nuclear bomb in an American city.

Nuclear terrorism may be the ultimate catastrophe, but it is also the ultimate preventable catastrophe—if we have the will to make it so.

PART ONE

INEVITABLE

1

WHO COULD BE PLANNING
A NUCLEAR TERRORIST ATTACK?

It is the duty of Muslims to prepare as much force as
possible to terrorize the enemies of God.

OSAMA BIN LADEN,
"The Nuclear Bomb of Islam"

"WHY DO YOU use an axe when you can use a bulldozer?" That was
Osama bin Laden's question in 1996 to Khalid Sheikh Mohammed,
the chief planner of what grew into the most deadly attack on the
American homeland in the nation's history. Mohammed is now in
American custody, the highest-ranking Al Qaeda leader captured to
date in the war on terrorism. He has told interrogators that the
"axe" to which bin Laden referred was his proposal to charter a
small plane, fill it with explosives, and crash it into CIA headquarters in Langley, Virginia. Bin Laden sent him back to the drawing
board with a charge to devise a more dramatic, devastating blow
against the "hated enemy."[1]

In the months that followed, Mohammed proposed a number of
"bulldozer" options for bin Laden's review. As he explained in an Al
Jazeera interview in April 2002, just before he was seized, he and
his colleagues "first thought of striking a couple of nuclear facilities." But with regret, he noted, "it was eventually decided to leave
out the nuclear targets—for now." When the interviewer asked:

"What do you mean 'for now'?" he replied sharply: "For now means for *now.*"[2]

AL QAEDA'S "MANHATTAN PROJECT"

In August 2001, during the final countdown to what Al Qaeda calls the "Holy Tuesday" attack, bin Laden received two key former officials from Pakistan's nuclear weapons program at his secret headquarters near Kabul. Over the course of three days of intense conversation, he and his second-in-command, the Egyptian surgeon and organizational mastermind Ayman al-Zawahiri, quizzed Sultan Bashiruddin Mahmood and Abdul Majeed about chemical, biological, and, especially, nuclear weapons. Bin Laden, al-Zawahiri, and two other as yet unidentified top-level Al Qaeda operatives who participated in these conversations had clearly moved beyond the impending assault on the World Trade Center to visions of grander attacks to follow.[3]

Mahmood and Majeed's meeting with the leaders of Al Qaeda came at the end of months of prior meetings with subordinates. Al Qaeda had sought out Mahmood, one of Pakistan's leading specialists in uranium enrichment, for his capabilities, his convictions, and his connections. Mahmood's career spanned thirty years at the Pakistani Atomic Energy Commission, and he had been a key figure at the Kahuta plant, which had produced the enriched uranium for Pakistan's first nuclear bomb test. Thereafter, he headed the Khosib reactor in the Punjab that produces weapons-grade plutonium.[4] In 1999, however, he was forced to resign abruptly for describing Pakistan's nuclear capability as "the property of a whole Muslim community" and for publicly advocating that Pakistan provide enriched uranium and weapons-grade plutonium to arm other Muslim states.[5] But even though the government of Pakistan vehemently denounced Mahmood's views, it had been surreptitiously following a similar policy, having offered or supplied uranium enrich-ment technology and know-how to Iraq, Libya, Iran, and even North Korea.

Mahmood is representative of a significant faction of Pakistani "nuclear hawks" who through the 1990s grew increasingly estranged from the country's more moderate leadership. Under the leader-ship of Dr. Abdul Qadeer Khan, the revered "father of the Islamic bomb," these scientists had thrust Pakistan into the ranks of the declared nuclear powers, and through their work they became some of the most respected members of Pakistani society. But for many of them, the mission was not only to overcome India's con-ventional superiority but to stand up for the Muslim world. As Prime Minister Zulfiqar Ali Bhutto revealed in his memoir (written from prison just before his execution in 1979), these scientists were ordered in January 1972 to "achieve a full nuclear capability" in order to demonstrate that "Islamic Civilization" was the full equal of "Christian, Jewish, and Hindu Civilizations."[6]

Mahmood was—and is today—an Islamic extremist. In the late 1980s, Mahmood published an essay titled "Mechanics of Dooms-day and Life after Death," in which he argued that natural catastro-phes are inevitable in countries that succumb to moral decay. In contrast, he later praised the virtues of the Taliban government in Afghanistan, which he called the vanguard of the "renaissance of Islam." His spiritual leader, the Lahore-based Islamic radical cleric Israr Ahmad, declared in the fall of 2001 that the U.S. attack on Afghanistan was the beginning of "the final war between Islam and the infidels." Ahmad condemned the U.S. war on terrorism as a "materialistic jihad," in contrast to the Muslims' jihad, which he characterized as being for "the sole purpose to gain the pleasure of Allah and for the preservation of justice and equality."[7] Ominously, Ahmad's student Mahmood predicted in an essay that, "by 2002, millions may die through mass destruction weapons, terrorist attacks, and suicide."

After his forced departure from Pakistan's Atomic Energy Commission in 1999, Mahmood founded a "charitable agency" that he named Ummah Tamer-e-Nau (Reconstruction of the Muslim Community) to support projects in Afghanistan. Majeed also retired in 1999 and joined Mahmood's organization. Under this cover, they traveled frequently to Afghanistan to develop projects, one of which called for mining uranium from rich deposits in that country. Other members of the board of Mahmood's foundation included a fellow nuclear scientist knowledgeable about weapons construction, two Pakistani Air Force generals, one Army general, and an industrialist who owned Pakistan's largest foundry.[8]

At the time of Mahmood and Majeed's visit to bin Laden in the summer of 2001, relations between the United States and Pakistan were still in a deep freeze, in response to Pakistan's test of a nuclear weapon in 1998. The United States had immediately imposed economic sanctions on the country, and President Bill Clinton denounced the Pakistani government for its decision, saying, "I cannot believe that we are about to start the 21st century by having the Indian subcontinent repeat the worst mistakes of the 20th century when we know it is not necessary to peace, to security, to prosperity, to national greatness or personal fulfillment."[9] In 1999, relations deteriorated further when General Pervez Musharraf seized power in a coup d'état that ousted the democratically elected prime minister, Nawaz Sharif.

When reports about the August 2001 meeting reached CIA headquarters at Langley after the attacks on the World Trade Center and the Pentagon, alarm bells sounded. Analysts at the Counterterrorism Center recognized the story line. In 1997, Pakistani nuclear scientists had made secret trips to North Korea, the result of which was that Pakistan would provide North Korea with technical assistance for its nuclear weapons program in exchange for North Korean assistance in Pakistan's development of long-range missiles. The CIA had additional information about a third Pakistani nuclear scientist, who had been negotiating with Libyan intelligence agents over the price for which he would sell nuclear bomb designs. CIA director George Tenet was so alarmed by the report of Mahmood's meeting with bin Laden that he flew directly to Islamabad to confront President Musharraf.

On October 23, Mahmood and Majeed were arrested by Pakistani authorities and questioned by joint Pakistani–CIA teams. Mahmood claimed that he had never met bin Laden, but repeatedly failed polygraph tests in which he was asked about his trips to Afghanistan. His memory improved, however, after his son Asim told authorities that bin Laden had asked his father about "how to make a nuclear bomb and things like that."[10] According to Mahmood, bin Laden was particularly interested in nuclear weapons. Bin Laden's colleagues told the Pakistani scientists that Al Qaeda had succeeded in acquiring nuclear material for a bomb from the Islamic Movement of Uzbekistan. Mahmood explained to his hosts that the material in question could be used in a dirty bomb but could not produce a nuclear explosion. Al-Zawahiri and the others then sought Mahmood's help in recruiting other Pakistani nuclear experts who could provide uranium of the required purity, as well as assistance in constructing a nuclear weapon. Though Mahmood characterized the discussions as "academic,"[11] Pakistani officials indicated that Mahmood and Majeed "spoke extensively about weapons of mass destruction," and provided detailed responses to bin Laden's questions about the manufacture of nuclear, biological, and chemical weapons.[12]

After their arrest and interrogation, Mahmood and Majeed were found to have violated Pakistan's official secrets act. Their passports were lifted and they remain, in effect, under house arrest. Nonetheless, the Pakistani government refused to bring the two to trial for fear of what they might reveal about Pakistan's other secret nuclear activities.[13] This was not an idle fear. In a prescient article published less than a month before he was kidnapped and executed while investigating the "shoe bomber" Richard Reid, Daniel Pearl of the *Wall Street Journal* revealed that Pakistani military authorities found it "inconceivable that a nuclear scientist would travel to Afghanistan without getting clearance from Pakistani officials," because Pakistan "maintains a strict watch on many of its nuclear scientists, using a special arm of the Army's general headquarters to monitor them even after retirement."[14]

In the end, U.S. intelligence agencies concluded that Mahmood and Majeed had provided bin Laden with a blueprint for constructing nuclear weapons. Thereafter, sometimes in collaboration with the Pakistani intelligence agency, Inter-Services Intelligence (ISI), and otherwise unilaterally, American operatives have sought to intercept further "vacations" in Afghanistan by Pakistani nuclear physicists and engineers. The CIA's summary of the matter, submitted to President Bush, concluded that while Mahmood and his charity claimed "to serve the hungry and needy of Afghanistan," in fact, it "provided information about nuclear weapons to Al Qaeda."[15]

PATIENCE, THOUGHTFULNESS, AND EXPERTISE

Andrew Marshall, director of net assessments at the Department of Defense and one of the wise men among national security insiders, has long warned that "if the U.S. ever faced a serious enemy, we would be in deep trouble." Al Qaeda qualifies as a formidable foe. With an annual budget of over $200 million during the 1990s, Al Qaeda brought more than sixty thousand international recruits to Afghanistan for training in terrorist attacks. It established cells, including sleeper cells, in approximately sixty countries. It created affiliate relationships with major terrorist groups around the world, from Chechnya to Indonesia, from Saudi Arabia to Germany, and within the United States itself. Indeed, an Al Qaeda sleeper cell in Singapore, among the most secure and watchful societies in the world, was narrowly prevented from launching an attack on the U.S. and Israeli embassies there, with ten times the amount of explosives used by Timothy McVeigh in Oklahoma City. As one

Singaporean official observed, "If they could do it here, they could do it anywhere."[16]

Even before 9/11, Al Qaeda's attacks demonstrated an organizational capacity to plan, coordinate, and implement operations well above the threshold of competence necessary to acquire and use a nuclear weapon. Veterans of the most successful U.S. covert actions agree with Tenet's bottom line: the attack on the World Trade Center and the Pentagon was "professionally conceived and executed—it showed patience, thoughtfulness, and expertise."[17] As an analyst conducting the postmortem on that attack observed: Who else could have found four scheduled American flights that took off on time?

After 9/11, terrorism analysts and other specialists within the U.S. government reexamined the pattern of Al Qaeda's earlier attacks in an effort to connect the dots. When those dots are connected, they reveal a dagger pointed from Al Qaeda's February 1993 attack on the World Trade Center, through the August 1998 attacks on the U.S. embassies in Kenya and Tanzania and the bombing of the warship USS *Cole* in October 2000, to the massive attack of 9/11. Indeed, the dagger points beyond what was achieved in that case to further mega-terrorist attacks with chemical, biological, and nuclear weapons.

When U.S. Special Forces, CIA operatives, and Afghan warlords toppled the Taliban government in Afghanistan in late 2001, the U.S. government and American journalists learned more about Al Qaeda than most had imagined they wanted to know. Overrunning hundreds of headquarters buildings, safe houses, training camps, and caves, they recovered tens of thousands of pages of documents, plans, videos, computers, and disks. Secretary of Defense Donald Rumsfeld found in this evidence "a number of things that show an appetite for WMD."[18] Together with information extracted through interrogation of captured Al Qaeda operatives, these findings now provide a solid base for assessing Al Qaeda as a nuclear threat.

One of the untold stories of this drama has been the key role played by journalists in acquiring critical information. In December 2001, the *Wall Street Journal* purchased a desktop computer and a laptop computer looted from an Al Qaeda safe house that turned out to have been used by several top bin Laden lieutenants, including al-Zawahiri and bin Laden's former military commander, the late Mohammed Atef. In addition to hundreds of routine letters and memos dealing with the daily administration of Al Qaeda's terrorist network, the computers' hard drives contained password-protected files on a project code-named "al Zabadi," Arabic for "curdled milk." The curdled milk project sought to acquire chemical and biological weapons, and it had reached the point of testing nerve gas recipes on dogs and rabbits.[19]

CNN discovered perhaps the most disturbing piece of evidence in the Kabul home of Abu Khabab, a senior Al Qaeda official—a twenty-five-page essay titled "Superbomb," which included information on types of nuclear weapons, the physics and effects of nuclear explosions, and the properties of nuclear materials. David Albright, a former nuclear weapons inspector who reviewed the document, concluded that "the author understood shortcuts to making crude nuclear explosives." Combined with other documents diagramming and describing the manufacture of nuclear weapons and their effects, the essay led Albright to conclude that "Al Qaeda was intensifying its long-term goal to acquire nuclear weapons and would likely have succeeded, if it had remained powerful in Afghanistan for several more years."[20]

The CIA's intelligence file on Al Qaeda's nuclear activities contains several thousand items. As early as 1993, Jamal al-Fadl, a senior Al Qaeda figure, met with a former Sudanese government minister and military officer named Salah Abdel al-Mobruk, who was offering a cache of weapons-usable uranium for $1.5 million. When al-Fadl reported to his superiors that the offer appeared serious, he was joined by another top bin Laden aide, Abu Rida al-Suri, and the two were shown a cylinder of South African origin that was said to contain the uranium. Al-Suri agreed to buy the uranium at the price offered, subject to its being tested by Al Qaeda experts, but at that point al-Fadl dropped out of the transaction. While he could not confirm whether the uranium actually changed hands, al-Fadl was paid $10,000 for arranging the purchase.[21]

In the early 1990s, as the former Soviet Union disintegrated, Al Qaeda operatives made repeated trips to three central Asian states, seeking the purchase of a complete warhead or weapons-usable nuclear material. Moreover, according to the National Intelligence Council, there were at least four occasions between 1992 and 1999 when "weapons-usable nuclear materials [were] stolen from some Russian institutes,"[22] though all were later recovered. In September 1998, Israeli intelligence sources told *Time* magazine that bin Laden had paid $2 million to a man in Kazakhstan who promised to deliver a Soviet suitcase nuclear device. One month later, the Arabic-language magazine *Al Watan Al Arabi* reported that bin Laden's followers had purchased twenty nuclear warheads from Chechen mobsters in exchange for $30 million in cash and two tons of opium.[23] In filing court papers to extradite a senior bin Laden deputy from Germany that December, the United States charged him with attempting to purchase enriched uranium for nuclear weapons.[24]

According to Hamid Mir, Osama bin Laden's biographer, these efforts may have already succeeded. In March 2004, Mir told the Australian Broadcasting Corporation that Ayman al-Zawahiri boasted to him three years earlier that Al Qaeda aleady possessed nuclear weapons. Al-Zawahiri reportedly told him, "If you have $30 million, go to the black market in central Asia, contact any disgruntled Soviet scientist and . . . dozens of smart briefcase bombs are available. They have contacted us, we sent our people to Moscow, to Tashkent [the capital of Uzbekistan], to other Central Asian states, and they negotiated, and we purchased some suitcase bombs."[25] A month earlier, the London-based *Al-Hayat* newspaper reported that Al Qaeda bought tactical nuclear weapons "from Ukrainian scientists who were visting Kandahar, Afghanistan, in 1998."[26] Even if one dismisses such unconfirmed claims, they illustrate how this relatively simple recipe for acquiring a nuclear weapon has become common knowledge.

Despite all of these reports—whose accuracy remains a matter of conjecture—some American intelligence analysts find grounds for optimism in bin Laden's conversations with the Pakistani nuclear experts Mahmood and Majeed. While confirming bin Laden's intent to acquire nuclear weapons, the content of the discussion, at least as reported by Mahmood, indicates a striking lack of technical expertise on Al Qaeda's part. It also suggests that in the summer of 2001, Al Qaeda was closer to the beginning rather than to the end of the road in acquiring the capacity to conduct a nuclear terrorist attack. And with Al Qaeda on the run since then, most experts doubt that it has acquired or assembled a nuclear weapon.

Yet other analysts at the CIA and elsewhere in the U.S. government believe that Al Qaeda already has a nuclear weapon. They observe that Al Qaeda has demonstrated a great capacity for what intelligence operatives call "compartmentalization." When speaking with bin Laden in August 2001, for example, Mahmood and Majeed had no inkling of what was in store in New York and Washington a month later. Other branches of Al Qaeda could thus be the vanguard of the organization's nuclear jihad. And to the optimists' claim that the failure of U.S. forces to find any abandoned nuclear weapons material in Afghanistan is a positive sign, pessimists reply, "We haven't found most of the Al Qaeda leadership either, and we know that they exist."[27]

No student of Al Qaeda, optimist or pessimist, inside or outside the U.S. government, questions the proposition that weapons of mass destruction, in particular nuclear weapons, fit Al Qaeda's profile, philosophy, and cause. The consensus view within the U.S. intelligence community is that Al Qaeda has experimented with chemical weapons (including nerve gas), biological weapons (anthrax), and nuclear radiological dispersal devices (dirty bombs). But some combination of technical problems (especially in dispersal) and disappointment with the damage that can be done by such weapons has so far sidetracked these efforts. Many fear that bin Laden's demand for an attack that will shock Americans as profoundly as 9/11 can be satisfied only by the real thing.

JEMAAH ISLAMIYAH

If we awake tomorrow to news of a nuclear terrorist attack, Al Qaeda will certainly be the most probable perpetrator. Unfortunately, however, the list of potential attackers does not stop there. There exists a rogues' gallery of other terrorist groups that have actively explored nuclear options or, on current trend lines, could do so in the next few years. Secretary of State Colin Powell has described Al Qaeda as a "holding company," within which are "terrorist cells and organizations in dozens of countries around the world, any one of them capable of committing a terrorist act."[28] This structure has allowed the organization to adapt to the loss of its sanctuary in Afghanistan. As Eliza Manningham-Buller, the director general of Britain's MI5 intelligence service, has observed, "There are many Al Qaedas rather than a monolithic organization with the leadership organizing every facet of the organization's activities."[29] Sophisticated, ruthless, and ambitious, these groups all have their own regional aims but share one strategic vision: they see defeating America as the means of achieving their goals. Seen through their eyes, American power makes possible the local injustices they suffer. Only by driving the United States out of their region, and out of all Muslim lands, can their goals be obtained. Even without Al Qaeda's direction or funds, these groups have embraced Osama bin Laden's banner of jihad against America and incorporated it into their own aspirations.

The most active Al Qaeda affiliate in Southeast Asia is Jemaah Islamiyah, which has been responsible for planning and carrying out attacks in the Philippines, Indonesia, and Singapore. Jemaah

Islamiyah gained international notoriety with its October 2002 bombing of a Bali nightclub, which killed 202 people, mostly Western tourists.[30] A year later, in August 2003, its car-bomb attack on the Marriott Hotel in Jakarta killed twelve and injured more than one hundred people.[31] Jemaah Islamiyah's stated goal is to create a pan-Islamic nation encompassing Indonesia, Malaysia, Singapore, and a portion of the Philippines. Many members of the group fought in Afghanistan against the Soviets before returning to Southeast Asia to take up their own jihads.

The Bali bombing, the deadliest terrorist attack in the world since 9/11, stunned Indonesian and American authorities with its size, sophistication, and target selection. The Sari nightclub was a known gathering place for Westerners, located in a neighborhood popular with tourists. The attack consisted of two bombs, the first comparatively small, 2.2 pounds of TNT. The second, much more powerful bomb was made from 330 pounds of ammonium nitrate, the same fertilizer used in the Oklahoma City bombing.[32] The first explosion was designed to induce panic, forcing people out of the building and into the full brunt of the second blast. The second bomb not only leveled the nightclub but destroyed much of the surrounding block as well.

The subsequent explosion at the Marriott sent an even clearer message. The hotel was the most visible American building in Jakarta and was considered to be among the most secure buildings in the city. Yet the SUV that delivered the explosives was able to charge up the driveway to the hotel's coffee shop before detonating.[33] In less than a year, Jemaah Islamiyah had moved from attacking a symbol of Western decadence in a Hindu-dominated region of Indonesia to attacking an American symbol in the heart of the capital.

The man behind these attacks was the group's operations officer, Riduan Isamuddin, better known as Hambali. Hambali had met and become good friends with Khalid Sheikh Mohammed, the architect of 9/11, in the jihad against the Soviets in Afghanistan.

Thereafter, Hambali was a coconspirator in the plot by Mohammed and his nephew, Ramzi Yousef, to simultaneously blow up eleven American jetliners over the Pacific Ocean in 1995. In January 2000, Hambali hosted an Al Qaeda meeting in Kuala Lumpur at which a dozen senior members planned the USS *Cole* and 9/11 attacks. A rare non-Arab in bin Laden's inner circle, Hambali was considered a master strategist. "There are very few people in the world who can put big operations together," explains Rohan Gunaratna, the former principal investigator of the United Nations' Terrorism Prevention Branch. "You need years of experience and a certain mind-set. Khalid Sheikh Mohammed and Hambali have that mind-set."[34]

Fortunately, Hambali was captured in Thailand in August 2003 and can no longer utilize his skills for either Jemaah Islamiyah or Al Qaeda. While hundreds of the group's members have been rounded up, however, hundreds more are still free and plotting further attacks, perhaps on a broader scale, aimed at the destruction of large American military bases or even an attack on the U.S. homeland.

NUCLEAR GANGSTERISM IN CHECHNYA

To date, the only confirmed case of attempted nuclear terrorism occurred in Russia, on November 23, 1995, when Chechen separatists put a crude bomb containing seventy pounds of a mixture of cesium-137 and dynamite in Moscow's Ismailovsky Park. The rebels decided not to detonate this dirty bomb but instead alerted a national television station to its location. This demonstration of the Chechen insurgents' capability to commit ruthless terror underlined their long-standing interest in all things nuclear.[35] As early as 1992, Chechnya's first rebel president, Dzhokhar Dudayev, began planning for nuclear terrorism, including a specific initiative to hijack a Russian nuclear submarine from the Pacific Fleet in the Far East.[36] The plan called for seven Slavic-looking Chechens to seize a submarine from the naval base near Vladivostok, attach explosive devices to the nuclear reactor section and to one of the nuclear-tipped missiles on board, and then demand withdrawal of Russian troops from Chechnya. After the plot was discovered, Russian authorities disparaged it, and yet it is ominous to note that the former chief of staff of the Chechen rebel army, Islam Khasukhanov, had once served as second-in-command of a Pacific Fleet nuclear submarine.[37]

Chechen separatists have been engaged for more than a decade in a deadly fight for independence from Russia. This war, the bloodiest conflict in the former Soviet Union, has left more than 100,000 civilians dead and nearly half of the region's population homeless. Most recently, the separatists attracted international attention when a group of forty rebels stormed the Dubrovka Theater in Moscow on October 23, 2002, taking eight hundred hostages. The heavily armed group demanded immediate withdrawal of Russian troops from Chechnya. After two days of failed negotiations, Russian commandos assaulted the theater in a rescue effort that killed the terrorists but also resulted in over one hundred civilian deaths.

For Movsar Barayev, the leader of the Chechen attack, the Dubrovka Theater was his second-choice target. Initially, Barayev planned to seize the Kurchatov Institute, one of Russia's leading nuclear design centers, with twenty-six operating nuclear reactors and enough highly enriched uranium to make thousands of nuclear weapons. Though far from optimal, the security at Kurchatov proved formidable enough for Barayev to pass up the nuclear facility for a softer target.[38]

Barayev's success in ambushing a theater only a ten-minute walk from the Kremlin was facilitated in part by the Chechen criminal network that extends far into Russia. The long war has transformed Chechnya from a proud mountainous community of Muslim villages to a breeding ground for criminal activity of all forms. Ransom kidnappings, robberies, and drug and arms trade have become the brutal hallmarks of Chechen separatism. Barayev's terrorist faction, the Special Purpose Islamic Regiment, funded its activities through kidnapping, extortion, and contract killings.[39]

Just as important, the impoverished and disenfranchised Chechens have proved a ready audience for Islamic extremism, particularly the militant Islam espoused by Ibn Al-Khattab, the Saudi Arabian–born, self-proclaimed commander of the foreign mujahedeen in Chechnya. Khattab, who was first indoctrinated in Islamic jihad when he joined the fight against the Soviet Union in Afghanistan in the 1980s, gained notoriety and respect among Chechens for his warring skills and cruelty, leading to greater ties between the Chechen separatist cause and Islamic extremist organizations.

Among international terrorists, Chechen rebels have achieved a reputation for extreme ruthlessness, including torture, executions, and beheadings. In 1998, four foreign workers from Britain's Granger Telecom were kidnapped and held for over two months before their severed heads were found in a sack on the side of the road. The militant Islamic group responsible for the deed had reportedly been receiving financial support from Osama bin Laden.[40]

Chechen separatists have a long-standing interest in acquiring nuclear weapons and material to use in their campaign against Russia. Aside from the submarine plot, Chechen militants made off with radioactive materials from a Grozny nuclear waste plant in January 2000; stole radioactive metals—possibly including some plutonium—from the Volgodonskaya nuclear power station in the southern region of Rostov between July 2001 and July 2002; and cased the railway system and special trains designed for shipping nuclear weapons across Russia.[41] Al Qaeda and other Islamic extremist organizations are among their largest sources of financial support. While the Chechens' target of choice for their first nuclear terrorist attack will surely be Moscow, that fact provides little comfort for Americans. If the Chechens are successful in acquiring several nuclear bombs, their Al Qaeda brethren could well find themselves the means to match their motivation.

THE A-TEAM OF ISLAMIC TERRORISTS

Before 9/11, the group responsible for the single deadliest terrorist attack on Americans in history was not Al Qaeda but Hezbollah. A violent Islamic terrorist organization, funded mainly by Syria and Iran, Hezbollah was responsible for the truck-bomb attack on the U.S. Marine barracks near the Beirut Airport on October 23, 1983, which killed 241 servicemen. Soon thereafter, President Ronald Reagan announced a "strategic redeployment" and withdrew U.S. troops from Lebanon. To this day, the group remains active and powerful in the Middle East. Deputy Secretary of State Richard Armitage has called Hezbollah the "A-team of terrorists," and CIA director Tenet testified in February 2003 that "as an organization with capability and worldwide presence," Hezbollah is Al Qaeda's "equal, if not a far more capable organization."[42]

Hezbollah's activities have been concentrated in Lebanon. The Israeli army had moved into southern Lebanon in 1982 to expel the Palestine Liberation Organization from the region and continued to occupy part of the country even after that goal was achieved. When Lebanon's Shiites realized that the Israelis intended to stay, they took up arms. Hezbollah launched a sustained guerrilla war against the Israelis, eventually forcing them to withdraw from Lebanon in May 2000. It was the first time that Arab arms had successfully ousted Israel from occupied territory anywhere in the Middle East, and Hezbollah attained heroic status throughout the Arab world. As Lebanon's president, Emile Lahoud, a Christian, told 60 Minutes: "If it wasn't for them, we couldn't have liberated our land. And because of that, we have big esteem for the Hezbollah movement."[43] Flush with victory, the group's leader, Sayyid Hassan Nasrallah, drew one conclusion: "This 'Israel' that owns nuclear weapons and the strongest air force in this region is more fragile than a spider web."[44]

Hezbollah's rhetoric, and its military success, raise the issue of whether the group might be motivated to carry out a nuclear terrorist attack against Tel Aviv or even New York, which Islamic fundamentalists have called "the Jewish capital of the world." Some analysts discount the possibility, observing a pattern of growing pragmatism as Hezbollah becomes further invested in day-to-day Lebanese politics.[45] (Hezbollah currently holds twelve seats in Lebanon's parliament.) Indeed, the group has turned part of its energies to providing social services to destitute Shiites in southern Lebanon, a "bombs and schools" strategy that has served other terrorist groups well, including the Irish Republican Army.

But as with Al Qaeda, it is important to examine carefully what Hezbollah says. The group's 1985 manifesto includes a section titled "The Necessity for the Destruction of Israel," which declares: "Our struggle will end only when this entity is obliterated. We recognize no treaty with it, no cease-fire, no peace agreements." Hezbollah's hatred of Israel extends to the United States: "We see in Israel the vanguard of the United States in our Islamic world."[46] Moreover, this rhetoric cannot be dismissed as out of date. As Nasrallah reiterated in 2003, "Death to America was, is, and will stay our slogan."[47] The CIA has concluded that Hezbollah "would likely react to an attack against it, Syria, or Iran with attacks against U.S. and Israeli targets worldwide."[48]

In 2002, Israeli security services foiled two attempts by Hezbollah to explode so-called mega-bombs, able to demolish office towers on the scale of the World Trade Center. One of these plots targeted the Azrieli Towers, two of Tel Aviv's tallest buildings, in what could have been a sequel to the attacks of 9/11. As Gal Luft, one of Israel's most thoughtful counterterrorism experts, has observed, it is only a matter of time before a "mega-attack" succeeds.[49]

Under what conditions might Hezbollah escalate to nuclear violence? One possibility involves the Iranian connection. In the early

1980s, Iran created Hezbollah as a proxy force against Israel, and it continues to give the group some $100 million a year. Iran also provides training, weapons, and explosives, as well as political, diplomatic, and organizational aid. With Iran actively building the infrastructure of a nuclear weapons program, its leaders fear that Israel could preemptively attack the facilities before they are completed, as it did in 1981 when Israeli aircraft bombed Saddam Hussein's nuclear reactor at Osirak. Iran has thought carefully about how it could deter such an attack. The Iranian defense minister warned in December 2003: "We will strike Israel with all weapons at our disposal if the Zionist regime ventures to do so."[50] If Hezbollah had a suitcase nuclear device and were able credibly to threaten Tel Aviv, would Israel be so quick to attack Iran's nuclear facilities?

Another possibility is that a splinter group from within Hezbollah could make the move toward nuclear terror. As the current leadership of Hezbollah becomes further entrenched in domestic Lebanese politics, the group's more militant operatives may well strike out on their own. Could a plausible threat to destroy Tel Aviv compel Israel to withdraw from the West Bank and Gaza or change its behavior?

Revenge against the United States for supporting Israel could also spur senseless destruction. For this purpose, Hezbollah might join forces with Al Qaeda, as it did in the 1996 attack on a U.S. military installation, the Khobar Towers, in Saudi Arabia. Hezbollah's security chief, Imad Mughniyah (believed to be behind the Marine barracks bombing in 1983 and the hijacking of TWA Flight 847 to Beirut in 1985), has reportedly met more than once with bin Laden and his top aides to establish their common goal of forcing the United States to withdraw from the Middle East. Ali Mohamed, a former U.S. Special Forces member who pled guilty to conspiring with bin Laden on the 1998 bombings of two American embassies in Africa, testified in October 2000, before a U.S. federal district court, that Hezbollah has provided Al Qaeda with explosives training and that he provided security for meetings between Mughniyah and bin

Laden.[51] If Hezbollah perceives U.S. policy as threatening its most vital interests, then it could begin to adopt Al Qaeda's more radical agenda. With its unrivaled technical terror expertise, Hezbollah would be well positioned to escalate to nuclear terrorism.

MUSHARRAF'S TIGHTROPE

Pakistan remains a source of nuclear worries for the United States, despite President Musharraf's declaration (within forty-eight hours of the 9/11 attacks) of "unstinted cooperation in the fight against terrorism." Despite strong domestic opposition, Musharraf imprisoned many known Al Qaeda sympathizers and demanded that the Taliban surrender Osama bin Laden. And yet Musharraf's about-face did not change the hearts and minds of the Pakistani people or the leadership of the country's key institutions. The uneasy contradiction of Musharraf's pro-American foreign policy and widespread anti-Americanism within Pakistan has forced him to walk a tightrope. On the one hand, he needs to pacify the Americans on whose financial support he depends. On the other hand, extremists are everywhere: in the *madrassas* (Islamic schools), in the intelligence services, in the military, and among the general public. With each day, he faces a growing threat of assassination or coup d'état.

In local elections held in October 2002, a coalition of fundamentalist parties was victorious and took over the government in the North-West Frontier Province. The group, known as Muttahida Majlis-e-Amal (MMA), offered a simple platform: pro-Taliban, anti-American, and against all Pakistani involvement in the war on terror. It is now the third largest party in Pakistan's national parliament, and controls the very region where the CIA believes Osama bin Laden, Ayman al-Zawahiri, and Mullah Muhammad Omar (the former Taliban leader of Afghanistan) are hiding. From its new position of strength, the MMA has spoken at length of the need to regain the honor that Pakistan has lost through its concessions to the

United States, and more recently to India, by whatever means necessary—an ominous threat, given the country's nuclear capability.

Musharraf's alignment with the United States has brought him into confrontation not just with the Pakistani people but with some of the most respected figures from the country's most powerful institutions. It is a widely held belief among Pakistan's scientific and military elite that Pakistan, as the home of the first Islamic bomb, has a duty to share its knowledge. General Hamid Gul, the former head of ISI, has been unrepentant in his belief that Osama bin Laden was not responsible for 9/11 and that it is Pakistan's duty to develop an Islamic nuclear infrastructure to protect Muslims in the future. In his own words, "We have the nuclear capability that can destroy Madras; surely the same missile can do the same to Tel Aviv. Washington cannot stop Muslim suicidal attacks. . . . Taliban are still alive and along with 'friends' they will continue the holy jihad against the U.S."[52] Just as troubling, in January 2004, the *New York Times* obtained a brochure advertising different types of nuclear technology available to other nations from the Khan Research Laboratories. The booklet, emblazoned with a Pakistani government stamp, was one of a batch that had been in circulation to the world's nuclear aspirants for several years. Not until the brochure was leaked to the press did Musharraf's government reluctantly call in Dr. Khan, who held the post of special adviser to the president, for questioning, leading very quickly to his arrest, confession, and pardon— another attempt by Musharraf to walk the line between addressing American security concerns and placating hard-line elements within his country.

Further revelations about the sale of nuclear materials and expertise to Iraq, Iran, Libya, and North Korea (Khan made thirteen visits to North Korea beginning in the 1990s)[53] have brought these ominous developments to a head. The nuclear sales took place either with Musharraf's approval or without his knowledge. It is unclear which scenario is worse. Musharraf has also made a deal with the Islamist parties to step down as head of the military by

December 2004 in exchange for a vote of confidence to serve out his presidential term until 2007, raising questions of whether he will be able to maintain control of the country without control of the Army. Musharraf's dilemma is compounded by the fact that he is now under American pressure to take a more conciliatory position on the Kashmir dispute with India, another political stand that contravenes public opinion in Pakistan.

Several terrorist organizations nominally focused on the Kashmir conflict are already operating beyond Musharraf's control. One such group, Jaish-e-Mohammed (JEM), has been linked to several major terror attacks, including the bombing of the Indian parliament in December 2001 and an attack in October 2000 on the local legislature in Indian-held Kashmir that killed thirty-eight people. JEM is a splinter group of an older jihadist organization, Harkat-ul-Mujahideen, with close ties to Osama bin Laden. JEM has ties to the Pakistani establishment as well: Brigadier Abdullah, the former head of the ISI's Kashmir department, is believed to have played a critical role in promoting JEM when it broke away from Harkat.[54] But JEM is hardly following orders from Islamabad. Pakistan officially banned the group in 2002 but has had limited success in rooting it out. American intelligence officials believe that JEM was behind two separate assassination attempts aimed at Musharraf in December 2003, including an attempt by two suicide bombers to ram pickup trucks filled with explosives into the president's motorcade on Christmas Day.[55]

Under these conditions, the emergence of a splinter group armed with nuclear expertise and access from within the Pakistani establishment looks increasingly feasible. We know that such a group would have the requisite organizational competence and nuclear know-how. But it now seems they also have a plausible purpose to pursue nuclear terrorism, either to express anger that Musharraf has become a puppet of the United States, to rid the country of the American infidel, or to answer bin Laden's call "to prepare as much force as possible to terrorize the enemies of God." Indeed, one can imagine elements

within the military or nuclear establishment proudly concluding that
they are the only ones who can carry out bin Laden's vision.

NOT ON ANYBODY'S RADAR SCREEN

We conclude this lineup of possible suspects with the countless
doomsday cults around the world, of which only a handful can be
considered dangerous. Few rival even the Branch Davidians, the
group headed by David Koresh that amassed a small arsenal before
meeting a fiery end in a standoff with federal officials in Waco,
Texas, in April 1993. Yet the inexorable spread of scientific knowledge, combined with a growing appeal of apocalyptic worldviews,
make it possible to imagine cults armed with weapons of mass
destruction.

Aum Shinrikyo, or Supreme Truth, offers the most chilling example of what a doomsday cult can achieve. Aum was founded in 1987
by Shoko Asahara, a blind former yoga teacher, and its members
were waiting for the end of the world, which Asahara prophesied
would come in the late 1990s through a nuclear apocalypse.[56] In a
bid to protect itself by overthrowing the Japanese government, the
cult actively recruited physicists, chemists, biologists, and engineers to build an astonishing arsenal. With its financial assets and a
technical knowledge base, Aum began experimenting with and producing chemical agents such as sarin, VX, phosgene, and sodium
cyanide, and biological weapons including anthrax, botulism, and
Q fever.[57]

Aum grabbed the world's attention on the morning of March 20,
1995, when its members carried pouches of sarin nerve gas onto
trains entering subway stations in central Tokyo. They placed the
pouches on the floor, pierced them, and fled. Soon commuters
began sweating, had difficulty breathing, and began vomiting. Those
closest to the pouches lost consciousness and collapsed into convul-
sions. Panic ensued as the trains continued on their way, creating

new victims at every stop. In the end, twelve people died and more than five thousand were injured.[58] Aum's larger goal—that the attack would destabilize the Japanese government—was not achieved, however.

As Japanese and American authorities began investigating the group in the wake of the attack, they discovered that Aum Shinrikyo owned a twelve-acre chemical weapons factory in Tokyo, had $1 billion in its bank accounts, operated a farm in Australia where it practiced gassing sheep, and claimed sixty thousand adherents worldwide. But as CIA officials told the Senate Government Affairs Permanent Subcommittee on Investigations, the name of the group did not appear on U.S. intelligence agencies' lists. They "simply were not on anybody's radar screen."[59] This ignorance was even more troubling when it became clear that Aum also had serious nuclear ambitions. The group's "construction minister," Kiyohide Hayakawa, was in charge of these efforts and had made numerous trips to Russia, where Aum had three times as many members as in Japan. While there, he successfully recruited physicists and engineers from the Kurchatov Institute. Documents seized from Hayakawa upon his arrest after the subway attack shed light on his other activities. One memo contained prices quoted for several nuclear warheads. Others showed how he spearheaded Aum's purchase of property in Australia that contained uranium deposits and how the group attempted to purchase mining licenses from the Australian government. Aum also imported a mechanical ditch digger and gasoline generators, rented heavy earthmoving equipment, and made plans to ship the uranium back to Japan for the development of nuclear weapons. In the United States, Aum purchased equipment that could likewise be used in the construction of a nuclear bomb. Hayakawa attempted to buy a Mark IVxp Interforometer from the Zygo Corporation in Connecticut, a laser system used for measuring flat and spherical surfaces. This equipment could have been used to measure the spherical surface of a fissile core used in nuclear weapons.[60]

Aum spent half a decade building weapons of mass destruction without arousing concern. Some analysts point to their lack of success in carrying out massively destructive attacks as proof that for a nonstate group, even one with Aum's financial and technical resources, such weapons are out of reach. Yet in the course of five years, Aum was able to produce a substantial chemical and biological weapons arsenal, and even though Asahara, Hayakawa, and other top members were jailed in Japan (Asahara was sentenced to death in February 2004), thousands of the group's adherents drifted back into other lives. The fate of many of those with specialized weapons knowledge is unknown.

WHAT ALL OF these groups have in common is a hatred of the United States or the West, along with sophisticated organizational structures and access to technical know-how. Though some observers may argue that a shift in American policies or activities might stem this hatred and thus diminish the threat, the uncomfortable fact is that being the world's only superpower is inevitably going to breed resentment of one form or another—and it is impossible to mollify every single group. The challenge to the United States is to prevent these organizations from acquiring the means to threaten us with a nuclear attack. Focusing our minds on that task will require a newfound appreciation and understanding of the unique destructive power of these terrible weapons.

2

WHAT NUCLEAR WEAPONS COULD TERRORISTS USE?

> A blinding flash swept across my eyes. In a fraction of a
> second, I looked out the window towards the garden as a
> huge band of light fell from the sky down to the trees. A
> thunderous explosion gripped the earth and shook it.
> There seemed no alternative to death as the earth heaved.
>
> A SURVIVOR OF HIROSHIMA, 1945

IN MAY 1997, during a private meeting with a delegation of American members of Congress, General Alexander Lebed, the national security adviser to Russian president Boris Yeltsin, acknowledged that the Russian government could not account for eighty-four one-kiloton Soviet suitcase nuclear devices. That revelation ignited a firestorm of controversy that continues to this day. Four months after his meeting with the members of Congress, Lebed was interviewed on *60 Minutes*, where the correspondent Steve Kroft grilled him about the missing weapons:[1]

KROFT: Are you confident that all of these weapons are secure and accounted for?

GENERAL LEBED: Not at all. Not at all.

KROFT: How easy would it be to steal one?

GENERAL LEBED: It's suitcase-sized.

KROFT: You could put it in a suitcase and carry it off?

GENERAL LEBED: It is made in the form of a suitcase. It is a suitcase, actually. You could carry it. You can put it into another suitcase if you want to.

KROFT: But it's already a suitcase.

GENERAL LEBED: Yes.

KROFT: I could walk down the streets of Moscow or Washington or New York, and people would think I'm carrying a suitcase?

GENERAL LEBED: Yes, indeed.

KROFT: How easy is it to detonate?

GENERAL LEBED: It would take twenty, thirty minutes to prepare.

KROFT: But you don't need secret codes from the Kremlin or anything like that.

GENERAL LEBED: No.

KROFT: You are saying that there are a significant number that are missing and unaccounted for?

GENERAL LEBED: Yes, there is. More than one hundred.

KROFT: Where are they?

GENERAL LEBED: Somewhere in Georgia, somewhere in Ukraine, somewhere in the Baltic countries? Perhaps some of them are even outside those countries? One person is capable of triggering this nuclear weapon—one person.

KROFT: So you're saying these weapons are no longer under the control of the Russian military.

GENERAL LEBED: I'm saying that more than 100 weapons out of the supposed number of 250 are not under the control of the armed forces of Russia. I don't know their location. I don't know whether they have been destroyed or whether they are stored or whether they've been sold or stolen. I don't know.

The Russian government reacted to Lebed's claim in classic Soviet style, combining wholesale denial with efforts to discredit the messenger. In the days and months that followed, official government spokesmen claimed that (1) no such weapons ever existed; (2) any weapons of this sort had been destroyed; (3) all Russian weapons were secure and properly accounted for; and (4) it was inconceivable that the Russian government could lose a nuclear weapon. Assertions to the contrary, or even questions about the matter, were dismissed as anti-Russian propaganda or efforts at personal aggrandizement.

U.S. government sources have never succeeded in getting to the bottom of this matter. Unquestionably, the U.S. nuclear arsenal has included Special Atomic Demolition Munitions (SADMs) that could be carried by one person in a backpack. Since Soviet nuclear programs followed America's lead—frequently using designs stolen from the U.S. nuclear designers by spies—it is likely that they possessed similar weapons. Moreover, Soviet war-fighting strategies included plans in which small nuclear devices would have been the weapon of choice. In the hours before Soviet troops would launch an attack on NATO forces in Europe, Special Forces units called Spetsnaz would blow up headquarters, communications, and political leaders behind enemy lines. KGB Special Forces, like the Alpha Group, had also prepared to conduct preemptive attacks on the U.S. president and other key targets in the American homeland if war was imminent.

The best evidence against Lebed's claim is the fact that no suitcase nuclear devices have been detonated, and none have been discovered to date. The best evidence for his claims combines the logic of Soviet war planning and the specificity of a number of the official denials. For example, just after Lebed's disclosure, the Operations

Directorate of the GRU (Russian military intelligence) denied that "any 60 x 40 x 20 briefcases containing nuclear charges" existed. Americans can imagine a cagey spokesperson defending the truth of this statement with an explanation that it depends on the meaning of the word "existed"—or the fact that the weapons in question were a centimeter larger or smaller. In 2001, General Igor Valynkin, the commander of the organization that has physical control of all Ministry of Defense nuclear weapons, confirmed that the "RA-115" serial number cited by Lebed in the debate about suitcase nuclear weapons referred to a type of munition that had been in the Soviet arsenal, but, he said, it had been eliminated.[2]

The bottom line today is summarized best by an American intelligence officer who spent many years tracking this issue. In his words: "We don't know with any confidence what has gone missing, and neither do they."[3]

THE NUCLEAR INVENTORY

Technically, it is possible for terrorists to employ any of several hundred models of some twenty thousand nuclear bombs in the global inventory.[4] Realistically, nuclear terrorists are most likely to use a small weapon stolen from the arsenal of one of the nuclear states, or an elementary nuclear bomb made from stolen highly enriched uranium (HEU) or plutonium. Where terrorists might acquire weapons or materials is examined in chapter 3, and how they might use the fissile material to construct an elementary nuclear bomb is explored in chapter 4. Here we examine the specific characteristics of the nuclear weapons that terrorists might wield and the consequences of their use.

A nuclear weapon is, in essence, a device that uses atomic fission to create a huge explosion. Fission occurs when an atom is split into two or more parts, releasing energy and neutrons. These neutrons then split more atoms, which release more energy, in a cascade called a chain reaction. To achieve a nuclear explosion, a minimum of thirty-five pounds of HEU, or nine pounds of plutonium, is required. Fissile material—HEU or plutonium—is thus the essential building block for a nuclear weapon. Without it, there can be no nuclear explosion.

When U.S. and British scientists exploded the first nuclear bomb, at Alamogordo, New Mexico, in 1945, they multiplied mankind's destructive power a million-fold. This phenomenon so far exceeded anything previously known in human experience that it required a new language that invented new metrics. Explosions from nuclear bombs are thus measured in kilotons, which are equivalent to the destructive power of thousands of tons of dynamite or TNT. A megaton is equivalent to one million tons of TNT. A single stick of dynamite weighs five pounds; a kiloton thus equals 400,000 sticks of TNT. Detonated in an SUV, one stick of dynamite will raise the air temperature to 2,700 degrees Fahrenheit, torching every passenger in an instant. The energy released is the equivalent of sitting in a car at a red light and being struck by a ten-ton truck traveling sixty-five miles per hour.[5]

The Hiroshima blast measured twelve kilotons, just slightly larger than the ten-kiloton weapon that Dragonfire reported was allegedly in New York on October 11, 2001. Packed tightly in a column one foot square, twelve thousand tons of dynamite (4.8 million sticks) would reach a height of two and a half miles. Superpower Cold War arsenals also include thermonuclear bombs, or hydrogen bombs, whose explosive power is thousands of times greater than the Hiroshima bomb. Indeed, the arsenals of both the United States and Russia today contain individual weapons that have more destructive power than all the nonnuclear bombs dropped by all the air forces of the world in all the wars in human history, including the recent bombing campaign against Iraq. These modern warheads sit atop intercontinental ballistic missiles (ICBMs) capable of deliver-

Davy Crockett tactical nuclear weapon. Note the nuclear warhead at the end of the silver barrel.

ing their payload in less than an hour to targets thousands of miles away. Standing six feet high, some of these weigh as little as eight hundred pounds and can be carried in the back of a pickup truck.[6]

More likely to be of interest to terrorists, however, are the tactical nuclear weapons designed to be delivered, in many cases, by a single soldier on battlefields in Europe and Asia. The American version of a suitcase nuclear device was the 60-pound W-54 SADM, crafted to be parachuted into enemy territory with Navy SEALs, where it would be detonated to destroy bridges, tunnels, command posts, and ports.[7] To halt a Soviet blitzkrieg into Western Europe, the United States also deployed more than two thousand Davy Crockett warheads, which could be fired from a 120- or 155-millimeter recoilless rifle mounted onto a jeep.[8] Weighing only 50 pounds, the Davy Crockett's 0.25-kiloton yield made it the baby of the U.S. nuclear family, though still a baby equivalent to 100,000 sticks of dynamite.[9] Atomic artillery shells like the W-82 are three feet long, six inches wide, and weigh 95 pounds. The 120-pound W-48 is two feet long and can be carried in a backpack.[10] In Europe and elsewhere, the United States also deployed thousands of atomic demolition munitions, with yields of 1 to 15 kilotons, for use in destroying airfields, communications facilities, and petroleum depots.[11]

Moscow's arsenal of tactical nuclear weapons was even larger and much more widely dispersed. These bombs included suitcase nuclear devices; backpack weapons, such as the Army's RA-155 and Navy's RA-115-01 (to be used underwater), which weighed as little as 65 pounds and could be detonated by one solider in ten minutes, producing a yield of between 0.5 and 2 kilotons;[12] atomic land mines weighing 200 pounds; air-defense warheads; and 120-pound atomic artillery shells designed to destroy an enemy force at a two-hundred-mile range.[13] The public museum at Russia's largest nuclear weapons design center, Chelyabinsk-70, displays what it claims is the world's smallest nuclear weapon, an artillery shell eighteen inches long and six inches in diameter.[14] A picture of this mini-nuke, standing next to the largest bomb in history, the Tsar Bomba (King of Bombs), a 100-megaton weapon, can be viewed on the Web.[15] Soviet military forces deployed 22,000 tactical nuclear warheads as part of the standard equipment of Red Army units stationed across the former Soviet Union, as well as in East Germany, Hungary, Poland, Bulgaria, and Czechoslovakia.[16] While each weapon in the American tactical nuclear force was identified by a unique serial number, Russia's tactical arsenal was produced by type, without identification numbers on individual weapons.[17]

LEST WE FORGET

In the six decades since their invention, nuclear weapons have been used against humans only twice, at Hiroshima and Nagasaki, in 1945. These cities are now almost mythological symbols of the nuclear age. Yet firsthand accounts by victims of what they saw and suffered speak to us today:

> When the blow came, I closed my eyes but I could still feel the extreme heat. It was like being roasted alive many times over. I noticed that the side of my body was very hot. It was on fire. I tried to put it out, but it would not go out so easily. You could hardly recognize me, my lips and my face were all popped up and I had to force my eyes open with my fingers in order to see.

> The blast was so intense it felt like hundreds of needles were stabbing me all at once.

> People had no hair because their hair was burned, and at a glance you couldn't tell whether you were looking at them from in front or in back.

> There were lots of naked people who were so badly burned that the skin of their whole body was hanging from them like rags.

> A tremendous blast wave struck our ship. A giant ball of fire rose as though from the bowels of the earth, belching forth enormous white smoke rings. Next we saw a giant pillar of purple fire, ten thousand feet high, shooting skyward with enormous speed. Awestruck, we watched it shoot upward like a meteor coming from the earth instead of from outer space. It was a living thing, a new species of being, born right before our incredulous eyes. It was a living totem pole, carved with many grotesque masks grimacing at the earth.

I looked at the face to see if I knew her. It was a woman of about forty. A gold tooth gleamed in the wide open mouth. A handful of singed hair hung down from the left temple over her cheek, dangling in her mouth. Her eyelids were drawn up, showing black holes where the eyes had been burned out.[18]

After the fires of Hiroshima subsided, a history professor climbed a hill on the southern edge of the city and described what he saw looking down on the ruins: "That experience, looking down and finding nothing left of Hiroshima—was so shocking that I simply can't express what I felt. Hiroshima didn't exist—that was mainly what I saw—Hiroshima just didn't exist."[19] Inspecting Nagasaki one month after the event, a U.S. naval officer reported: "The general impression is one of deadness, the absolute essence of death in the sense of finality without hope of resurrection. Like the ancient Sodom and Gomorrah, its site has been sown with salt and ichabod is written over its gates."[20] Hiroshima, a city with a population equivalent to that of Sacramento, California, lost more than one-half of its 400,000 citizens within five years from the nuclear blast. In Nagasaki, 140,000 died.[21]

All of us have seen photographs or films of nuclear explosions. Eyewitnesses to this phenomenon, however, never forget. The first nuclear explosion at Alamogordo, on July 16, 1945, created something new under the sun. Watching that event, J. Robert Oppenheimer, the head of the Manhattan Project, was speechless. Then from some distant recess of his memory, he recalled a line from the Hindu scripture, the Bhagavad Gita: "Now I am become Death, the destroyer of worlds."

The principal consequences of a nuclear explosion are heat, blast, and radiation. Because light travels faster than sound, thousands of victims of Hiroshima and Nagasaki were incinerated before they could hear what killed them. At ground zero, the temperature spikes to more than 10 million degrees Fahrenheit, vaporizing the bomb's content, metal casing, and all surrounding structures out to a quarter mile. As the fireball expands, its temperature drops to that of the surface of the sun, 13,500 degrees Fahrenheit, scorching anything in its path.[22] Birds ignite in midair. Everyone within a half mile of the blast is scorched to blackened char.[23]

Some burn victims who survive never see again. As a Japanese optometrist who treated flash blindness victims in Hiroshima observed: "Those who watched the plane had their eye grounds burned. The flash of light apparently went through the pupils and left them with a blind area in the central portion of their visual fields. Most of the eye-ground burns are third degree, so cure is impossible."[24] The expanding shock wave sucks oxygen into the fire, propelling it from the epicenter of the explosion. As the flames spread, gas lines, heating fuel, gasoline, and other combustibles ignite a ring of secondary fires. But most within this ring will be killed not by fire but by intensive asphyxiation and lung burns or by overpressure from the blast itself. Ordinarily our bodies experience 14.7 pounds per square inch of atmospheric pressure; a ten-kiloton bomb creates overpressure twice the normal level over a quarter-mile diameter from the blast, collapsing human bodies. The over-pressure also flattens buildings, hurls objects, and levels houses up to a mile from the epicenter.[25]

Radiation from a nuclear bomb keeps on killing in the years following the explosion and beyond to future generations. Effects of radiation on human beings are measured in millirems (abbreviated MREM). A five-hour airplane ride delivers 3 MREM to each passenger; a chest X-ray, 10 MREM.[26] In a ten-kiloton explosion, a dose of 10,000,000 MREM of radiation kills every human being within one-half mile from ground zero. People three-quarters of a mile away receive a 1,000,000 MREM dose, meaning a certain death within days. Farther out, 500,000 MREM doses kill half of those exposed; 100,000 MREM kill up to 5 percent.[27] One in a hundred people exposed to as little as 12,500 MREM will develop cancer.[28]

Following a nuclear explosion, airborne poisons fall like black rain around the region and on communities downwind. At Hiroshima, the entire downtown was contaminated from radioactive fallout, rendering it uninhabitable for many years. Fallout from American and Soviet atmospheric nuclear tests during the 1950s and 1960s can still be detected today.[29] According to an analysis of government studies by the Institute for Energy and Environmental Research, an estimated eighty thousand people who lived in or were born in the United States between the years 1951 and 2000 will contract cancer as a direct result of the fallout caused by atmospheric nuclear weapons testing.[30] Radiation from a nuclear explosion also transmits genetic defects to future generations. In the esteemed journal *Science,* a research team led by Yuri Dubrova found that more than half of all children of parents exposed to Soviet nuclear tests between 1949 and 1956 have damaged genetic material.[31]

Perhaps because the bomb has not been used in war for almost sixty years, the catalog of horrors that people will suffer from a nuclear explosion seems to have been forgotten. Some policy makers and even military officials talk as if nuclear weapons were just another option in the toolbox. Graphic vignettes of the effects of nuclear weapons shock our consciousness and force us to face the horrifying fact that if even a small nuclear weapon was detonated in any city in the United States, it would cause suffering and devastation far beyond anything we can imagine, including the terror attacks of 9/11.

ACCIDENTS WAITING TO HAPPEN

Nuclear weapons occupy the top of the pyramid of threats, but as we all learned on 9/11, even the everyday instruments of modern life (like airplanes) can be turned into weapons. High on the list of potential dangers are the nation's nuclear power plants. The prospect of a terrorist crashing an airplane into a nuclear plant or detonating a powerful truck bomb next to a vulnerable area is among many people's worst nightmares.

Nuclear plants have long been the focus of wariness, especially after the frightening incidents at Three Mile Island and Chernobyl. On March 28, 1979, Americans faced the prospect of a nuclear reactor meltdown at the Three Mile Island power plant in Pennsylvania. A combination of technical and human error caused America's worst nuclear accident. Failure of a valve that drained water from the core went unnoticed by the technicians on duty, who turned off the emergency cooling pumps, which in turn led the reactor to overheat. By the time the operators noticed the problem, the core was less than an hour from complete meltdown. That would have meant a breach of the concrete walls around a container building and the release of massive amounts of radiation into the environment.[32] Fortunately, the actual release of radiation was small, exposing two million people in the area to only one MREM.[33] Nonetheless, during the crisis, hundreds of thousands of residents from surrounding areas fled for safer ground.

Much more deadly was the explosion at Reactor Unit 4 at the Chernobyl nuclear power plant in Ukraine on April 26, 1986. The 1,000-ton steel and concrete roof capping the reactor building blew off, temperatures inside rose to 3,632 degrees Fahrenheit, and 50 tons of radioactive material began spewing into the air. For twelve days, while military helicopters flew overhead dropping sand, lead, and boron onto the burning reactor, valiant firefighters on the ground waged a suicidal battle to put out the flames, even as the plant spread radioactive debris across wide swaths of the Soviet Union. Air currents carried fallout across the Baltic states into Sweden, Norway, Finland, and other parts of eastern and central Europe. Polish authorities banned the sale of milk; in Austria the government advised pregnant women and children to stay indoors; and many Western Europeans refused to eat fruit and vegetables grown in areas clouded by the plume.

This disaster killed six thousand people directly and continues to claim thousands of additional victims annually through cancer.[34] An area the size of Kentucky, covering territory in Ukraine, Russia, and

Belarus, is contaminated with enough cesium-137 to warrant regular cancer examinations.[35] The eighteen square miles around the plant have been designated an "exclusion zone" from which everyone was evacuated and, to this day, no one has been allowed to return.

Chernobyl and Three Mile Island were accidents. Accidents happen. Thus nuclear power plants are designed with multiple safeguards—what is called a "belt-and-suspenders" approach. Redundant safety systems ensure that even extreme cases of multiple failures will not cause a meltdown of the core or any other catastrophic release of radiation. When these reactors and safety systems were designed, however, experts focused on "normal" failures, not intentional sabotage or attack.

Before 9/11, few considered the possibility that a jetliner could crash into a nuclear reactor. In a dispute about a proposed plutonium plant on the Savannah River, a group called Georgians against Nuclear Energy (GANE) argued that the risks of a "malevolent act" had not been taken into account in designing the facility. The Nuclear Regulatory Commission (NRC) responded that "federal agencies need only address reasonably foreseeable environmental impacts" and that "GANE does not establish that terrorist acts . . . fall within the realm of 'reasonably foreseeable' events." After the shock of 9/11, a commission spokesman reversed course, confessing, "I'd like to tell you that everything's going to be okay, but I can't do that."[36] Power plants are designed to withstand earthquakes, tornadoes, and other natural disasters but, according to the NRC, none of the 103 operating U.S. nuclear reactors was designed to withstand the impact of a Boeing 767 jetliner. Twenty-one of these reactors are located within five miles of an airport.

The pools of water where spent nuclear fuel is stored present an even softer target than the thick containment domes. Simply draining the water from the pools can lead to combustion of the spent fuel. The Union of Concerned Scientists, using deliberately provocative language, calls the storage pools "Kmarts without neon" for terrorists.

According to an authoritative report from the Brookhaven National Laboratory, a severe release from such a pool could cause as many as 28,000 cancer fatalities and $59 billion in damage, and render about 188 square miles of land unfit for habitation.[37] And that's just from one attack.

A recent report on security at the Indian Point nuclear power plant, located twenty miles north of New York City, highlights other vulnerabilities as well. Keith Logan, a former investigator for the NRC, found that only 19 percent of security officers at Indian Point believed they could adequately defend the plant against a terrorist attack and that only half the security force was physically fit enough to thwart terrorists. Moreover, critical equipment, such as alarms and surveillance systems, was found to be defective.[38] In the words of Senator Charles E. Schumer of New York, "Security at Indian Point has more holes than Swiss cheese."[39] While the official evacuation plan covers only the surrounding communities, in the case of a Chernobyl-like release of radiation, most of New York City would empty out—a challenge itself, given the limited exit points at bridges and tunnels. Iodine pills, useful in preventing thyroid cancer caused by radioactive elements found in abundance in nuclear power plants, have been distributed only to those local residents living within ten miles of the plant.[40]

DIRTY POOL

Just before Christmas 2003, the U.S. government raised the national threat level from yellow (elevated) to orange (high). Media and public attention, which focused on stories of Al Qaeda plots to hijack passenger planes, led to several canceled transatlantic flights. Out of public view, however, scientists from the Department of Energy were deployed to cities across the United States, armed with radiation detectors. Walking the streets of New York, Washington, Baltimore, Las Vegas, and Los Angeles, these nuclear sleuths carried briefcases, golf bags, and backpacks filled with equipment designed to register the slightest spike in unnatural radiation levels. Fortunately, only a homeless man's cigar-size radium pellet, found in the garbage and kept as a charm, set off alarms. The immediate threat passed and the alert level was eventually lowered to yellow, but the fear of a dirty bomb attack did not disappear.[41]

Dirty bombs, which experts call radiological dispersal devices, are mechanisms designed to scatter radioactive material without triggering a nuclear explosion. Radiation bombs can take many forms—from sticks of dynamite packed in a briefcase with cesium to a fertilizer-based truck bomb wrapped in cobalt. Upon detonation, the radioactive material is pulverized and spewed into the environment. If it is exploded in the open air, tens or hundreds of square miles can be contaminated by radioactive matter. The amount and type of radioactive material used will determine the number of casualties, the extent of evacuations, and the area of contamination. Material such as cesium, which emits gamma rays (a form of electromagnetic radiation similar to X-rays), can cause tissue damage and radiation poisoning to those exposed to intense radiation close to the point of detonation. Those at a distance can be exposed to long-term, low levels of gamma rays, leading to cancer. Plutonium and other materials emitting alpha particles (which are the nuclei of helium atoms) are dangerous only when ingested into the body. They cannot pass through clothes or skin, but even small amounts, once inside the lungs or stomach, will cause cancer; larger doses will bring about radiation poisoning and death.

In March 2002, an industrial gauge with a significant quantity of cesium was found at a scrap-metal plant near Hertford, North Carolina. The Federation of American Scientists examined the consequences of detonating a radiation bomb constructed with that cesium and ten pounds (two sticks) of TNT in Washington. The initial radioactive cloud, the group found, would not require immediate evacuation. But if weather conditions were favorable for the attackers, a one-mile-long area of the city would be polluted to levels that would require its evacuation until possible decontamination. If the bomb was exploded at the National Gallery of Art, the affected area could include the Capitol and the Supreme Court building. In another scenario, the federation examined the consequences of a radiation bomb built with cobalt exploding in Manhattan. According to their calculations, that case required the evacuation of the entire borough for years, as one in every one hundred people would develop cancer due to the residual radiation. Decontamination of such an extensive urban landscape has never been attempted, so massive demolition and resettlement would be required.[42]

Though a radiation bomb attack has never occurred, an event from September 1987 offers insight into potential consequences. Two men scavenging for scrap metal broke into an abandoned cancer clinic in Goiânia, Brazil, and stole a medical device containing nineteen grams of cesium-137. After puncturing the protective capsule that contained the cesium, the men sold the device to a junkyard. Fascinated by the "glowing blue powder," the junkyard operator showed off the material to family and friends. They, in turn, took samples into their homes, on public transportation, and even sprinkled it on their bodies. Soon, people began falling violently ill. After diagnosing radiation sickness, the Brazilian authorities realized the enormity of the contamination and began monitoring over 112,000 people for radiation exposure. A total of 249 people were identified as contaminated, 151 both internally and externally, and 49 were admitted to hospitals. The internally contaminated were themselves radioactive, thereby complicating their treatment. In the end, 28 people suffered radiation burns and 5 people died. Because of the wide dispersal of the radioactive material, buildings were destroyed and topsoil removed. A total of 124,000 cubic feet of radioactive waste was collected and trucked to a temporary disposal site.[43]

The anthrax attacks of October 2001 offer further clues about some likely effects of a radiation bomb. Letters containing finely milled anthrax spores were sent to network news anchors Tom

Brokaw and Dan Rather, to a tabloid newspaper in Florida, and to the offices of Senators Tom Daschle and Patrick J. Leahy. In the Hart Office Building, where Senator Daschle's office was located, anthrax spores spread through the ventilation system, contaminating the entire building. Three months later, after extensive disinfection with chlorine dioxide gas, at a cost of $20 million, the building finally reopened. But it took over two years to reopen the post office facility that had handled the anthrax letters destined for Capitol Hill. Upon hearing the news of anthrax-laced letters, thousands began taking ciprofloxacin (the antibiotic used to treat anthrax infection), though they may have never come anywhere near anthrax spores. In cities across the country, false alarms, white-powder hoaxes, and runs on the antibiotic multiplied. By January 2002, more than twelve hundred samples of suspected anthrax had been sent to the Indiana State Department of Health alone.[44] Many people ironed and microwaved incoming envelopes, hoping to kill any anthrax spores they feared clung to their mail.

After a radiation bomb attack, the panic will likely be even more widespread. Fear of radiation exposure and resulting cancers will prompt many people to flee their homes. It has been estimated that more immediate deaths will occur in traffic accidents during the rush to escape the radiation than from the radiation itself. If large amounts or especially strong radioactive material is used, those closest to the bomb will require immediate medical attention to treat radiation poisoning. In the long term, entire city blocks will have to be decontaminated. Radioactive dust particles will require vacuuming or pressure washing to remove. Sandblasting and acid will be needed where radioactive material has penetrated deeply. Concrete, asphalt, vegetation, and topsoil might have to be carted away and disposed of safely. Thousands of people will have to relocate, and some might never be allowed to return.

Terrorists hoping to inflict nuclear terror may choose to detonate a radiation bomb in a metropolitan area or attack a nuclear power plant. But those looking to kill as many as they can and wreak unprecedented destruction will seek nuclear weapons. No other weapon of mass destruction, whether chemical or biological, sits in the same class. Thousands of nuclear weapons and potential nuclear weapons remain vulnerable at poorly secured storage sites throughout Russia. Any one of these weapons could kill hundreds of thousands of people immediately. Unfortunately, Russia is not the only place where terrorists can obtain a nuclear bomb.

3

WHERE COULD TERRORISTS
ACQUIRE A NUCLEAR BOMB?

If the Soviets do an excellent job at retaining control over
their stockpile of nuclear weapons—let's assume they've
got 25,000 to 30,000; that's a ballpark figure—and they are
99 percent successful, that would mean you could still
have as many as 250 that they were not able to control.

DICK CHENEY,
Meet the Press, December 1991

IN OCTOBER 2003, American intelligence agents boarded a cargo ship
en route from Malaysia to Libya via Dubai. As they examined the
containers in the hull, they located a number of large boxes from
Malaysia crudely labeled "USED MACHINERY." Inside they found
thousands of centrifuge parts for enriching uranium. The buyer was
Libya's Muammar el-Qaddafi; the seller, Dr. A. Q. Khan, the developer of Pakistan's nuclear bomb.

The interception of this one shipment uncovered the dark under-
side of globalization—a worldwide, decades-old black market in
nuclear materials, designs, and technologies that the head of the
International Atomic Energy Agency (IAEA) has called a "Wal-
Mart of private-sector proliferation."[1] The catalog of products offered
by Khan's network included the following:

- A comprehensive "starter kit" for Iraq's uranium enrichment program
- Rudimentary P-1 centrifuge blueprints that Khan had stolen from the European nuclear consortium Urenco, where he worked in the 1970s
- More sophisticated P-2 centrifuge designs
- Necessary components to build P-2 centrifuges
- State-of-the-art P-3 centrifuges
- Blueprints of Chinese-designed nuclear warheads
- Nearly two tons of uranium hexafluoride, enough for one nuclear bomb if sufficiently enriched
- Contact information for consulting services in assembly and repair

The range of customers was even more frightening. In late 1990, on the eve of the Gulf War, one of Khan's intermediaries offered Saddam Hussein centrifuges and designs to jump-start his ongoing nuclear program. Suspecting a sting operation, Iraq turned it down. Libya purchased both P-1 and P-2 centrifuge designs; parts for ten thousand advanced centrifuges—enough to make ten bombs a year; Chinese warhead blueprints; and uranium hexafluoride gas. Iran bought P-1 and P-2 centrifuge designs and parts as well, while North Korea traded its own ballistic missile technology in exchange for what were most likely Pakistan's P-3 designs.[2]

Khan himself, a Pakistani national hero, led the operation. George W. Bush has since described him as the "director of the network, its leading scientific mind, as well as its primary salesman."[3] In his retirement, while serving as an honorary government adviser and founding charities, Khan simultaneously established the greatest nuclear export business the world has ever seen, amassing a personal fortune of tens of millions of dollars in cash and real estate holdings. B. S. A. Tahir, a Sri Lankan national based in Dubai, was the network's "chief lieutenant and money launderer."[4] Tahir was a top executive at a successful engineering company that manufactured

parts in Malaysia, providing the perfect cover for producing centrifuge components and shipping them to Khan's customers around
the world. Other middlemen came from Turkey, Switzerland, and
Britain, some of whom were unaware of their involvement in the
network. As one investigator explained, "A Swedish firm sold vac-
uum pumps to a man in Switzerland that it thought were for Coca-
Cola. Then the Swiss sent them to Dubai, which sent them on to
Libya."[5]

In January 2004, the *New York Times* published excerpts of a
glossy sales brochure from Pakistan's Khan Research Laboratories,
offering Khan's personal consulting on a range of nuclear services.
Stamped with a "Government of Pakistan" seal, the cover of the
brochure superimposed a photograph of Khan over a mushroom
cloud. Hundreds of copies of the booklet were delivered around
the world. Whether the brochure, or the products it listed, found
their way into terrorists' hands remains an open question.[6]

Khan himself quickly sank from a national hero to an international disgrace. He was removed from his position as scientific
adviser to the prime minister, a largely honorary post given to him
after his retirement as head of Khan Research Laboratories in
2001. Then in February 2004, after enduring weeks under house
arrest, he presented a plea for clemency directly to President
Musharraf and delivered an official televised apology to his country
on Pakistan's state-run television. Khan not only accepted full responsibility for his proliferation network; he also absolved Musharraf's
government of any potential complicity in the scandal, saying,
"There was never ever any kind of authorization for these activities
by the government." But most analysts believed that in order to
avoid prison, Khan essentially fell on his sword, taking the blame
for a program in which many figures participated. As one Pakistani
cabinet minister told the *Washington Post*, "[Khan] has made tons
of money, but no one in the government believes that he was the
only one to milk the program."[7]

While the scope and audacity of Khan's black-market dealings were unprecedented, the problem of loose nuclear weapons or materials had long been familiar to American officials. In June 1993, Bill Courtney, the U.S. ambassador to Kazakhstan, received an urgent phone call from the national security adviser to the president of that newly independent former Soviet republic. The official informed Courtney that Kazakh security officers had recently discovered a warehouse full of nuclear material that they believed could be used to make nuclear weapons.

Courtney immediately grasped the significance of the report. He knew that several thousand nuclear weapons and potential nuclear weapons remained at various places in Kazakhstan. At Semi-palatinsk, in the eastern part of the country, the Soviet Union had conducted 468 nuclear and thermonuclear test explosions, and at the Derzhavinsk and Zhangiz-Tobe bases in northeast Kazakhstan, 1,410 nuclear warheads from the former Soviet strategic arsenal remained on alert atop 104 SS-18 ICBMs.[8] Moreover, Courtney had learned from earlier U.S. intelligence briefings that a number of eager buyers were on the hunt, including Saddam Hussein's operatives, who had successfully purchased Scud missiles and taken them to Iraq; Iranian agents, who had established an import-export business for cover in Almaty, then the capital of Kazakhstan; and Chechen militants seeking nuclear weapons for a then-obscure terrorist group run by a Saudi named Osama bin Laden.[9]

Courtney called Washington. Within days, experts arrived from the Department of Energy (DOE) and from U.S. weapons labs. In an abandoned building at the Ulba Metallurgy Plant in the mountain town of Ust-Kamenogorsk, they found 1,278 pounds of highly enriched uranium. With that material, terrorists could make an arsenal of twenty crude nuclear weapons. This HEU had been produced as fuel for nuclear-powered submarines of the Soviet Navy. But when the Soviet Ministry of Atomic Energy (Minatom) closed the production line in the late 1980s, the facility, including the material, was essentially abandoned. Security at the warehouse consisted of a single padlock, which DOE technicians easily removed with an ordinary bolt cutter.

When told of this discovery, Minatom rejected all efforts to return the material. In fact, Minatom denied that the material in question could be HEU, or that it could have belonged to the former Soviet ministry. The U.S. government then agreed to remove it, paying Kazakhstan about $1 million per potential weapon. In a secret operation code-named Sapphire, the material was packed into 1,300 steel canisters, flown by American C-5 transport planes to Dover Air Force base in Delaware, and driven in unmarked DOE tractor-trailers to the Oak Ridge National Laboratory in Tennessee. When experts examined the purchase, they found even more of the material than they had expected—enough to make two additional nuclear weapons.

Two years earlier in Podolsk, a city twenty-five miles south of Moscow, Yuri Smirnov was arrested for stealing HEU from the Luch Scientific Production plant, which produced nuclear reactors for the Soviet Union's space program. Police recovered three pounds of bomb-usable HEU from the balcony of Smirnov's fourth-floor apartment, where he had stored it in a metal container. Between May and September 1992, while his fellow employees took smoking breaks, he filled a fifty-gram vial with HEU powder. Like many Soviet enterprises, Luch had accepted a certain percentage of "irretrievable losses" when accounting for nuclear materials each month, so the small amounts Smirnov took each day were never detected. Employees did not pass through radiation detectors or undergo physical inspections as they entered or exited the plant. Smirnov had no problem filling his vial, wrapping it in a rag, and carrying it out in a duffel bag.

In a rare interview with a convicted nuclear thief, journalists from the PBS program *Frontline* asked Smirnov why he did it. Though he expressed mild regrets, he defended his actions as a rational response to difficult circumstances. According to his story, he was adequately paid for his work before Russia's currency reform of 1992. But when Soviet price controls were abolished in that year, inflation skyrocketed at a rate of over 2,000 percent. He could no longer make ends meet, much less replace the decrepit, forty-year-old refrigerator and stove in his apartment. "I just needed to live through that time when I wanted to buy something but couldn't because of inflation," he explained. After reading an article in the newspaper about someone stealing uranium from another Minatom plant, he realized that the material he worked with must have some value, so he began taking home a vial of HEU a day. "I thought the maximum I'd make was five hundred dollars," he said. "But that was my salary for two years."[10]

Five months into the project, he decided that he had enough material to take the train to Moscow to see if he could find a buyer. At the Podolsk train station, he happened upon one of his neighbors who was sharing a bottle of vodka with friends. As the group waited on the train platform, the police, acting on an anonymous tip, arrested them all for stealing batteries from the factory where they worked. Smirnov was swept up with the group, even though he was not involved in the battery scheme. During questioning, Smirnov admitted that he had stolen the uranium and intended to sell it to a buyer in Moscow. But having never encountered a case of nuclear smuggling before, the Podolsk police had little idea of its significance. After keeping him in jail for several weeks, they gave him a slap on the wrist and released him on three months' probation.

A decade later, in 2002, fissile material sufficient to build three nuclear weapons was recovered from the Vinca Institute of Nuclear Science, a facility in the suburbs of Belgrade, Yugoslavia, which had operated a nuclear research reactor fueled by more than one hundred pounds of HEU supplied by the Soviet Union in the 1970s.[11] But as Yugoslavia unraveled and its economy sank, the facility's workers stopped receiving paychecks. To make up for the shortfall, some managed to clock in and then leave to work second jobs, if they could find them.[12]

During the 1999 U.S. bombing campaign against Yugoslavia, Vinca was prominently marked on Air Force no-fire lists to prevent American explosives from dispersing the HEU and spent nuclear fuel at the facility to create a massive dirty bomb.[13] While the Air Force's precaution was commendable, it makes the previous—and, even more, the subsequent—lack of urgency about eliminating this risk puzzling. During the war and for months afterward, nothing prevented Yugoslav president Slobodan Milosevic, an alleged war criminal under fire by American smart bombs, from selling this material to terrorists. Nonetheless, the question of what to do about it remained stuck in the bowels of the Departments of State and Energy for three years after the war's end. Officials in charge could not get the approval to spend the $5 million demanded by the Yugoslav government for closure and cleanup before they would agree to withdrawal of the material. To break through this bureaucratic logjam, a private foundation, Ted Turner's Nuclear Threat Initiative, provided the money. But as former senator Sam Nunn, now chief executive of the foundation, has cautioned, "There are 100 nuclear research reactors and other facilities in 40 countries using highly enriched uranium—the raw material of nuclear terrorism. Some of it is secured by nothing more than an underpaid guard sitting inside a chain-link fence."[14]

THE SUPPLY SIDE EQUATION

If a nuclear terrorist attack occurs tomorrow morning, the first question will be *Who did it?*; the second question will be *Where did they get the bomb, and are they likely to have more?* Today there are more than two hundred addresses around the world from which terrorists could acquire a nuclear weapon or the fissile material from which one could be made. Some sites are clearly more dangerous than others, as a result of the quantity of weapons and materials, the lack of physical protection of these items from criminal or terrorist raids, and the corruption and corruptibility of nuclear guardians. Russia is the most likely source, not because the Russian government would intentionally sell or lose weapons or materials, but simply as an instance of the Willie Sutton principle. When asked why he robbed banks, Sutton answered: "Because that's where the money is." Russia's eleven-time-zone expanse contains more nuclear weapons and materials than any other country in the world, much of it vulnerable to theft.

Pakistan is a close second. Intricate links between Pakistani security services and Al Qaeda magnify uncertainties about the chain of custody of its nuclear arsenal, and Pakistan's top nuclear scientist has been caught red-handed as the kingpin of a black market in nuclear technology and materials stretching back for decades. The third most likely source is North Korea, already the world's most promiscuous proliferator of delivery systems for weapons of mass destruction. Over the past decade, North Korea has sold long-range missiles to Iraq, Iran, Pakistan, Saudi Arabia, Yemen—and to anyone else able to pay. In 2003 it abrogated its 1994 agreement with the United States not to produce material for nuclear weapons, and it is currently producing additional fissile material and constructing production lines that will, when completed, turn out enough HEU and plutonium for a dozen bombs a year. Fourth place goes to the twenty-odd research reactors in developing or transitional countries around the globe with quantities of HEU sufficient for one or more nuclear weapons. Most of these reactors, like Vinca, were provided by Minatom to clients and friends of the Soviet Union during the Cold War and remain in Ukraine, Uzbekistan, and a number of other countries today. Instructively, Saddam's Iraq would not have made the top twenty most likely suppliers of nuclear material.

Russia

At the end of the Cold War, 22,000 tactical nuclear weapons remained in fourteen of the fifteen newly independent states of the former Soviet Union, as an integral part of the standard equipment of the military units stationed there.[15] The equipment included nuclear warheads for surface-to-air missiles at air defense posts around the Soviet border, as well as nuclear bombs for fighter aircraft in several hundred storage depots. As the tentacles of Moscow's command-and-control society weakened, and conflicts emerged along the Soviet periphery, the Soviet Union's tactical weapons arsenal presented an acute risk. With this danger in mind, in the fall of 1991 President George H. W. Bush announced that the United States would unilaterally withdraw all tactical nuclear weapons from its forces around the world and challenged the Soviet leader, Mikhail Gorbachev, to do likewise. Gorbachev accepted the challenge, and by the end of May 1992, the Russian Ministry of Defense declared that all tactical weapons had been removed and were now securely stored in Russia. This process was facilitated by assistance from the Nunn-Lugar Soviet Nuclear Threat Reduction Act of 1991, which allowed the United States to provide funding for secure containers, rail cars, and equipment needed to move tactical nuclear weapons from their storage depots to the railheads and eventually to Russia.

Under the most favorable conditions, Federal Express or DHL would find it challenging to move so many items from so many sites in so little time without losing any. But the Soviet Ministry of Defense had to do this as the country was coming apart at the seams, and in fact dissolved in December 1991. Inflation had jumped over 2,000 percent, fueling corruption and criminality throughout Russian society. In the slogan of that era, "Everything is for sale." Managers of state enterprises found themselves in charge of vast entities liberated from the control of crumbling Soviet ministries. In many cases, they concluded that the assets of these enterprises must belong to them. At steel, aluminum, palladium, and other plants, general directors decided to sell these commodities on the international market to the highest bidder and pocket the profits themselves. More troubling for the disarmament efforts, the military officers charged with extracting nuclear weapons and returning them to Russia were not receiving regular paychecks. In light of these realities, is it conceivable that 22,000 nuclear weapons—which are much more valuable than steel or aluminum—were recovered without a single loss? As Secretary of Defense Cheney observed in 1991, recovery of 99 percent of the weapons would constitute "excellent" performance.[16] But even that level of efficiency would leave 220 highly portable nuclear weapons lost, stolen, or otherwise unaccounted for.

The problem comes into sharper focus as one recalls the ways in which many Russian military commanders were exercising their newfound freedom in the 1990s to enrich themselves. As commanders of bases, fleets, and divisions with thousands of aircraft, tanks, and artillery, they sold items from every category. Indeed, as Russian soldiers continued to fight a bloody war in Chechnya, some Russian commanders were willing to sell guns and artillery shells to their own enemy. In the words of one Chechen militant, "Wave some cash at a soldier and he will give you the tank he is sitting in."[17] In 1999, a sailor serving on a nuclear attack submarine in Murmansk stole twenty-four rings of valuable palladium-vanadium wire from the submarine's reactor. After the sailor was caught trying to sell the material to a petty officer, officials discovered that he had broken into the control station of the reactor while on duty guarding the submarine.[18]

The most celebrated case of such behavior involved the commander of the Russian Pacific Fleet, Admiral Igor Khmelnov. In 1997, rumors surfaced that entire ships were being sold in a scam in which they were decommissioned, declared scrap, and sold to foreign buyers for low prices and a hefty bribe. Russian authorities denied these rumors for months until they discovered that a 900-foot-long, 47,000-ton aircraft carrier was no longer in service. After an extensive investigation, Admiral Khmelnov was charged and convicted of selling sixty-four decommissioned ships, including two aircraft carriers, to South Korea and India, and keeping the proceeds for himself. The official price for the aircraft carrier was $5 million.

In its campaign to discredit General Lebed's revelations in 1997 about suitcase nuclear devices, the Russian government insisted that the loss of a nuclear weapon was unthinkable. No responsible party could lose something so important. And yet we know that not only the Soviet Union but also the United States lost numbers of nuclear weapons during the Cold War. At least four Soviet submarines, armed with a total of forty nuclear weapons, sank during the Cold War. According to press reports, one of these was partially recovered from the Pacific Ocean floor by a unique deep-ocean mining ship, the *Glomar Explorer,* owned by the reclusive billionaire Howard Hughes. Three nuclear missiles and two nuclear torpedoes were recovered.[19] The Department of Defense has acknowledged a number of what it calls "broken arrows" (accidents involving a nuclear weapon, including loss), although it has never said how many. The confirmed reports include a 1965 case in which an aircraft loaded with a B43 nuclear bomb rolled off a carrier stationed near Japan. Neither the aircraft nor the weapon was ever recovered. A year later, the U.S. Air Force accidentally dropped a twenty-megaton nuclear bomb in the Mediterranean Sea during a high-altitude refueling mission near Palomares, Spain. After three months of frantic search, it was found. Given the sensitivity of such events, it is reasonable to infer that the few official confirmations are merely the tip of this iceberg.[20]

Terrorists would find it easiest to steal fissile material because it is smaller, lighter, more abundant, and less protected than the weapons themselves. In the first three years after the fall of the Soviet Union, the German government reported more than seven hundred cases of attempted nuclear sales, including sixty instances that involved seizure of nuclear materials. The catalog of unambiguous cases of nuclear smuggling includes:[21]

- **November 1993:** Russian Navy captain Alexei Tikhomirov entered the Sevmorput shipyard near Murmansk through an unguarded gate, broke into a building used to store nuclear submarine fuel, and stole three pieces of a reactor core containing about ten pounds of HEU. He put the fuel in a bag and then walked out of the shipyard the way he came in. Tikhomirov was arrested eight months later when he sought help selling the material. His asking price was $50,000. The lead Russian prosecutor in the case noted that "potatoes were guarded better" than the nuclear fuel at Murmansk.[22]

- **May 1994:** German police found a small but worrisome quantity of supergrade plutonium in the garage of Adolf Jackle in Tengen, Germany. Extremely expensive to produce, this rare item probably came from Arzamas-16, one of Russia's two premier nuclear weapons labs.[23]

- **December 1994:** In Prague, Czech police seized over eight pounds of HEU, which was found inside a metal container in the backseat of a car parked on a side street. A Czech nuclear scientist, a Russian, and a Belarusian were arrested for the theft.

- **December 1997:** A delegation from Russia's Minatom visited the Vekua Institute of Physics and Technology in the war-torn region of Abkhazia, Georgia. The facility and its fissile material had been abandoned five years earlier when separatist fighting broke out. Minatom confirmed that 1.7 pounds of HEU was missing; other Russian sources put the figure at closer to 4.5 pounds.[24]

- **December 1998:** The FSB (the successor to the KGB) broke up a conspiracy by nuclear insiders at Chelyabinsk, the second of Russia's leading nuclear weapons labs. According to the testimony of Victor Yerastov, chief of nuclear accounting and control for Russia's Ministry of Atomic Energy, the planned theft involved "quite sufficient material to produce an atomic bomb."[25]

- **April 2000:** Four Georgian nationals were arrested with about two pounds of HEU outside Batumi, the capital of the chaotic Adzhariya Autonomous Republic in Georgia.

- **November 2003:** A Russian court sentenced a top official at Atomflot, the enterprise that maintains Russia's fleet of nuclear-powered icebreakers, to eighteen months in a penal colony for possession of two pounds of uranium "yellowcake," a key precursor to HEU. He was attempting to sell the material for $55,000.

In its February 2002 report to Congress on nuclear risks from Russia, the National Intelligence Council—the organization responsible for the U.S. intelligence community's most authoritative judgments—confirmed four cases, between 1992 and 1999, in which "weapons-grade and weapons-usable nuclear materials have been stolen from some Russian institutes." Summarizing the bottom line, the council said: "Undetected smuggling has occurred, although we do not know the extent or magnitude."[26]

More recently, Russian authorities have acknowledged two incidents in 2001 in which terrorist groups penetrated security systems to identify locations of secret Russian nuclear weapons storage facilities and carried out active surveillance of the sites. The Russian government revealed two further incidents in which terrorists were found tracking nuclear warhead transport trains, presumably with plans to derail the train and steal the weapons (as terrorists did in the 1997 film *The Peacemaker*).[27]

During the Cold War, the Soviet Union established a vast nuclear enterprise under its Ministry of Atomic Energy that employed more than a million people in ten "closed" cities requiring special entry and exit visas. The scientists and technicians in these cities designed and built weapons and produced uranium and plutonium not only for weapons but also for the fuel that powered the nation's fleet of nuclear-powered submarines and its nuclear power plants. The material recovered from Kazakhstan in Operation Sapphire, for instance, had been part of this far-flung network. U.S. experts have estimated that Russia possesses over two million pounds of weapons-usable material, or enough for more than eighty thousand weapons.[28] Yet a dozen years after the dissolution of the Soviet Union, much of this vast stockpile remains dangerously insecure.

Recent evidence includes a February 2001 report from the U.S. General Accounting Office, describing its inspectors' visit to a Russian nuclear facility at which the door to the main area with nuclear material was left wide open, and another in which guards did not respond when metal detectors went off.[29] In March 2001, former senator Howard Baker testified to Congress about what he had seen firsthand as head of a U.S. delegation that examined security conditions at Russian naval bases near Murmansk: "In Russia, I'm talking about kilograms of material. I'm talking about finished weapons that are barely protected. I'm talking about doors that have an ordinary padlock on them and sometimes not even that."[30] In October 2001, Yuri Volodin, chief of safeguards for the Russian nuclear regulatory agency, admitted dozens of violations of regulations for securing and accounting for nuclear material. In one case, a nuclear facility received much less of a shipment of nuclear material than documents indicated it should have, suggesting possible theft while in transit.[31] Russian customs chief Nikolai Kravchenko reported more than five hundred incidents of illegal transportation of nuclear and radioactive materials across Russian state borders in the year 2000 alone.[32]

From outright nuclear theft and smuggling to more general problems of inadequate resources for nuclear security systems, and low pay and morale for nuclear workers and military forces, reports of nuclear insecurity in Russia continue to emerge at an alarming rate today. If we know about these lapses, terrorist groups likely know about them, too.

Pakistan

In the summer of 2002, American spy satellites detected a Pakistani C-130 cargo plane loading missile parts near Pyongyang, the capital of North Korea. Intelligence analysts recognized immediately what was happening: Pakistan was trading nuclear centrifuge technology for North Korean ballistic missile parts in order to enhance its nuclear deterrent against its archrival, India. But the Pakistani–North Korean quid pro quo was just the first trickle of a flood of evidence that has led nonproliferation experts to award Pakistan the dubious prize as "the world's No. 1 nuclear proliferator."[33] As a senior Bush administration official observed in January 2004 about recent Pakistani deals with North Korea, Iran, and Libya, "These guys are now three for three as supplier to the biggest proliferation problems we have."[34]

Pakistan is thought to possess as many as fifty nuclear weapons and enough HEU for fifty more, plus production lines that can reliably supply five to ten new bombs a year.[35] Its clandestine networks for procuring and selling nuclear technology span the globe from China, North Korea, Malaysia, and Myanmar, to the Netherlands and Germany, and on to Iran, Iraq, Saudi Arabia, and the United Arab Emirates. A recently declassified State Department memo confirms that Pakistan originally acquired the technology for "fissile material production and possibly also nuclear device design" from China.[36] Following a pattern of reciprocal back-scratching that characterizes much of its nuclear proliferation activities, Pakistan offered China improved centrifuge designs years later, designs that A. Q. Khan had stolen from the Dutch centrifuge plant where he worked during the 1970s.

Pakistan's centrifuge plans also gave a boost to the Iranian nuclear program as early as 1987, when Pakistan was officially an American ally helping to expel the Soviet Union from Afghanistan. During the 1980s, Iran sought to master uranium enrichment technology independently but made little headway. Though the details of the Iranian-Pakistani connection remain murky, it appears that a Dubai intermediary relayed Dr. Khan's centrifuge design to the Iranians, allowing them "to skip many difficult research steps," in the words of former UN inspector David Albright.[37] Though the Musharraf regime denies knowledge of the transfers to Iran, the Center for Nonproliferation Studies reports that "Pakistani government sources have admitted that scientists from Khan Research Laboratories likely shared technologies and know-how with Iran for personal monetary and career gains."[38] A Dubai middleman also reportedly offered Dr. Khan's nuclear help to Saddam Hussein in late 1990, just before the first Gulf War.

When Libya's Muammar el-Qaddafi announced in December 2003 that he would voluntarily dismantle his weapons of mass destruction program, it quickly became clear that Pakistan had been the source for yet another rogue regime's centrifuge designs. Qaddafi's decision was at least partly affected by the fact that his activities had been discovered three months before his announcement. In September of that year, U.S. and British intelligence officers learned that a German ship heading from an interim port in Dubai through the Suez Canal to Libya was hauling thousands of centrifuge parts. In cooperation with the German shipping company, officials diverted the ship to a port in southern Italy and seized the materials two days before it docked in Libya.[39] Though the parts themselves had been manufactured in Malaysia, they were based on the same Pakistani plans that Dr. Khan had stolen from the Dutch centrifuge plant decades earlier. Those plans were likely offered as compensation for many years of financial support that Libya provided for Pakistan's nuclear program, support for which former Pakistani prime minister Zulfiqar Ali Bhutto named the nation's largest cricket arena Qaddafi Stadium.

Clues have even trickled out of possible nuclear collusion between Pakistan and Saudi Arabia, leading some to worry that there might be an as-yet-undiscovered "oil for nukes" deal between the two countries.[40] Like Libya, Saudi Arabia certainly supplied much of the funding for Pakistan's nuclear program under Dr. Khan, as confirmed by Prime Minister Bhutto's press adviser, Khalid Hasan.[41] In 1999, the Saudi defense minister, Prince Sultan, was given a tour of Pakistan's nuclear enrichment facilities, at which time he invited Dr. Khan to visit Saudi Arabia. After Dr. Khan's visit to the desert kingdom, a Saudi nuclear expert declared, "Saudi Arabia must make plans aimed at making a quick response to face the possibilities of nuclear warfare agents being used against the Saudi population, cities, or armed forces."[42] Over the past decade, Riyadh has also given Islamabad roughly $1.2 billion worth of oil annually, for which it has not been paid.[43] While this fact is admittedly circumstantial evidence, it does raise questions about the nature of the relationship between the two countries, especially in light of Pakistan's use of nuclear technology as its most valuable export.

In January 2004, an Israeli businessman based in South Africa was detained in Denver for exporting nuclear trigger devices to Pakistan. The triggers were a classic "dual-use" product, used not only by hospitals to break apart kidney stones but also by weapons builders to detonate nuclear explosions. U.S. authorities became suspicious when they realized that the Israeli had ordered two hundred of these items from an American company, even though hospitals usually need no more than a handful, and had sent them to a man in Pakistan with links to the military. As usual, the Pakistani government flatly denied any involvement in the transfer.

The most troubling question of all remains how and to what extent Pakistan's free-market approach to proliferation has allowed terrorist groups like Al Qaeda to acquire nuclear materials and technology. U.S. officials fear that Al Qaeda's ideological soul mates are increasingly active in Pakistan's military, intelligence cadres, and nuclear establishment, and may be playing a role in nuclear transfers to terrorist groups. Pakistan's hard-line Islamist parties have long called Musharraf a puppet of the United States. His acquiescence to American demands that Pakistan crack down on the Khan Research Laboratories' proliferation activities and his removal of Dr. Khan from his government post may serve to inflame them further.[44] And while Pakistan's Army, which is the dominant institution in the country, has traditionally held a moderate, secular view of the world, a recently declassified U.S. intelligence report found that "high-ranking [Pakistani] officials are worried that radical Islam is slowly seeping into the officer corps."[45] In chapter 1, we saw how

Musharraf's decision to back the United States in its war against the Taliban and Al Qaeda fueled Pakistan's fundamentalist flames. As the terrorism analyst Peter Bergen has noted, "Killing Musharraf has been a central objective [of Al Qaeda and militant Pakistani groups] since after 9/11."[46] In December 2003, Musharraf came within seconds of assassination twice in two weeks, which led counterterrorism experts to conclude that "the inner security circle for Musharraf has been breached."[47]

Should the assassins succeed in a subsequent attempt, the specter arises of a radical Islamist government in possession of a major nuclear arsenal. U.S. officials admit that they do not know where all of Pakistan's nuclear arsenal—weapons or fissile material—is located, because Pakistan has dispersed its weapons to multiple locations in an effort to reduce its vulnerability to an Indian preemptive attack. Seizure of the arsenal in the event of a coup would thus be impossible. As one senior Bush administration official observed candidly, "It's what we don't know that worries us, including the critical question of how much fissile material Pakistan now holds—and where it holds it."[48] A coup in Pakistan would raise the stakes considerably in any effort to contain and prevent nuclear terrorism.

North Korea

In April 2003, the 40,000-ton French cargo ship *Ville de Virgo* left the German port of Hamburg on its way to Asia with a seemingly innocuous delivery on board: 214 aluminum tubes purchased by a Chinese aircraft company. After the ship set sail, German intelligence officials discovered that the tubes were bound not for China but for North Korea. When German authorities tracked down the ship and seized the cargo, they pieced together a greater plot by North Korea to obtain as many as 2,000 tubes to make gas centrifuges for enriching uranium. Put simply, the tubes were for making nuclear weapons.[49]

The *Ville de Virgo* shipment offers a classic example of how North

Korea has used front companies and third countries to procure the necessary parts for a nuclear weapons program. In the case of the 214 aluminum tubes, a North Korean "businessman" contacted the owner of a small German export company called Optronic. The German agreed to supply the tubes, which he was told were being purchased for China's Shenyang Aircraft Corporation. The deal was brilliant in its simplicity. As a German investigator put it, "With only a phone and an Internet connection, you can send such materials across the world."[50] And the North Koreans have set up shop elsewhere: in the summer of 2002, Slovakian police raided New World Trading Slovakia, a "company" established by two North Korean operatives in Bratislava to buy materials for their own nuclear program and to sell missile technology to countries such as Egypt, Libya, Iran, Syria, and Vietnam.[51]

North Korea first acquired basic nuclear technology when the former Soviet Union supplied a small research reactor in 1967. A decade later, it built a thirty-megawatt thermal reactor capable of generating enough plutonium for one bomb per year, the first of what would grow into seven plutonium production sites.[52] In the early 1990s, Pyongyang violated the Nuclear Nonproliferation Treaty it had signed years earlier and began to reprocess plutonium to weapons-usable form, likely producing enough material for one or two bombs, according to CIA estimates. In 1994, the Clinton administration negotiated the so-called Agreed Framework, according to which North Korea promised to freeze its plutonium production in exchange for two light-water nuclear reactors administered under IAEA safeguards, as well as fuel and food assistance provided by Japan and South Korea.

But when the Bush administration came to power in 2001, it brought with it a newly confrontational posture toward North Korea. Foreign policy hawks such as Vice President Cheney and Defense Secretary Donald Rumsfeld believed that North Korea had been cheating on its obligations and that the Agreed Framework merely gave the rogue regime more time to build a nuclear arsenal. In October 2002, the North Koreans admitted to Bush administration envoys that they had developed a secret uranium enrichment program (almost certainly based on Pakistan's centrifuge blueprint). By the end of the year, they expelled IAEA inspectors from the country, withdrew from the Nuclear Nonproliferation Treaty, and began reprocessing the eight thousand spent fuel rods from the Yongbyon nuclear reactor that they had agreed to freeze in 1994—enough for about five or six bombs, not counting the one or two the CIA estimated that North Korea already possessed. As Washington and Pyongyang have remained at a stalemate, the North Koreans have been reprocessing plutonium, enriching uranium, and completing construction of facilities that possibly will be able to produce about a dozen nuclear warheads a year.[53]

North Korea is a country wracked by food shortages, a stagnant economy, and mass deprivation. The country has lapsed into a preindustrial past. Satellite pictures from above the Korean peninsula show sparkling lights in the South and utter darkness in the North. As a South Korean businessman put it, "North Korea's No. 1 problem is electricity."[54] Human rights groups estimate that as many as two million people starved from widespread famine in the early 1990s. Notwithstanding its official ideology of *juche* ("self-reliance"), the regime depends heavily on imported oil and food. The government in Pyongyang has demonstrated for a decade that it is willing to sell anything for cash to stave off economic collapse. Even at the height of the diplomatic crisis over Iraq in December 2002, North Korea had the chutzpah to send a shipload of ballistic missiles to Yemen amid a growing U.S. military buildup in the Middle East.

A nuclear-armed North Korea with a serial production line for an additional dozen weapons per year could become a Nukes R' Us for developing nations, "rogue states," and terrorist groups. Its top leadership has openly boasted that it intends to sell fissile material and even nuclear weapons—for the right price. In April 2003, during talks in Beijing among American, North Korean, and Chinese officials, North Korea's chief representative, Li Gun, told Assistant

Secretary of State James Kelly that Pyongyang will "export nuclear weapons, add to its current arsenal, or test a nuclear device."[55]

While missiles are North Korea's major cash crop, bringing in about $500 million annually, they are just one product in a catalog that includes drug running and counterfeiting as well. In essence, North Korea is a mafia state. Some of the regime's ambassadors fund their embassies through black-market dealings in methamphetamine, heroin, and cocaine. The *New Republic* reported that Japanese officials interdicted $335 million worth of North Korean methamphetamine in just one bust. In July 2002, Taiwanese police seized 175 pounds of heroin that had been smuggled through an official diplomatic channel. Throughout the 1990s, North Korean envoys working with European and Asian organized-crime groups were caught with thousands of fake $100 bills in Mongolia, Russia, and Cambodia.[56] This extensive experience in illicit international trade leaves North Korea supremely qualified to move fissile material around the globe to willing buyers.

Nuclear Research Reactors

In 1972, General Atomics, a San Diego–based company specializing in civilian nuclear energy, sent uranium bar no. 6916 to the Triga II research reactor it designed in Kinshasa, Zaire (present-day Congo). The reactor was part of America's Atoms for Peace program, started under President Dwight D. Eisenhower, through which the United States exported 1,650 pounds of plutonium and 60,000 pounds of HEU to thirty-nine countries over thirty years.[57] But as with many research reactors given to Third World countries during the Cold War, Zaire's Triga II reactor fell into disarray. Funding for the reactor ceased in 1988, and it was shut down in 1992. Five years later, when rebels overthrew the dictator Mobutu Sese Seko, eight uranium bars, including no. 6916, were spirited out of the country and into the black market.

The uranium found its way into the hands of the Sicilian Mafia.

In a high-stakes sting operation, an Italian police agent posing as an Egyptian businessman agreed to purchase the uranium for $12.2 million. As the exchange of dollars for uranium was being made, Italian police stormed in and arrested the nuclear mafiosi. Happily, as it turned out, the uranium was only 19.9 percent enriched—not quite pure enough to create a nuclear explosion.[58] But that was a fortunate coincidence, since it just as easily might have come from the Vinca reactor in Yugoslavia or one of several dozen other reactors fueled with more highly enriched uranium.

There are at least 130 operating research reactors fueled with HEU in more than forty countries, all but a handful of which were supplied by either the United States or the Soviet Union during the Cold War.[59] Some are located at universities, where a revolving crew of low-paid students provides what passes for security. After the clean-out of Vinca, the State Department identified two dozen remaining Soviet-supplied sites, some with enough HEU for at least one bomb. Since then, three more reactors have been secured in Romania, Bulgaria, and Libya, leaving over twenty sites of serious concern. The question is, Who will get to them first: the nuclear clean-out teams or the terrorists?

Project Vinca was a watershed, removing three bombs' worth of HEU within easy reach of terrorists or organized criminals. In September 2003, Russia collaborated with U.S. authorities to take back thirty pounds of weapons-grade uranium from Romania. When describing the conditions of the uranium outside the Romanian capital of Bucharest, a Department of Energy official said, "You could throw it in the back of a truck and drive away with it."[60] Three months later, another joint U.S.–Russian team recovered thirty-seven pounds of HEU from a Bulgarian reactor. Because the Bulgarian HEU was "fresh fuel," or nonirradiated, the same DOE official noted that it would have been "quite useful to a terrorist [since] you can handle it without protection."[61]

Though U.S. officials are appropriately tight-lipped about the locations of the more than twenty remaining reactors of greatest concern, nonproliferation experts have fingered former Soviet republics like Uzbekistan (home to a terrorist group with close ties to Al Qaeda), Ukraine (where arms trafficking and drug smuggling are endemic), and Belarus (a decaying semi-Stalinist state). Shut-down facilities in Belarus are said to have over 600 pounds of HEU; those in Ukraine, over 150 pounds. While DOE has announced a goal of finishing the twenty-odd Soviet-supplied sites by the end of 2005, it has thus far been moving at a rate of about one per year. At that pace, over two decades will pass before all of these most troubling reactors have been cleaned out, and beyond those, there remain an additional one hundred sites with less than a bomb's worth of HEU.

The United States

For most people, one of the last places that springs to mind as a potential source of nuclear weapons or material is the United States. Yet in 1997, one of the most heavily guarded areas of the Los Alamos National Laboratory in New Mexico, known as Technical Area-18 (TA-18), was breached. As guards rushed to the scene, snipers shot them from the surrounding hills while their compatriots located multiple canisters of HEU inside the facility. When the canisters proved too heavy for an individual to carry, the attackers used a Home Depot garden cart to haul enough HEU for numerous nuclear weapons out of TA-18 and into the woods of Santa Fe. Department of Energy security planners refer to the now-notorious heist as the Garden Cart incident.

Fortunately, the "terrorists" were a team of Army Special Forces commandos carrying out a planned security exercise, using lasers instead of real bullets.[62] Still, the Special Forces team beat the Los Alamos guards handily, even though the odds had been stacked against them. A typical nuclear terrorist war game would have required the commandos to steal only enough fissile material for one weapon, which would fit in an individual rucksack. But by design, this exercise required them to take more than one person could carry.[63] When the Special Forces solved that problem by a quick trip to Home Depot, Los Alamos officials objected, calling this "unfair," since, in their words, "the Home Depot cart was not on DOE's approved list of weapons for war games."[64] One wonders if the box cutters used by the 9/11 hijackers would have been prohibited as well.

In 1998, Navy SEALs conducted a similar drill at the Rocky Flats Nuclear Laboratory in Denver, Colorado, and successfully stole several bombs' worth of plutonium without getting caught. When they repeated the test, Rocky Flats officials demanded that the terrorists not leave through the same hole in the perimeter fence through which they had entered, but rather climb a guard tower and rope the plutonium over the fence.[65] The captain of the Navy SEAL team later derided the test for its unrealistic constraints, which had clearly been set up in the guards' favor. Richard Levernier, a former nuclear security expert who has run war games at various nuclear labs, eventually blew the whistle. "Some of these facilities would fail year after year," he said. "In more than 50 percent of our tests of the Los Alamos facility, we got in, captured the plutonium, got out again, and in some cases didn't fire a shot, because we didn't encounter any guards."[66]

There are ten major sites in the United States with enough weapons-grade plutonium or HEU for a nuclear weapon, including Los Alamos and Rocky Flats as well as Lawrence Livermore, near San Francisco, and Sandia, in Albuquerque, New Mexico.[67] According to the Institute for Science and International Security, there are 1.27 million pounds of HEU and 200,000 pounds of plutonium stored in America's nuclear complex.[68] But the insufficient security around these stockpiles continues to draw bipartisan fire. In the summer of 2003, Senator Charles Grassley of Iowa, a Republican, issued a damning critique of America's nuclear labs: "Security is lax. Our nuclear secrets are not safe. . . . To criminals and spies, the labs must be like a candy store with the front door left wide open and nobody at the register. And the terrorists must be licking their chops."[69] Representative

Edward Markey of Massachusetts, a Democrat, echoed these concerns. "Terrorists," he said, "could find what they needed to launch a nuclear attack right here in the United States of America."[70]

Reports have also surfaced of disturbing insider activity. At two labs, master keys leading all the way to the reactors themselves have gone missing. Computer hard drives with classified weapons research data have disappeared. An FBI sting operation has turned up numerous stolen laptops and CIA computers at a "chop shop" selling spare computer parts outside the Sandia labs. An FBI surveillance video caught one member of the guard force stealing such computer parts; he later sold them to his supervisors.[71]

The case of the FBI agent Robert Hanssen, who sold state secrets to the Soviet Union over a span of twenty-two years, reminds us that greed, as well as the intrigue of international crime and espionage, can draw even high government officials to betray the interests of their country. Hanssen's crime was particularly unsettling for the American security community because he was the FBI's number one counterintelligence officer in charge of rooting out Communist moles. For $1.4 million, Hanssen betrayed at least three Soviet spies working for the United States, two of whom were ultimately executed, and revealed an untold number of secrets that compromised his fellow citizens' security. In 1985, the legendary CIA turncoat Aldrich Ames gave up the identities of all twenty-five spies working for the United States in Russia, in exchange for $4 million.

THE POTENTIAL SOURCES of a terrorist nuclear bomb span the globe. Many assume that nuclear weapons or materials are either too well guarded for a thief to obtain or too dangerous for an insider to contemplate selling. But, as we have already seen, both insiders and intruders are far less constrained than common sense would suggest. From Pakistani nuclear scientists' meetings with Al Qaeda, to A. Q. Khan's nuclear import-export business, to impoverished Russian scientists' schemes for making an extra ruble—the list of insider activity is disturbingly long. For intruders, a nuclear heist at many Russian facilities would be easier than robbing a bank. Most people have never laid eyes on a nuclear storage facility, much less actual nuclear weapons or materials, so they remain a largely abstract fear. But while it is easy to forget the sheer magnitude of the global nuclear arsenal, terrorists surely have not.

4

WHEN COULD TERRORISTS LAUNCH
THE FIRST NUCLEAR ATTACK?

If the Iraqi regime is able to produce, buy, or steal an
amount of uranium a little bigger than a softball, it could
have a nuclear weapon in less than a year.

PRESIDENT GEORGE W. BUSH

TOM RIDGE, the secretary of homeland security, has repeatedly
warned Americans to expect future terrorist attacks that "will rival
or exceed the attacks on New York and the Pentagon."[1] In his
words, "The question is not if, but when."[2]

If the Dragonfire report of a ten-kiloton nuclear bomb in New
York City had been confirmed, the answer to "when" could have
been October 2001. If Al Qaeda had acquired one hundred pounds
of HEU that same October, it could have exploded a crude nuclear
bomb a year later, on the first anniversary of 9/11. Had the hijackers of American Airlines Flight 77 targeted New York's Indian Point
nuclear power plant instead of the World Trade Center, local residents would have been the victims of a massive dirty bomb on the
morning of September 11.

Over a quarter of a century ago, in 1977, a Princeton undergraduate named John Aristotle Phillips demonstrated the truth of President Bush's assertion that with fissile material on hand, a nuclear
bomb could be built in "less than a year." An aerospace science

major with a senior thesis to write, Phillips decided to investigate whether he could design a nuclear weapon from publicly available information. He began with basic college textbooks on nuclear physics, but later turned to the U.S. government for more specifics about nuclear bombs. For $25 he purchased copies of *The Los Alamos Primer: The First Lectures on How to Build an Atomic Bomb* and other technical papers, written during the Manhattan Project, from the National Technical Information Service, the central depository for government-funded scientific, technical, and business information. When he read the first draft of the thesis, Phillips's academic adviser, Freeman Dyson, a physicist with nuclear weapons experience, was shocked to find that such detail had somehow been declassified.[3]

Phillips had approached his assignment as if he were a terrorist. His bomb had to be inexpensive, simple, and small enough to be transported by car or truck. Hoping to draw attention to the dangers of plutonium produced by the civilian nuclear power industry, he chose to design an implosion bomb that utilized plutonium. As he developed his weapon, Phillips identified and solved the most difficult problem facing any terrorist trying to build an implosion bomb: calculating the arrangement of explosives needed to collapse the plutonium core and cause a nuclear explosion. Knowing little about explosives, he called the DuPont Company for help. When he asked the chemical explosives division what materials would be useful for compressing high-density metals, a DuPont engineer told him the exact type that the company had sold the U.S. government for use in nuclear weapons.[4] With this information in hand, he completed his thesis in five months. The resulting design was a perfect terrorist weapon: a bomb the size of a beach ball, with a ten-kiloton yield and a price tag of $2,000.[5] His thesis, "An Assessment of the Problems and Possibilities Confronting a Terrorist Group or Non-nuclear Nation Attempting to Design a Crude Pu239 Fission Bomb," received an "A." Members of the physics department at Princeton who had worked on the Manhattan Project more than three decades earlier believed that Phillips's bomb would work. Concerned that the paper might fall into the wrong hands, they turned it over to the U.S. government, where it was immediately classified "secret."

SAFEGUARDS WILL NOT SAVE US

Once terrorists have bought or stolen a nuclear weapon in good working condition, they can explode it as soon as it reaches their target. If the weapon has a lock, the date of detonation can be delayed for several days. If the bomb has not been properly maintained, weeks of reconditioning may be required to ensure the maximum blast. Many of the most vulnerable weapons in the former Soviet arsenal are "beyond warranty" and thus might need maintenance before becoming operational. But the arsenals of India and Pakistan were constructed much more recently and have no integral locking mechanisms.

In the 1960s, America's nuclear guardians recognized the risk of nuclear theft or unauthorized detonation and began equipping the nation's weapons with safety devices. The most successful product was called a permissive action link (PAL). PALs are locks that make it especially challenging to explode a nuclear weapon without first entering a top-secret code.[6] In 1962, the original PALs—five-digit mechanical locks—were retrofitted onto the arming circuits of America's tactical nuclear weapons, such as atomic demolition munitions, the miniature Davy Crockett warhead, and the W-33 and W-48 artillery shells.[7]

Early PALs were little more than combination locks that could be easily opened or removed. Subsequent designs culminated in twelve-digit "Category F" locks, which have a total of one trillion possible combinations and a "limited try" feature that permanently disables the electrical circuits of the warhead after several false attempts at cracking the code.[8] Category F's almost guarantee that a terrorist without access to the codes would find it impossible to activate the bomb. Unfortunately, these advanced safety features are found only on America's most recent nuclear warheads.[9]

Additional nuclear safety features called environmental sensing devices (ESDs) can also be overcome with limited imagination. These devices measure the altitude, atmospheric pressure, or air temperature of the weapon as it is delivered to its target, and block detonation until the correct environment is achieved. But as the U.S. Office of Technology Assessment determined, ESDs can be bypassed with limited imagination.[10] Depending on the sophistication of the lock and the technical abilities of the nuclear thieves, it could take as little as a few days for them to work around these safety features and activate the weapon.

During the Cold War, Soviet officials rebuffed multiple efforts by American officials to share PAL and ESD technologies.[11] Skeptical of the Americans' preoccupation with technological solutions, the Soviet Union counted on people rather than on technology to control its nuclear arsenal. Consequently, many of Russia's nuclear warheads mounted on long-range ballistic missiles, and most of its small tactical weapons, today lack any technical protections.[12] In 1996, a leaked Top Secret CIA report assessed that Russia's tactical nuclear weapons "appear to be . . . most at risk," noting that even the few locks that did exist—on the Russian Navy's nuclear-tipped torpedoes, for example—could easily be removed.[13] The report concluded that "all technical [security] measures can be circumvented—probably within weeks or days depending on the weapons involved."[14]

In the Hollywood version of the way nuclear weapons work, the president and his Russian counterpart have a "nuclear football" by their side at all times, with the activation codes to all nuclear devices. Without these codes, the story goes, weapons cannot be launched. But no classified information is required for us to understand why this picture is incomplete. Imagine a nuclear first strike that kills the president and destroys the football. Would a responsible government allow itself to be disarmed by such a surgical decapitation?

Must the president remember a twelve-digit code for the nation's nuclear deterrent to be usable? What if he was drunk, as Russian president Boris Yeltsin demonstrably was on a number of public occasions in the 1990s, or unconscious, or simply forgot the code?

In real life, governments have prepared for such contingencies by giving the nuclear codes to other key personnel in the chain of command. While this ensures the viability of the nuclear arsenal, it also means that each of these individuals may be a "weak link"— vulnerable to coercion, bribery, or blackmail. Moreover, as anyone with a home security system knows, the technicians who develop and maintain the locks also have the ability to unlock them.

In the graphic description of one weapons designer: "Bypassing a PAL should be about as complex as performing tonsillectomy while entering the patient from the wrong end." [15] Yet this is not always the case. The bottom line is that PALs and ESDs can temporarily delay, but cannot prevent, terrorists from using a stolen nuclear weapon.

A further barrier to terrorists' use of a nuclear weapon may be the readiness of the weapon itself. Warheads are designed to perform in extreme environments: plunging from an aircraft or hurtling on a missile at twenty times the speed of sound. But to assure maximum performance, Russian weapons must be serviced approximately every seven years.[16] Extended exposure to the radioactivity from the fissile material can cause weapons components to lose their intended shapes and can cause the conventional explosives to dry out, degrading the performance of the weapon.[17] Annually, as many as 10 percent of all U.S.- and Russian-deployed weapons are returned to a warhead production facility to be taken apart, tested, reassembled, and then delivered back to the field.[18]

If a stolen nuclear weapon is beyond warranty or has not been properly maintained, it may not perform as designed, reducing the bomb's blast. And yet even this possibility offers little comfort. If a ten-kiloton nuclear warhead was to misfire (known to nuclear scientists as a "fizzle") and produce a one-kiloton blast, bystanders near ground zero would not know the difference. Such an explosion would torch anyone one-tenth of a mile from the epicenter, and topple buildings up to one-third of a mile out.[19] In Times Square on a normal workday, this "disappointing" one-kiloton explosion would kill up to 250,000 people within a week, from the combined effects of heat, blast, and radiation—as opposed to 1,000,000 people if it had detonated at full strength.[20] But bomb designers would designate such an explosion a "failure."

Even if sophisticated locking devices, poor maintenance, or damage in transit rendered a stolen weapon inoperable, it would still be useful to a terrorist. They could "cannibalize" the weapon, mining it for fissile material with which they could make a crude nuclear bomb. Moreover, in the case of the two newest nuclear weapons states—Pakistan and India—the need to bypass a lock, service a poorly maintained weapon, or cannibalize its fissile material would be moot. Neither country's weapons are fitted with locks, nor are most old enough to require reconditioning. Moreover, each of these arsenals has been deployed with an eye, first, to preventing the other from disarming it in a preemptive attack, and only secondarily to preventing insider theft. If terrorists obtain a bomb from the Asian subcontinent, they will be able to use it immediately.[21]

BUILD IT YOURSELF

National security experts agree that the most likely way terrorists will obtain a nuclear bomb will not be to steal or purchase a fully operational device but to buy fissile material and construct their own. President Bush was correct when he argued that if Saddam Hussein had obtained a softball-size lump of HEU, he "could have a nuclear weapon in less than a year." With the same quantity of HEU, Al Qaeda or another terrorist group could do the same.

It took the genius of Albert Einstein and numerous other Nobel Prize–winning physicists to imagine and construct the first nuclear weapon. But that was sixty years ago. Nonetheless, in the popular imagination, the belief persists that building a nuclear weapon requires Manhattan Project–style science. Those who work with nuclear weapons have always known better. David Lilienthal, the first chairman of the Atomic Energy Commission, acknowledged in 1948 that the myth of a secret formula was "nothing less than a gigantic hoax."[22] And Theodore Taylor, the nuclear physicist who designed America's smallest and largest atomic bombs, has repeatedly stated that given fissile material, building a bomb is "very easy. Double underline. Very easy."[23]

In 1979, Secretary of Energy James R. Schlesinger asked for a federal court injunction to prevent the publication of an article in the *Progressive* magazine titled "The H-Bomb Secret."[24] For only the second time in American history—the first being the Nixon administration's attempted censorship of the Pentagon Papers— the government sought to exercise "prior restraint" to block a publication it judged damaging to the national interest. The article described the physics of the hydrogen bomb in such detail that it would have been classified Top Secret if it had been a government document. But after a six-month court battle, the article appeared in the *Progressive* exactly as originally written, complete with schematics of a thermonuclear weapon. It is now available on the Internet.[25] Recent revelations about A. Q. Khan's nuclear network demonstrated that complete fission bomb designs are now available for sale on the black market.[26] An official at the International Atomic Energy Agency who reviewed plans confiscated in Libya remarked to the journalist Seymour Hersh that the design in question was "a sweet little bomb" that would be "too big and too heavy for a Scud, but it'll go into a family car"—a "terrorist's dream."[27]

As far back as 1964, U.S. government scientists at the Lawrence Livermore National Laboratory, one of the nation's premier nuclear weapons design labs, devised an experiment to test the proposition that the nuclear genie was out of the bottle. "The purpose of the so-called 'Nth Country Experiment,'" as the official project design states, "is to find out if a credible nuclear explosive can be designed, with a modest effort, by a few well-trained people without contact with classified information."[28] The few "well-trained people" in this case were two recent physics Ph.D. students, chosen deliberately for their lack of knowledge of nuclear physics. One of the students, Dave Dobson, admitted having only a "high school understanding of nuclear fission."[29] The other, Bob Selden, was interviewed for the job by Edward Teller, the creator of the hydrogen bomb, who quizzed him on nuclear bomb physics. Selden was initially discouraged: "I didn't know anything. As the evening wore on, I knew less and less."[30] Two days later he was invited to join the project. The experiment assumed that they resided in a fictitious country with decent university libraries, machinists like those found in auto-engine repair shops, and conventional explosives like dynamite.

Early in the project, Dobson and Selden concluded that a gun-type bomb design (the straightforward design used in the Hiroshima bomb) would be too easy. They elected, instead, to pursue a more challenging path: to create an implosion bomb using plutonium. Surveying the relevant scientific literature, the two men quickly found essential information on nuclear fission, the shaping of conventional explosives, and even charts and tables of nuclear data from the first Los Alamos experiments. Armed with this knowledge, they performed calculations on primitive punch-card computers with less computing power than today's cell phones. In the end, they produced a document with such precise details on how to build the bomb, and what materials would be required, that Selden remarked that it "could have been made by Joe's Machine Shop downtown."[31] Nuclear weapons experts at Livermore judged that the design, if built, would explode with Hiroshima-like power. Though the device would have been too large to fit on a missile, it could have been easily carried in a cargo container or in a van.

That was forty years ago. Since then, the technology and tools available to would-be bomb makers have improved immensely. Over the past several years, a team of scientists at the Los Alamos

National Laboratory complex in New Mexico has developed a catalog of crude nuclear weapons designs in order to assist the government's Nuclear Emergency Support Teams, who would be called on to try to disarm a terrorist weapon. The scientists' assignment is to use "technology found on the shelves of Radio Shack and the type of nuclear fuel sold on the black market to construct homemade bombs."[32] Reportedly, they have produced several dozen alternative bomb designs, which they maintain in "a comprehensive computer database of nuclear weapon design information—from reports in scientific journals to passages from spy novels."[33]

Senator Joseph R. Biden, the ranking Democrat on the Foreign Relations Committee, has conducted his own experiment. "I gathered the heads of all the national laboratories and asked them a simple question," he recalled in January 2004. "I said, 'I would like you to go back to your laboratory and try to assume for a moment you are a relatively informed terrorist group with access to some nuclear scientists. Could you build, off the shelf, a nuclear device? Not a dirty bomb, but something that would start a nuclear reaction—an atomic bomb. Could you build one?' They came back several months later and said, 'We built one.' They put it in a room and explained how—literally off the shelf, without doing anything illegal—they actually constructed this device."[34]

How could it be so easy? It all goes back to the basic design that was developed at Los Alamos during World War II. A nuclear explosion occurs when a chain reaction within a critical mass (the smallest amount required to sustain a steady chain reaction) of fissile material, either HEU or plutonium, accelerates and becomes "supercritical," and thus, over a short period of time, the fission rate and the resulting release of nuclear energy multiplies. If enough HEU is at hand (approximately 100 pounds), a gun-type design is simple to plan, build, and detonate. In its basic form, a "bullet" of HEU is fired down a gun barrel into a hollowed HEU "target" fastened to the other end of the barrel. Fused together, the two pieces of HEU form a supercritical mass and detonate. The gun in the Hiroshima

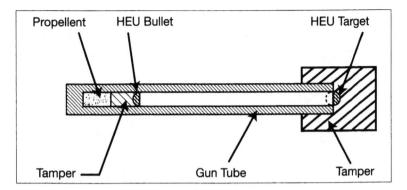

Concept for a simple "gun-type" nuclear bomb.
Source: NATO

bomb was a 76.2-millimeter antiaircraft barrel, 6.5 inches wide, 6 feet long, weighing about 1,000 pounds. A smokeless powder called cordite, normally found in conventional artillery pieces, was used to propel the 56-pound HEU bullet into the 85-pound HEU target.[35]

The main attractions of the gun-type weapon are simplicity and reliability. Manhattan Project scientists were so confident about this design that they persuaded military authorities to drop the bomb, untested, on Hiroshima. South Africa also used this model in building its covert nuclear arsenal without even conducting a test. If terrorists develop an elementary nuclear weapon of their own, they will almost certainly use this design. Two declassified U.S. government publications based on the work of Manhattan Project scientists and engineers in the 1940s, *The Los Alamos Primer* and *Atomic Energy for Military Purposes,* offer instruction on building such a device. Both are available from Amazon.com for a combined price of $40.76, plus shipping. While the books do not quite provide blueprints, they do summarize in detail the hurdles that Manhattan Project scientists faced and explain how they overcame them.

Of course, 100 pounds of HEU is a large amount to acquire through theft or smuggling. But that is only a modest barrier for a determined nuclear terrorist. If a terrorist group obtained plutonium, or an amount of HEU too small to utilize in the gun design, it could attempt to build an implosion-based bomb. The implosion method requires less fissile material than the gun-type bomb, but it is more complex. In this design, precisely shaped explosives are arranged around a less-than-critical mass of fissile material. When the bomb is detonated, the explosion compresses the fissile material, causing a sudden increase in density, which, in turn, increases the number of free neutrons that strike other atoms, triggering a chain reaction. A mass that was subcritical at normal density thus becomes supercritical after sufficient compression.

For an implosion bomb to work, the compression must be symmetrical—the inward force must strike the fissile core equally at every point. The high explosives must detonate simultaneously at points spaced uniformly around the core, with materials of different densities utilized to focus the resulting shock wave. The entire structure of the explosives and firing system resembles a soccer ball. Constructing such a package is technically challenging, but it can be perfected through tests using ordinary metal cores that do not undergo fission. Moreover, a group can easily acquire shaped explosive lenses, which did not exist before the Manhattan Project, because these now have various military and commercial applications (boring holes for oil wells, demolition work, ice-breaking) and are found throughout the world. And as the Princeton student John Aristotle Phillips showed in 1977, the implosion design now lies within the grasp of undergraduate science majors.[36]

If it is so easy for terrorists to build a nuclear bomb, why has it proved so difficult for states like Iraq, Iran, or Libya to do so? The answer is that terrorists and states have different aspirations. For terrorists' purposes, a single, crude nuclear bomb will suffice. Most terrorists will be satisfied with a large, cumbersome, unsafe, unreliable, unpredictable, and inefficient device. In contrast, states seek not a single weapon but a weapons production line, including their

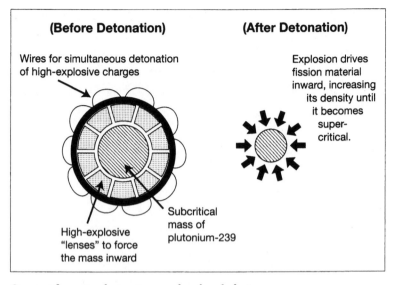

Concept for an implosion-type nuclear bomb design.
Source: NATO

own capacity to make fissile material. But fissile material production is the most technically challenging and expensive hurdle to building nuclear weapons, requiring a substantial industrial enterprise with large buildings, complex precision equipment, and technological expertise. Moreover, while terrorists can deliver weapons by truck or cargo container, states want warheads that can be used for military purposes, particularly smaller weapons that can be delivered on top of a missile.

ENRICHING AND REPROCESSING

Producing fissile material from scratch is likely to prove too difficult for terrorists. The technology, the industrial infrastructure, and the financial commitment for such a project essentially require the resources of a state. But if a terrorist group can rent a state, as Al

Qaeda did in Afghanistan from 1996 to 2001, this undertaking might be feasible, particularly with assistance from the international black market.

A nuclear explosion requires one of two essential elements: uranium-235 and plutonium. Uranium consists naturally of three isotopes, or variants: uranium-234, uranium-235, and uranium-238, of which only uranium-235 is useful for bomb making. However, when extracted from the earth's crust, uranium is composed of less than 1 percent uranium-235 and more than 99 percent uranium-238 (uranium-234 exists only in minute amounts). The goal of a nuclear aspirant is to separate the rare uranium-235 from the more abundant uranium-238, using an arduous process called "enrichment," which takes advantage of the fact that uranium-235 is fractionally lighter than uranium-238. Here is how enrichment works. First, thousands of tons of natural rock must be extracted from the ground, of which 1 to 20 percent is uranium ore. The uranium ore must then be milled by massive crushers and grinders, and soaked with sulfuric acid to leach out the pure uranium. Next, the pure uranium is dried and filtered into a coarse powder called "yellowcake." The yellowcake is then chemically converted into a volatile gaseous compound, uranium hexafluoride, by exposing the yellowcake to fluorine gas and heating it to a temperature of 133 degrees Fahrenheit. The uranium hexafluoride gas is then sent through to high-speed rotational machines called gaseous centrifuges.[37] These sophisticated machines spin at the speed of sound, and each consists of approximately one hundred components that must be manufactured to stringent specifications or else the centrifuges would literally fly apart. As the tubes spin, the different weights of the uranium isotopes cause them to separate, with the heavier uranium-238 being thrown to the outer wall of the centrifuge and the lighter uranium-235 staying near the inside. *New York Times* reporter William Broad has compared these "slender and elegant" machines to "a washing machine on spin cycle."[38] The gas from the inside wall then passes from centrifuge to centrifuge, each step extracting more uranium-235. The process requires about fifteen hundred centrifuges, working in a chain called a "cascade," for about one year to gather enough uranium-235 for a single bomb.[39] The enriched uranium-235 gas is then converted into a metal powder, uranium oxide, which can be shaped into a nuclear bomb charge through a chemical process involving the use of hydrogen and temperatures of 1,500 degrees Fahrenheit.[40]

According to international standards, uranium containing more than 20 percent of the isotope uranium-235 is "highly enriched." While highly enriched uranium is principally used in nuclear weapons, it is also utilized in some nuclear research reactors and submarine propulsion systems. For use in bombs, uranium is generally enriched to a level of 90 percent. The amount required depends on whether a reflector surrounding the fissile material is used to intensify the explosion by forcing neutrons back into the chain reaction. With a reflector made from the element beryllium, a softball-size core of 35 pounds of HEU is required for achieving a critical mass. Without such a reflector, a terrorist would need a lump almost as large as a football, weighing 100 pounds.[41]

The second element that can be used in a nuclear bomb is plutonium-239, a synthetic element. Plutonium is produced during a nuclear reaction when a slow-moving neutron strikes a uranium-238 atom; instead of splitting apart, the uranium absorbs the neutron. This initiates a subatomic reaction, transforming the uranium into plutonium-239. Most plutonium is produced in ordinary nuclear reactors and appears as part of the waste, or spent fuel. The process of extracting the plutonium-239 from spent reactor fuel is known as "reprocessing." Reprocessing involves removing spent fuel rods from the reactor, chopping them up, and dissolving them in nitric acid. The resulting liquid is separated into three streams: plutonium, uranium, and highly radioactive waste products. The solidified plutonium-239 is then usually purified to a concentration of over 90 percent for nuclear weapons, referred to as "weapons-grade." Like enriched uranium, the amount of plutonium required for a nuclear weapon can be reduced when surrounded by a reflector. With a beryllium reflector, 9 pounds of plutonium is sufficient to achieve a critical mass; without a reflector, 33 pounds is necessary.[42]

The recent case histories of Pakistan and North Korea illustrate the obstacles and opportunities along these two paths to a nuclear bomb. As discussed in chapter 3, Pakistan initiated its nuclear program under the tutelage of A. Q. Khan, who had worked at a Dutch uranium enrichment facility in the mid-1970s, where he stole gas centrifuge blueprints. But even with the assistance of a cadre of Western-educated Pakistani scientists who had received advanced degrees in nuclear physics and engineering from MIT, Harvard, and Oxford, it took nearly ten years for Pakistan's centrifuges to begin producing highly enriched uranium. It would be another ten years before the country actually tested a weapon.[43]

North Korea took another direction, focusing on weapons-grade plutonium rather than on highly enriched uranium. The construction, with Soviet assistance, of a thirty-megawatt graphite reactor at Yongbyon in 1979 enabled North Korea to move toward plutonium production, and by 1986 it was producing spent reactor fuel. By the end of that decade, it had diverted enough spent fuel to make one or two nuclear weapons, according to CIA estimates. When North Korea froze its weapons program after a diplomatic showdown with the United States in 1994, eight thousand spent fuel rods were left at Yongbyon under active monitoring by the International Atomic Energy Agency.

In January 2003, North Korea withdrew from the Nuclear Nonproliferation Treaty, evicted IAEA inspectors, ended the monitoring program, and removed an estimated sixty pounds of plutonium-239 from the Yongbyon reprocessing facility. Ten months later, U.S. intelligence detected the telltale release of krypton-85 gas, the by-product of the chemical process that extracts the plutonium-239 from spent reactor fuel.[44] Pyongyang initially admitted and subsequently denied having a secret uranium enrichment facility, reportedly based on Pakistan's P-2 high-speed centrifuge designs, which had been provided in 1997 in exchange for North Korean ballistic missile components.[45]

The sustained financial and political commitment of North Korea and Pakistan illustrates the difficulty involved in enriching uranium and reprocessing plutonium. While they are within the reach of states, especially those left unhindered by the international community, the technology, industrial base, and costs required for producing fissile material present an almost insurmountable obstacle for terrorist organizations without state sanctuary and support. In the post-9/11 world, buying fissile material in the black market is a more attractive option.

buy or steal a nuclear weapon or fissile material, but intent on nuclear terror, could attack a nuclear power plant or detonate a dirty bomb. The only time constraints here are logistical: planning the operation and assembling the necessary materials, explosives, and weapons. An attack on a nuclear power plant could occur whenever terrorists hijack a commercial airplane or charter a private one and fill it with conventional explosives. Dynamite is readily available on the open market, and explosives can be made from materials such as ammonium nitrate fertilizer, which was used in the 1995 Oklahoma City bombing and the 1993 World Trade Center attack. Given the abundance of radioactive sources and availability of conventional explosives, a dirty bomb attack is long overdue. In fact, in the spring of 2002, captured senior Al Qaeda member Abu Zubaydah revealed to interrogators that Al Qaeda not only was interested in dirty bombs, but that they already possessed the knowledge to build them as well.[46] Government analysts believe that Al Qaeda most likely has also acquired radioactive dirty-bomb ingredients such as cesium-137.[47]

Terrorists who acquire a nuclear weapon—whether ready to explode, requiring unlocking, or crudely built from scratch using illicitly acquired fissile material—will not likely use it to blackmail or make empty threats. Instead, seeking to inflict as much damage on the United States as possible, they will explode it. To do so, however, they will have to deliver the bomb to the American homeland. Unfortunately, as the next chapter shows, that may be the easiest step in the whole process.

5

HOW COULD TERRORISTS DELIVER A NUCLEAR WEAPON TO ITS TARGET?

In the spring of 1946, in a closed congressional hearing, J. Robert Oppenheimer was asked "whether three or four men couldn't smuggle units of an [atomic] bomb into New York and blow up the whole city." The father of the atomic bomb answered, "Of course it could be done, and people could destroy New York."

When a nervous senator then asked how such a weapon smuggled in a crate or even a suitcase could be detected, Oppenheimer quipped, "With a screwdriver."

JOHN VON NEUMAN,
letter to Lewis Strauss,
October 18, 1947

ON AUGUST 23, 2003, a suitcase containing fifteen pounds of nuclear material was successfully shipped from Jakarta, Indonesia, to the Port of Los Angeles inside a cargo container aboard the *Charlotte Maersk*. Container no. TEX 2409147, one of eleven thousand arriving at the port that Saturday, passed through Customs unopened and was stored in an adjacent bonded warehouse until it was picked up by Superior Dispatch Trucking. The driver for Superior paid the $60 Customs fee, took the 110 Freeway through downtown Los

Angeles, and delivered the cargo to a storage warehouse one mile from the Los Angeles Convention Center.[1]

The good news is that the nuclear material in question was depleted uranium, a harmless by-product of the uranium enrichment process. ("Depleted" means that nearly all of its uranium-235 has been extracted.) The bad news is that for purposes of detection, depleted uranium when shielded gives off a radioactive signature essentially identical to that of highly enriched uranium—the core of a nuclear bomb. The shipment was a test designed by ABC News investigative reporter Brian Ross to highlight the ease with which terrorists could smuggle nuclear material through U.S. borders. To make the case as realistic as possible, Ross consulted nuclear scientists to help him select a substance that closely resembled nuclear fissile material without threatening public safety or breaking the law. Transported inside a homemade, quarter-inch-thick steel pipe casing with a lead lining, the depleted uranium had an X-ray profile and a radioactive signature essentially equivalent to that of HEU. ABC selected Jakarta as the point of origin for the shipment because it was known to be an active Al Qaeda hot spot after the Bali bombing of October 2002, which killed 202 people. Coincidentally, Jemaah Islamiyah launched its deadly car bombing on the Jakarta Marriott Hotel around the time the material was being shipped (see chapter 1).

An amateur in the contraband game, Ross intentionally avoided sophisticated smuggling techniques. In Jakarta, he and his crew placed the pipe containing the depleted uranium inside an ordinary Samsonite suitcase, which went into a teak trunk. They then used the local yellow pages to locate a freight forwarding company named Maersk Logistics, which advertised full-service, door-to-door delivery from Jakarta to wherever. When Maersk arrived with a standard twenty-foot cargo container, the reporters packed the trunk inside, along with some wooden furniture and terra-cotta pots. The shippers sealed the container with a metal strip that would have to be broken to open it. They asked no questions about the contents of the trunk or the other items. Indeed, they repeatedly told Ross to "stuff anything you want inside the container and don't worry, we'll take care of the paperwork." The shipping agent then made a list of the items supposedly packed inside and gave it to U.S. Customs, again with no questions asked. A few weeks later, the ABC News team was filming the delivery of their unopened container at a warehouse in downtown Los Angeles.

In an interview for the ABC News special, Asa Hutchinson, the undersecretary of homeland defense for border and transportation security, insisted that security officials at the port had identified cargo container TEX 2409147, "targeted it, inspected it, and confirmed that it was not a danger to America." Authorities at the Port of Los Angeles did, in fact, scan the container with an X-ray machine. But like scanners at the airport, Customs' X-rays offer only a two-dimensional picture that traces the shape of a dense object, without any information about what is inside. As a scientific consultant to ABC testified on camera, "The only way to know that this is the real thing, or depleted uranium, is to actually open the container and take a look." Customs would have to follow Oppenheimer's advice and open the container with a screwdriver, unfasten the suitcase, and unscrew the cap on the end of the pipe. But when the ABC News crew received the container in Los Angeles, the metal seal was still intact.

Senator Dianne Feinstein of California called the ABC test "a case in point which established the soft underbelly of national security and homeland defense in the United States."[2] In response to the exposé, federal authorities threatened criminal charges against ABC's reporters, prompting an outcry from both journalists and politicians. As Senator Charles Grassley of Iowa wrote in a letter to Attorney General John Ashcroft, "If my neighbor told me my barn was on fire, my first instinct would be to thank my neighbor and get some water for the fire. I worry that the government's first instinct is to pour cold water on the neighbor."[3]

The nuclear weapon that terrorists would use in the first attack on the United States is far more likely to arrive in a cargo container than on the tip of a missile. In March 2001, six months before 9/11, national intelligence officer Robert Walpole testified to a Senate subcommittee: "Nonmissile delivery means are less costly, easier to acquire, and more reliable and accurate."[4] In addressing Dragonfire's report of a ten-kiloton nuclear weapon in New York in October 2001, the CIA's counterterrorism experts found themselves overwhelmed by the number of nonmissile possibilities. The weapon could have arrived in any of the ways items of similar size and weight reach American cities every day. A football-size lump of HEU enclosed in a lead camera bag and packed inside a suitcase would be indistinguishable from any other metal object of the same size. Every day, 30,000 trucks, 6,500 rail cars, and 140 ships deliver more than 50,000 cargo containers with more than 500,000 items from around the globe.[5] Approximately 21,000 pounds of cocaine and marijuana are smuggled into the country each day in bales, crates, car trunks—even FedEx boxes.[6] Any one of these containers could hold something far more deadly.

FOLLOW THE GOLF CLUBS

The odds are better than 99 in 100 that each of us has come into direct contact today with items shipped to the United States in cargo containers. From the coffee or orange juice we drink in the morning; to the socks, underwear, blouses, and shirts we wear; to the televisions we watch and the computers and cell phones that connect us to the world—the stuff of our daily lives arrives in one of the 200 million cargo containers that form the backbone of the vast international shipping system.[7] These familiar twenty- or forty-foot metal boxes hauled by trucks on the highway are referred to as "intermodal" because they can be transported by ship, rail, or truck. Efficient transportation networks have propelled a hundred-fold increase in global trade over the past fifty years—from $60 billion in 1950 to more than $6 trillion today. The intermodal transportation system moves anything anywhere at ever-increasing speed and shrinking costs. Wal-Mart has essentially become an American distribution arm for Chinese manufacturers, who sold $10 billion worth of goods to the company last year. Designers at the Gap's head-quarters in San Francisco order miniskirts in the color of the sea-son from factories in China, Malaysia, and Indonesia, and have them delivered in weeks to stores in every major American and European city.

Consider a friend who lives in Tokyo and plans to visit the United States next month. An avid golfer, she wants to send her golf clubs ahead, rather than lugging them through airport security. How would she get her clubs to the resort?

One way would be to use the same method that ABC News chose: having the clubs shipped by a freight forwarder. Forwarders are everywhere. The site www.freightnet.com lists such companies in 150 countries, from Algeria to Vanuatu, in the South Pacific. Freight forwarding companies help clients choose the best rates, routes, and modes for transporting goods, from cars and clothing to animals and basmati rice. As long as the sender provides a plausible description of the contents of her shipment—say, a bag of golf clubs—few questions are asked. As Brian Ross found with the Jakarta yellow pages, anyone can pick up the phone and arrange to have items shipped around the world. Forwarders handle all the paperwork, pick up packages at the sender's doorstep, and person-ally deliver them to the port of departure. From there, cargo con-tainers are loaded onto ships bound for destinations all around the world.

Ninety percent of global trade moves through this intermodal shipping system.[8] In 2002, more than seven million seaborne con-tainers reached American shores at a rate of twenty thousand per day.[9] The Port of New York–New Jersey handled about a million of these, while the Port of Los Angeles received almost two million.[10] Even after 9/11, fewer than one in twenty of these containers is inspected upon arrival.[11] The process resembles the experience one has when arriving by air from a trip abroad. The chances of being stopped and inspected by Customs are less than 1 in 100 for ordinary travelers, even though the suitcase checked by the passenger who sat beside you could contain the material for a terrorist nuclear weapon.

Before a ship arrives, Customs officials review shipping manifests, points of origin, and intelligence leads to determine which (if any) of the ship's cargo should be considered "high risk." Customs then inspects these high-risk containers for contraband. In much the same way that airport security personnel go over your carry-on luggage, Customs officials scan the interior of cargo containers with X-ray machines or vehicle and cargo inspection system (VACIS) devices, which use gamma rays to produce a more precise image. When officials find something suspicious, they open the containers for physical inspection. As a rule of thumb, it takes five agents three hours to conduct a thorough physical inspection of a single fully loaded intermodal container. At that rate, in order to keep trade moving efficiently, only a tiny fraction of containers can be physically inspected.[12]

As illustrated by the ABC News test, current inspection methods fail to identify shielded nuclear material. A General Accounting Office study concluded that U.S. port programs "to detect illegal fissile material or nuclear weapons . . . are carried out without the use of adequate detection aids."[13] Currently, Customs officials scan for radiation with pager-size devices clipped to their belts. Department of Energy officials, however, regard these pagers not as search instruments to find fissile material but as personal safety devices to warn workers who might be exposed to major radiation sources.[14]

Customs has begun installing more X-ray and VACIS machines at major ports, along with larger radiation "portal detectors" that can scan entire cargo containers for traces of unshielded radioactivity in minutes.[15] But overall, improvements in port security have lagged far behind airport security and other homeland defense priorities.

During the 2003 debates over the Bush administration's $87 billion funding request for operations in Iraq, Senator Barbara Boxer criticized the proposal for committing "more money to protect the ports in Iraq than here."[16] The Coast Guard is currently doing vulnerability studies for the nation's fifty-five largest ports, but these are not due to be completed until 2008.[17] There is little doubt, however, about what the fundamental conclusion will be. After reviewing the holes in U.S. port security in the summer of 2003, Robert C. Bonner, the commissioner of the Bureau of Customs and Border Protection, acknowledged candidly that "the system of containerized shipping [is] vulnerable to terrorist exploitation."[18]

This vulnerability was first exposed less than a month after September 11, 2001, when an Egyptian Al Qaeda suspect was found hiding in a shipping container on its way from Egypt to Toronto. His possessions included a laptop computer, a satellite phone, airport maps, three security badges for airports in Canada, Egypt, and Thailand, and a certificate from a two-year course in airplane engine maintenance. The stowaway had even set up the cargo container with a bed and a bathroom. Intelligence agencies have also reported that Al Qaeda frequently uses cargo ships to transport conventional weapons, as it did before its attack on the U.S. embassies in Kenya and Tanzania in 1998.[19]

While most global trade moves via seaborne cargo containers, your friend with the golf clubs would probably just call FedEx or UPS. With a fleet of 662 airplanes, FedEx would offer her a simple option for delivery across the world. According to the company's Web site, senders can ship freight of up to 2,200 pounds for air delivery to most cities in the world in one to three days. The Web site even has a "Global Trade Manager" that takes the sender through all the paperwork.[20] FedEx's Tennessee-based operations have turned Memphis International Airport into the world's biggest air cargo hub, handling nearly 3.5 million tons of goods annually.[21] UPS, the next largest air cargo carrier, flies into more than 360 airports in the United States alone, from major airports to one-strip landings in rural outposts.[22]

Would your friend's golf clubs be subject to inspection if she shipped them via FedEx? Not likely. While federal regulations now require all baggage to be screened on passenger flights, they subject less than 10 percent of air cargo on passenger and all-cargo flights to random screening.[23] In January 2004, Senator Charles E. Schumer of New York noted that over 22,600 aircraft carrying unscreened cargo fly into New York airports each month.[24] Freight planes are also held to lower security standards than passenger planes when they are parked on the ground at airports, making their contents more vulnerable to tampering.

In September 2003, a homesick young man in the Bronx named Charles McKinley avoided the cost of an airline ticket by shipping himself to Texas on a cargo plane. McKinley asked a friend to pack him into a shipping crate with a tag declaring the contents to be computer equipment and clothing. Fifteen hours later, McKinley stunned a delivery man at his parents' home near Dallas when he kicked himself free of the box and thanked the man for dropping him off.[25] Because the company McKinley listed as the crate's sender was classified as a "known shipper," its cargo was never subject to inspection. Representative Edward J. Markey of Massachusetts suggested that airline passengers should "ask the TSA [Transportation Security Administration] guards whether there is anyone carrying a crowbar or a gun or a bomb in the cargo hold. If they're honest, they'll tell you, 'We don't know, 'cause we don't check.'"[26]

Even baggage on passenger flights continues to pose a threat. Despite intense scrutiny and billions of dollars in federal spending, screening of passengers and their luggage at American airports remains inadequate. Just over two years after Al Qaeda terrorists boarded Flights 11 and 175 at Logan International Airport in Boston, five undercover agents from the Department of Homeland Security successfully smuggled knives, a bomb, and a gun through several security checkpoints at that airport without being detected. TSA tests of checkpoint screeners have found that they miss as many as 30 percent of simulated bombs when the items are simply thrown in a suitcase, the way a traveler would pack a pair of socks.[27]

If your friend's golf destination is near the border with Mexico or Canada, UPS might fly her clubs into a major airport in that country and drive them across the border in one of its famous brown trucks. The bags would be unlikely to see the light of day until they arrived at their destination. Cargo shipped by truck is inspected by Customs officials at points of entry, using the same less-than-foolproof methods employed to inspect seaborne cargo. Here again, only a fraction of all cargo shipments ever gets physically inspected. Prior to the 9/11 attacks, nearly five thousand trucks passed daily through the world's busiest land-border crossing—Ambassador Bridge, between Detroit, Michigan, and Windsor, Ontario—leaving inspectors just two minutes on average to process each truck.[28] Recognizing this weakness, the United States has begun installing new detection equipment at major points of entry. At the Ambassador Bridge, trucks now drive through radiation-sniffing portals as they cross the border. In July 2003, after these devices were installed, inspectors became accustomed to finding trace amounts of radioactivity in three or four garbage trucks each week. But these detectors are currently in service at only a few of the many border crossings.

Elsewhere, Customs officials rely more on intuition than on technological devices. In December 1999, Customs agent Diana Dean, a nineteen-year veteran, asked a series of routine questions to a driver crossing the U.S.–Canadian border at Port Angeles in northern Washington state—his citizenship, his travel plans, the belongings in his car. But as Dean later put it, "After working on this job a while, you get a knack for knowing when something isn't right."[29] Her gut reaction proved correct: the driver, Ahmed Ressam, was carrying more than one hundred pounds of explosives that he intended to use in Al Qaeda's millennium plot to bomb Los Angeles International Airport. Had she not noticed his nervous behavior, or had Ressam been a better-trained terrorist, he could have entered the United States without a hitch. Following tests in 2002 of U.S. border security by government special investigators, Senator Grassley pointed out, "The border was tested by sea, by air, by car, and on foot. In every instance, our border was penetrated—sometimes the investigators didn't even need their fake IDs."[30]

In any good spy movie, a terrorist trying to sneak a nuclear weapon into the United States would smuggle it across the border under cover of darkness. But once packed into a shipping crate, that nuclear weapon is not so easily distinguished from a bag of golf clubs. Unfortunately, terrorists who do their homework will realize that they can simply ship their nuclear cargo by land, air, or sea to any address in the country and expect it to arrive uninspected up to 95 percent of the time.

FOLLOW THE DRUGS

Terrorists who insist on an even higher likelihood of success will follow the drugs. The Bush administration has declared that the United States is creating "a seamless air, land, and sea border that protects the United States against foreign threats while moving legitimate goods and people into and out of the country."[31] To see how far short of that aspiration current performance falls, one need only consider the tons of drugs and thousands of people who go around, over, under, and through established checkpoints every day.

Professional smugglers have used a wide array of tools and vehicles for delivering their goods: snowmobiles, all-terrain vehicles, night-vision optics, global positioning system (GPS) equipment, cabin cruisers, sailing vessels, private Cessna planes—even corporate jets. In recent years they have literally gone underground. In February 2002, officials from the Drug Enforcement Administration (DEA) discovered a four-foot-wide, 1,200-foot-long tunnel that ran twenty feet underground from Mexico to the small border town of Tecate, California, seventy miles east of San Diego. Through that tunnel, an underground rail system was used to "smuggle billions of dollars' worth of cocaine, marijuana, and other drugs into the United States for several years," according to these officials.[32] The tunnel included electrical lighting and a sophisticated ventilation system. DEA and Customs agents shut down six similar tunnels in the last nine months of 2002, but they know that many more exist, from simple shafts to more elaborate construction projects. The special agent in charge of the San Diego DEA office pointed out that such tunnels "would be a secure way to facilitate the movement of terrorists and weapons of mass destruction."[33]

The continental United States shares a 4,000-mile border with Canada and a 2,000-mile border with Mexico. With Alaska and Hawaii included, the borders stretch for 7,500 miles on land and 12,400 miles along the coastline. Roughly 300 border-crossing points, 360 deepwater seaports, and 430 commercial airports represent official points of entry into the United States. But they constitute less than 1 percent of America's entire 20,000-mile-long perimeter. To a smuggler, the U.S. border must look like a gigantic piece of Swiss cheese, with holes big enough to drive a truck through.

Indeed, in many places, the border disappears altogether. Twenty-one different American Indian reservations stretch across hundreds of miles of the northern and southern borders, and no state or federal agency has jurisdiction to patrol these lands. In New York, roughly ten miles of unpatrolled border crosses through the Akwesasne reservation of the St. Regis Mohawk nation, which has denied access to U.S. agents. As the local Franklin County district attorney remarked, "Over the years, everything has been smuggled through there, from Iranian rugs—when you weren't supposed to bring in Iranian rugs—to people, to drugs, to alcohol and cigarettes. . . . The bad guys have always known about it."[34] Four of the five Great Lakes also straddle the border with Canada. People who set out on the lakes for an afternoon of recreational boating or fishing find no line in the water when they pass from Canada to the United States or vice versa. In northern Maine, some houses are built right on the dividing line, with the living room or the kitchen table technically in two countries.

The 9/11 attacks led U.S. authorities to step up their vigilance at the Canadian border, causing such diplomatic tension that Secretary of State Colin Powell publicly addressed it during a visit to Ottawa in November 2002. A month before Secretary Powell's visit, a Canadian citizen named Michel Jalbert had crossed into Maine to fill up his pickup truck at the gas station before heading out on a hunting expedition. In and around tiny Estcourt Station, Maine—population 4—hundreds of Canadians had made a habit of ducking across the national line for cheaper American gasoline. This time, however, gassing up landed Jalbert in jail on weapons charges, because of the hunting rifle he had brought along in the back of his truck. As he pointed out in his defense, "There's not even a fence there. It was an invisible line. And crossing it was a habit."[35]

But while the political furor over the Jalbert case proved temporary, the incident illustrated the open and permeable nature of many of America's boundaries. Since 9/11, the number of Border Patrol agents assigned to the Canadian border has tripled, from 334 to 1,000. Unfortunately, this still leaves four miles of border per agent. As Kevin Haskew, head of the International Boundary Commission (the U.S. agency responsible for surveying the U.S.–Canadian border), concluded, "You can walk across the border, and nobody's going to know."[36] Even with a higher concentration of agents at the border with Mexico, approximately thirty backpackers carrying up to one hundred pounds of drugs still cross the Tohono O'odham Indian reservation along the Arizona–Mexico border each night. The hikers simply duck under the single strand of barbed wire that marks the line and walk about fifteen miles through the desert to the reservation's villages.[37]

America's coastline offers even greater opportunity. As one former Customs inspector noted in 2002, "less than 10 percent of noncommercial private vessels are inspected by Customs."[38] Sailboats, yachts, and fishing boats sail freely into San Diego or Miami all the time. For years, the Coast Guard has been trying to battle these smuggling tactics as part of its drug enforcement duties, but in 2000, it estimated that it interdicted just 11 percent of the total amount of cocaine smuggled into the United States by these methods. That year, while the U.S. government spent $18.8 billion trying to solve America's drug problem, the DEA said the nation nonetheless consumed 730,000 pounds of cocaine.

Drug trafficking is not the only trade exploiting the holes in America's Swiss-cheese borders. Sneaking illegal immigrants past the Border Patrol has also become a big business. Many migrants pay "coyotes"—professional human smugglers—thousands of dollars to help them enter the country. As many as 500,000 people successfully slip across the border—through tunnels, in the trunks of cars, or on foot overland across the southwestern deserts—and take up residence in the United States each year, despite the more than $9 billion that our government spends each year on border controls as part of the national homeland security effort. As one officer put it, "The best we can do is manage the border, not control it."[39]

Almost all the smuggling routes that are used in bringing illegal immigrants or drugs into the United States would be an equally effective way to transport a nuclear weapon across the border. After all, a nuclear weapon is smaller than a person, and the HEU or plutonium for a bomb's core could weigh less than the hundred-pound loads of drugs that smugglers bring in backpacks. It is not uncommon for migrants to get themselves deep into the United States without anyone noticing. Any sophisticated terrorist group can surely do better.

LOOKING FOR A NEEDLE IN A HAYSTACK
OF NEEDLES

In 1974, the FBI received a note threatening to explode a nuclear bomb somewhere in Boston if a $200,000 ransom was not paid. The threat caught authorities completely by surprise. A team of experts from the FBI was rushed to the city to search for the blackmailer's bomb. Scientists from the Atomic Energy Commission flew in to assist the FBI, but unfortunately their radiation detection gear arrived at a different airport.[40] Federal officials rented a fleet of vans to carry concealed radiation detectors around the city's streets, but forgot to bring the tools they needed to install the equipment.[41] Thankfully, the threat was a hoax. "If they were counting on us to save the good folk of Boston," one of the searchers later observed, "well, it was bye-bye Boston."[42]

The good news is that if the FBI received a similar threat today, the U.S. government would find itself much better prepared to respond. Following the false alarm in Boston, President Gerald Ford established the elite Nuclear Emergency Support Teams (NEST). A "volunteer fire department for the atomic age," NEST has as its mission to assess the likelihood of nuclear threats, find nuclear devices, and disable them. NEST personnel include one thousand highly trained volunteers, including physicists, engineers, chemists, and mathematicians, who work throughout the country in nuclear laboratories and with private contractors. When deployed to investigate a potential nuclear incident, these "nuclear ninjas" often disguise themselves as tourists or local residents, with their gamma ray and neutron detectors hidden inside briefcases, beer coolers, or golf bags.[43] Other searchers may ride around the area in vans specially outfitted with bulkier detection equipment and painted to blend in with commercial vehicles on the road.[44] To support the teams on the ground, NEST also maintains a fleet of planes and helicopters equipped with sophisticated radiological sensing systems at Nellis Air Force base, just outside Las Vegas.

Since 1975, NEST has been warned of 125 nuclear terror threats and has responded to around 30. All have been false alarms. Linton Brooks, head of the National Nuclear Safety Administration, told Congress in July 2002 that since the 9/11 attacks, "officials had performed approximately 70 assessments" of possible nuclear-related incidents.[45] In December 2003, technicians with radiation detectors wandered through Times Square and other crowded New Year's Eve venues in Washington, Los Angeles, and Las Vegas. While there was no specific intelligence pointing to an imminent radiological attack, officials decided to err on the side of caution. According to the Defense Department, similar techniques are in effect constantly within the Pentagon and around the president.[46]

If authorities learned tomorrow that terrorists had managed to smuggle a nuclear weapon into Washington, could they actually find it? If the searchers had to investigate the entire capital, then the answer would almost certainly be no. If intelligence sources specified that the bomb was hidden somewhere inside the Capitol building, however, then they would have a better-than-even chance of tracking it down.

The laws of physics give the hiders enormous advantages over the seekers. Despite their advanced degrees and technologies, NEST scientists face the same challenges in finding nuclear weapons as do border guards and customs officials: the low level of radioactivity emitted by HEU, the ease with which it is shielded, and the frequent false alarms caused by naturally occurring background radiation. As David Kay, the former U.S. chief nuclear weapons inspector in Iraq, has noted, "If you make very sensitive sensors, [background radiation is] going to start kicking off those sensors and then you're going to pull a lot of agricultural products and mineral products aside, and find absolutely nothing."[47] Indeed, there are any number of radioactive sources in the United States, including freshly paved roads, the polished granite used in most federal buildings in Washington, and even orange Fiesta Ware dinner plates. According to one NEST volunteer, distinguishing a bomb's radioactive signature from natural radiation "is like looking for a needle in a haystack of needles."[48]

Concern about a nuclear terrorist attack on the capital led to the construction in November 2001 of a "Ring around Washington." Using the best available technology, federal officials assembled a grid of hundreds of sophisticated radiation detection devices at major points of approach to the nation's capital, such as Interstate 95 and the Potomac River. Aircraft and ground vehicles also patrolled the city with mobile sensors. According to Bush administration officials, during large-scale operational trials the sensors repeatedly failed to identify threatening radioactive signatures. In other instances, the detectors raised false alarms by reading hazardous medical waste and granite monuments. After several months, the "Ring" was shut down.[49]

New York City also responded to the threat of nuclear terror by installing a network of radiation detection devices at its ports, toll-booths, bridges, and tunnels, on its garbage trucks, and in its subway system. But this network, too, has been bogged down by false positives. According to the *Journal of the American Medical Association*, a man who ingested radioactive iodine to treat Graves's disease set off alarms while riding on a Manhattan subway. After being interrogated and strip-searched, the man was sent on his way by police detectives.[50]

In addition to the problem of background radiation, NEST searchers are aware that terrorists could conceal a nuclear device within a container lined with lead or tungsten to shield detectable radiation emissions. Kay explains that "a nuclear weapon is a device . . . that has damn few signatures unless you're up really feeling it—I mean up close, personal."[51] For all of their modern equipment, a NEST squad searching the Capitol building for a shielded nuclear device would have to follow Oppenheimer's advice and take screwdrivers to every sealed container, access panel, and ventilation shaft, to get sensors within range of each potential hiding place.

The Bush administration acknowledges that technology will not save us from nuclear terrorism. As one official noted: "It's not going to be about technology. It's going to be about intelligence. I am 100 percent sure we will fail if you tell me there's a nuclear weapon 'somewhere in New York City.' If you tell me Lower Manhattan, the odds are a little bit better. If you tell me a neighborhood, we will probably find it."[52] Kay considers nuclear terrorism defenses based on radiation detectors and search teams a "fool's game." "You're going to try to interrupt the terrorist on his final run to target," he says, but "there are too many ways to get there; you don't often know the actual target until after the attack."[53] In the game of nuclear hide-and-seek, the odds are stacked against NEST producing a last-second rescue and a happy Hollywood ending.

THE PRECEDING FIVE chapters do not paint an encouraging picture. There are numerous terrorist groups, from Al Qaeda to Hezbollah to various doomsday cults, who would have the motive and capacity to seek out nuclear weapons. The deadly effects of these weapons far exceed those of conventional munitions. Nuclear material and weapons are poorly guarded in much of the former Soviet Union and in the developing world, and proliferators like Pakistan and North Korea are making this bad situation worse. If terrorists do get their hands on a nuclear device or on highly enriched uranium or plutonium, they could easily make a bomb operational within a year. And once they have a nuclear weapon in hand, America's porous border controls will offer little resistance as they seek to deliver the bomb to its target. Whether the question asked begins with who, what, where, when, or how, the answer comes back the same. If we continue along our present course, nuclear terrorism is inevitable.

But this is not a counsel of fatalism. Unlike the many intractable problems facing humankind, nuclear terrorism is preventable if we act now to make it so.

PART TWO

PREVENTABLE

6

THROUGH THE PRISM OF 9/11

Only slowly did it dawn upon us that the whole world
structure and the order we had inherited was gone. . . .
Over and over I had to learn how false were our postulates.

DEAN ACHESON,
Present at the Creation

We saw the existing evidence in a new light through the
prism of our experience on 9/11.

Secretary of Defense DONALD RUMSFELD

AL QAEDA'S ATTACK on September 11 awakened Americans to their
vulnerability to a catastrophic terrorist attack. The security bubble
in which we had lived burst, and ordinary men and women across
the country discovered fear—personal fear of attack by shadowy
figures in distant lands. And the threat of nuclear terrorism sud-
denly became incandescent. Skeptics who had long argued that no
one could seriously want to kill thousands of Americans shut up.
Preventing attacks vastly worse than 9/11 obviously deserved highest priority. Surely after 9/11 the Bush administration would do
everything in its power to minimize the threat of this ultimate catastrophe?

In the weeks and months that followed, Americans rallied
around the flag, behind the commander in chief, giving President

George W. Bush license to do whatever he deemed necessary to prevent future terrorist attacks. In ordering military attacks abroad and placing new constraints on freedoms at home, the president acted in confidence that he would have broad bipartisan support from Congress and the American people in prosecuting the war on terrorism. Three years later, the question is: Has the U.S. government kept its eye on the antiterrorism ball?

Through the prism of 9/11, the Bush administration saw that the status quo was fatally flawed. The inherited international order left America vulnerable to catastrophic terrorist attacks. Despite America's overwhelming military, political, and economic power, a determined band of terrorists toppled two of our tallest buildings in a flash. Absent fundamental changes in the international security system, terrorists would move on to what President Bush called his "nightmare scenario": a nuclear terrorist attack that would make 9/11 look like a minor tragedy. Such conditions were incompatible with our survival as a free nation, in which our fundamental institutions and values remained intact.

The president and leaders of Congress recognized that the United States and its allies had essentially stood by and let this happen. In the sanctuary of Afghanistan, behind the accepted legal shield of "sovereign immunity," Al Qaeda had trained thousands of terrorists for attacks like 9/11. It was now clear that the United States and the civilized world could no longer allow the presumption of sovereign immunity to permit developments inconsistent with our common survival. In a process of fits and starts, the Bush administration began inventing a "new" new world order. One essential requirement of that order is that it protect us from terrorists with weapons of mass destruction. And yet no coherent strategy for combating nuclear terrorism has emerged.

DECLARATION OF WAR ON TERRORISM

Nine days after the attacks on the World Trade Center and the Pentagon, President Bush officially declared war on terrorism. In an address to a joint session of Congress, he announced, "Enemies of freedom committed an act of war against our country."[1] The president's choice of words marked a dramatic shift from the language of law enforcement to the language of war. The Clinton administration had treated the bombings of American embassies in Kenya and Tanzania in 1998 and the attack on the USS *Cole* in 2000 primarily as criminal acts, to be dealt with by the Justice Department and the FBI. Some suggested that the Bush administration respond to the World Trade Center and Pentagon attacks in much the same way. Sir Michael Howard, a leading Anglo-American historian and strategist, argued that "the United States is not 'at war' in any recognizable sense of the word. . . . It is confronted with a hideous international crime."[2] But President Bush had no intention of turning over the 9/11 case to a team of lawyers. Instead, he unleashed the full might of the American military superpower, including Special Forces units and intelligence operatives, against Al Qaeda and its allies, the Taliban government in Afghanistan. As Cofer Black, the State Department's counterterrorism chief, testified to a joint Senate-House review of the attacks in New York and Washington, "After 9/11, the gloves came off."[3]

President Bush also insisted from the outset that the war extend beyond the perpetrators of 9/11 to include all terrorists with global reach: "Our war on terror begins with Al Qaeda, but it does not end there," he told Congress. "It will not end until every terrorist group of global reach has been found, stopped and defeated."[4] The ambitious scope of the new campaign would require every resource and ally the United States could muster, from the military and the CIA to foreign intelligence agencies and local police units around the globe. Neutrality was not an option. "Every nation, in every region, now has a decision to make," the president proclaimed. "Either you are with us, or you are with the terrorists."[5]

Despite discomfort with some of Bush's rhetoric, the international response was overwhelmingly positive. Universal sympathy for the victims of the terrorist attacks led governments and citizens around the world to proclaim solidarity under the banner "We are all Americans." A week after Bush's speech, the UN Security Council unanimously passed Resolution 1373, requiring member states to undertake affirmative obligations to freeze terrorist assets, deny terrorist groups support or safe havens, cooperate with other governments to prevent terrorist acts and prosecute those who commit them, and criminalize active and passive assistance for terrorist activity. The UN announced its "determination to take all necessary steps to ensure the full implementation of this resolution" and established a special Counterterrorism Committee, chaired by Sir Jeremy Greenstock, the British ambassador to the UN, to organize and monitor states' efforts to comply. Two years later, in October 2003, the U.S. deputy ambassador to the UN, James B. Cunningham, announced that the world organization had "achieved universal engagement in Resolution 1373, with all 191 Member States submitting reports on their counterterrorism capabilities and steps taken to implement the Resolution."[6]

Conceptually, the president's war on terrorism broke new ground in formulating what his staffers named the Bush Doctrine. "From this day forward," he declared, "any nation that continues to harbor or support terrorism will be regarded by the United States as a hostile regime."[7] The Bush Doctrine effectively revoked the sovereignty of states that provided sanctuary for terrorists. Sovereign immunity had been a central pillar of the international system established by the Treaty of Westphalia, which ended the Thirty Years' War in 1648 and made nation-states the principal actors in international affairs. Three hundred years later, this model of international order was reaffirmed in the UN Charter, expressed as "non-interference in the internal affairs of states."

When the UN was founded at the end of World War II, the great powers worried about wars of aggression by one country against another, like Hitler's invasion of Poland. Newly independent states worried equally about colonial domination. Member states from both camps, however, agreed that what happened within the borders of a sovereign state should remain a domestic affair, free from outside interference. Even as late as 1994, the genocide in Rwanda— in which hundreds of thousands were killed in a matter of weeks— was allowed to happen in part because the conflict between the Hutus and the Tutsis was considered an internal Rwandan affair. The standard of noninterference began to erode later in the decade, when the UN and NATO intervened in the Balkans in response to ethnic cleansing there. But the 9/11 attacks demonstrated, once and for all, that unconditional sovereignty was incompatible with basic national security. Al Qaeda's murder of nearly three thousand Americans on 9/11—hatched in the training camps in Afghanistan and abetted by the Taliban—opened Americans' eyes to an unacceptable vulnerability.

The war in Afghanistan served as the first application of the Bush Doctrine and the opening salvo of America's global war on terrorism. The invasion of Afghanistan had a clear military purpose: to overthrow the Taliban, replace it with a moderate pro-Western government, and capture or kill as many Al Qaeda operatives as possible. But it also heralded a new assertiveness in U.S. foreign policy and demonstrated America's unparalleled military dominance. The speed and efficiency with which U.S. forces dispatched the Taliban drove home both points. Hereafter, any government knowingly hosting Al Qaeda or equivalent groups would invite attack. Moreover, given America's overwhelming military dominance, it had the power to topple other regimes unilaterally, without requiring others' assistance or asking their permission.

Yet the war on terrorism has lacked a commander and a clear chain of command, even within the U.S. national security establishment. Tension between the Pentagon and the CIA over who was in charge in Afghanistan frequently flared up. As Bob Woodward's book *Bush at War* reveals, at a critical National Security Council meeting, Donald Rumsfeld said defensively, "This is the CIA's strategy. They developed the strategy. We're just executing the strategy." When a top CIA official disagreed, claiming that his agents were acting only in support of the Pentagon, Rumsfeld shot back: "No, you guys are in charge. You guys have the contacts. We're just following you in."[8] This tension stemmed from the two-pronged invasion strategy: an Air Force bombing campaign followed on the ground by Afghan opposition forces (the Northern Alliance) accompanied by CIA liaison officers. While this strategy minimized American casualties and succeeded in ousting the Taliban, it predictably increased the likelihood of Osama bin Laden and his associates escaping, since it extended the time line between the start of hostilities and the arrival of CIA operatives or Special Forces units who might have captured him. Moreover, the "rented" Northern Alliance fighters had multiple loyalties—giving bin Laden both time and warning to abandon his mountain hideout in Tora Bora. Had U.S. Special Forces taken the lead, bin Laden might have been captured in December 2001.

IDENTIFYING THE THREAT

Horrific as the attack on the World Trade Center was, the Bush administration rightly saw the potential for even worse attacks in the future. The false alarm in October 2001 of a nuclear bomb in New York City, as well as a sweeping reexamination of previous evidence through the prism of 9/11, alerted the president and his advisers to the scope of the nuclear danger. In a vivid line repeated in countless speeches and press briefings, Bush identified the defining threat for the foreseeable future: "the world's most destructive technologies" in the hands of "the world's most dangerous people."[9]

For most of recorded history, only states have had the capacity to kill citizens of other states on a massive scale. But the relentless advance of technology is now "democratizing" or "denationalizing" killing capabilities. On 9/11, in an operation that cost less than $500,000, a nongovernmental terrorist group executed a deadlier attack on the American homeland than any foreign government had managed in the country's previous two hundred years. As Vice President Cheney watched the chaos in New York following the collapse of the World Trade Center, he observed to an aide, "As unfathomable as this was, it could have been so much worse if they had weapons of mass destruction."[10]

National security experts agree that nuclear terrorism is the focal threat facing America today. As Robert Kagan has noted, the nexus between terrorism and weapons of mass destruction has become "the reigning foreign policy paradigm of the post-9/11 era."[11] Democrats and Republicans alike support the Bush administration's declaration that "our highest priority is to keep terrorists from acquiring weapons of mass destruction."[12] But the implications of such a major shift in attitudes about national security and nuclear nonproliferation are still unfolding. The realization that the nexus of terrorists and nuclear weapons represents the greatest danger to the United States has required a fundamental shift in strategic thinking about these weapons. Since the advent of the nuclear age, the greatest danger to the United States had always come from other states, particularly nuclear-armed nations like the former Soviet Union. While that danger has not gone away, with the end of the Cold War it has greatly diminished. Moreover, even during the most dangerous moments of the Cold War, a nation that attacked the United States with a nuclear-armed ballistic missile would know that it had signed its own death certificate, since U.S. retaliation would be immediate and overwhelming. For decades, this strategy of mutually assured destruction created a stable, if grotesque, stalemate between the U.S. and Soviet nuclear superpowers.

The 9/11 attacks radically changed our understanding of the nuclear equation. In the 1990s, new nuclear states were seen as a menace because they might take direct action against their regional rivals and ignite a nuclear war. Today, they are feared even more because of their potential as conduits of nuclear weapons and technology to terrorists. Indeed, the highest nonproliferation priority today is to prevent nonstate actors from acquiring nuclear weapons or nuclear technology—especially from new nuclear powers, like Pakistan, or from emerging nuclear powers, like North Korea or Iran. Another complicating factor is that the ground troops of Islamist terrorism are unaffected by a fear of death, making deterrence inoperable as a strategy. Even if Osama bin Laden and his deputies wish to stay alive to carry on the jihad, they operate in the dark alleys and caves of the world, without a home base against which the United States could retaliate, leaving them free to attack America with near impunity. A nuclear bomb smuggled into the country inside a ship or a truck and detonated by surprise would leave no return address. In the aftermath of a nuclear attack, America's leaders could find themselves with no idea of where it came from, or how and against whom to respond.

SEARCHING FOR A STRATEGY

Having identified the threat, the president and his team have struggled to devise an appropriate response. Three distinctive features of the administration's efforts to date have emerged. First, the administration decided to go on the offensive against terrorists. As the *Washington Post* editorial columnist Fred Hiatt summarized the president's view: "If the nation learned a single lesson from Sept. 11, it should be this: that the only way to defeat terrorists is to attack them."[13] Second, the administration chose to confront openly what it called the "axis of evil"—North Korea, Iran, and Iraq—threatening them with regime change. Third, and most controversial, the administration asserted a doctrine of "preemption," according to which it reserves the right to attack its adversaries before they attack the United States.

This preference for the offensive manifested itself on multiple levels. The Bush administration asserted America's global military dominance and its readiness to use its unique capability to protect and advance American interests. Since America's military could destroy just about any government in the world, leaders of other countries ruled at our sufferance. As one disillusioned State Department official wrote in a letter of resignation in February 2003, the administration seemed to have adopted the Roman emperor Caligula's dictum *Oderint dum metuant:* "Let them hate as long as they fear."[14]

The administration justified its focus on the axis of evil and adoption of a doctrine of preemption as necessary responses to a single unifying imperative: preventing another catastrophic terrorist attack on America. Singling out Iraq, Iran, and North Korea as threats in his 2002 State of the Union address, President Bush argued that "States like these, and their terrorist allies, constitute an axis of evil, arming to threaten the peace of the world."[15] "By seeking weapons of mass destruction," the president said, "these regimes pose a grave and growing danger. They could provide these arms to terrorists, giving them the means to match their hatred."[16]

In its attempt to fashion a coherent post-9/11 strategy for combating catastrophic terrorism, the Bush administration got a number of things right. First, it made the crucial conceptual breakthrough that "the gravest danger to freedom lies at the perilous crossroads of radicalism and technology"—terrorists armed with nuclear weapons. It rightly rejected a status quo that left the terrorist and WMD threats to international law. It recognized that unless America took the lead and carried most of the load, the war on terrorism would falter. It embraced the use of America's full-spectrum military dominance to defeat international terrorists wherever they were found. And it was willing to revise traditional Cold War policies of deterrence and containment in those cases where they no longer applied. Deterrence, which discouraged other states from launching a nuclear attack on the United States through the threat of overwhelming retaliation, was useless against nonstate terrorists who did not fear death. Nuclear terrorism required strategies different from the ones that had been designed to counter nuclear states.

And yet it missed almost entirely the "supply side" of this challenge: neutralizing the means by which terrorists might mount a nuclear terrorist attack. Nunn-Lugar funding for eliminating potential nuclear weapons in Russia remained at the same level established under the previous administration, and execution of the program continued at the same lethargic pre-9/11 pace. With the exception of the G8 initiative to enlist other states to help fund this activity, and the Proliferation Security Initiative to search vehicles suspected of transporting WMD cargo, no one observing the behavior of the U.S. government after 9/11 would note any significant changes in activity aimed at preventing terrorists from acquiring the world's most destructive technologies.

Imagine in contrast that the president's speech to the joint session of Congress on September 20, 2001, had included a page aimed directly at this threat. He might have said, "Today I am asking Congress for $10 billion to secure and eliminate vulnerable potential nuclear weapons in Russia and other states of the former Soviet Union over the next one hundred days. I have spoken with President Putin and we have agreed that there is no matter of greater urgency in U.S.–Russian relations than our joint effort to reduce the threat of nuclear terrorist attacks on our nations and the world. I have spoken to leaders of Congress and asked them to form a bipartisan panel that will work with me and the members of my administration to address the threat of nuclear terrorism. I have asked former senator Sam Nunn to become ambassador-at-large with responsibility for doing whatever it takes to protect America from nuclear terrorist attacks. He will head a task force within the White House charged with ensuring that the U.S. government is taking every feasible action without delay, and bringing to me on a daily basis any obstacle within the government, or between our government and other governments, that he is unable to overcome. At the end of this initial crash program, he and other key members of my national security team will propose an ongoing program by which we can prevent nuclear terrorism in our lifetime."

Unfortunately, the administration has failed to declare war on nuclear terrorism. As a result, Americans are no safer from a nuclear terrorist attack today than we were on September 10, 2001. A central reason for that can be summed up in one word: Iraq.

THE REAL COST OF THE WAR IN IRAQ

Whatever one thinks about the Bush administration's decision to go to war against Iraq, the fact remains that the stated reason for toppling Saddam Hussein—his possession of a cache of nuclear, biological, and chemical weapons—does not withstand close scrutiny. Deputy Secretary of Defense Paul Wolfowitz acknowledged as much in a candid *Vanity Fair* interview in which he explained: "For bureaucratic reasons, we settled on one issue, weapons of mass destruction, because it was the one reason everyone could agree on."[17] The WMD threat served as the administration's least common denominator and most effective sales pitch, not its top priority. In the campaign to prevent nuclear terrorism, Iraq was at best a strategic diversion and at worst a strategic blunder.

The diversion of scarce resources from war on terrorism to Iraq was evident across the spectrum of the U.S. government. Anything that required high-level attention, direction, and drive floundered as the president, the secretary of state, the secretary of defense, and the national security adviser focused on making the case for and conducting war against Iraq. Agendas for meetings at CIA and the Pentagon focused intensely on preparing for and adjudicating differences over Iraq—not terrorism. Like a company pursuing a hostile takeover, the leadership's bandwidth was consumed by this great undertaking.

Less than two months after the government in Kabul fell, the

U.S. Central Command—which directs military operations in both Afghanistan and Iraq—began complaining that Pentagon orders to shift key units and weapons to Iraq were draining its capacity for pursuing war against Al Qaeda. More than three hundred commandos from the Army's Arabic-speaking Fifth Special Forces Group were redeployed from Afghanistan to Iraq in February 2003,[18] replaced by a group that specialized in Latin America. As a result, intelligence liaisons with southern Afghan tribes were lost.[19] Unmanned Predator aircraft armed with Hellfire missiles, which in November 2002 located and killed a top Al Qaeda leader in Yemen, were also diverted to Iraq. After Saddam Hussein's regime was toppled, the CIA's station in Baghdad rapidly became its largest mission in the world. In February 2004, the *New York Times* reported that Task Force 121, a covert commando team that had played a major role in capturing Saddam, was only then moving back to Afghanistan in a push to capture Osama bin Laden.[20]

By devoting most of its energy and leverage to Iraq during 2002 and 2003, the United States neglected higher-priority threats to its national security. North Korea and Iran were essentially given breathing room to advance their own nuclear ambitions. Al Qaeda and affiliated terrorist groups had an opportunity to recover, adjust, and adapt following the war in Afghanistan, which was truly disruptive to their activities. While the U.S. government did not quite shut its eyes, it nonetheless blinked at evidence of Pakistani nuclear black marketeering.

In the immediate aftermath of 9/11, objective assessments of the danger of nuclear terrorism identified North Korea as a greater potential threat than Iraq. At that time, the American intelligence community believed that North Korea probably possessed one or two nuclear weapons, created in the early 1990s by reprocessing fuel rods from Yongbyon. In the fall of 2002, North Korea shrewdly seized its opportunity and announced that it would begin making more nuclear weapons, while U.S. attention was fixated on Iraq. The administration responded by repeating its mantra: "no crisis."

On *Meet the Press* in December 2002, Secretary of State Colin Powell conveyed the administration's sense of resignation: "Yes, the North Koreans have had these couple of weapons for many years, and if they have a few more, they have a few more, and they could have them for many years."[21] Such passivity in the face of a growing North Korean nuclear threat is dumbfounding.

In the State Department's annual report on terrorism, Iran holds the uncontested distinction as "the most active state sponsor of terrorism." America's preoccupation with Iraq provided Iran with a welcome respite during which it accelerated its secret programs to enrich uranium and reprocess plutonium in the quest for nuclear weapons. Intelligence about the secret facilities in Natanz and Arak was first revealed in August 2002, followed by satellite imagery in December 2002, and confirmed by an IAEA visit in February 2003. With U.S. energies focused on Iraq, Iran escaped diplomatic censure until October 2003, the deadline given by the IAEA for Iran to come clean. Meanwhile, it continued importing the equipment and material required to establish its own facilities to manufacture centrifuges for uranium enrichment.

The administration's pursuit of war with Iraq also undermined key alliances required for victory in the longer-term war on terrorism at a time when they most needed strengthening. As a result, America's strategic partnerships are today in worse shape than at any time since World War II. Europe, the second pillar of the transatlantic alliance, America's top trading partner, and a reservoir of shared values, now views the American government with deep suspicion. In the fall of 2003, a poll of citizens in all fifteen European Union nations produced results no one had anticipated, and that most Americans still find unbelievable. Asked which nations pose a "threat to world peace," citizens in every European country put the United States at the top of the list, alongside North Korea and Iran.[22] Similarly, a German Marshall Fund survey of June 2003 found that nine out of ten respondents in France and Germany thought that U.S. unilateralism would be an important threat to international peace in the next decade. In Britain and Poland, two of America's staunchest allies in the war against Iraq, two out of every three citizens agreed with this proposition.[23] Imagine mobilizing active support for blunting the nuclear threat from North Korea or Iran on such a footing.

America's standing in the Muslim world fell still further and faster. In Indonesia, the nation with the largest Muslim population in the world and a critical battleground in the war on terrorism, the U.S. favorability rating fell from 61 percent in early 2002 to 15 percent in the summer of 2003.[24] A year after the war in Iraq, a substantial majority of Pakistanis, Turks, Jordanians, and Moroccans found U.S. motives in the war on terrorism suspect, and believed that the United States was overreacting to the threat.[25] Asked whom they trust to "do the right thing in world affairs," more Pakistanis, Indonesians, and Jordanians chose Osama bin Laden than President Bush.[26]

Ironically, the U.S. war in Iraq realized bin Laden's vision, convincing majorities across the Muslim world that the "Christian-Zionist crusaders" had launched a war of civilizations against Muslims around the world. Strong majorities in Turkey, Pakistan, Indonesia, and Nigeria said they feared that the United States could become a military threat to them. As the former National Security Council official Richard Clarke put it in an interview with *60 Minutes,* "Osama bin Laden had been saying for years, 'America wants to invade an Arab country and occupy it, an oil-rich Arab country.' So what did we do after 9/11? We invade and occupy an oil-rich Arab country that was doing nothing to threaten us. In other words, we stepped right into bin Laden's propaganda."[27]

Finally, the decision to market the war against Iraq as a necessary response to an impending danger of WMD attacks on the United States and its allies discredited the larger case for a serious campaign to prevent nuclear terrorism. The argument for launching war against Iraq in the spring of 2003, rather than at some later date, after the inspectors finished their work or had been ejected by

Saddam, rested on two propositions: (1) Saddam was racing to acquire a nuclear capability that he could transfer to Al Qaeda or other terrorists; and (2) Saddam posed an imminent threat that required immediate action.

The assertions regarding Saddam's nuclear and other WMD programs were simply wrong. In a speech to the Veterans of Foreign Wars in August 2002, Vice President Cheney said, "Many of us are convinced that Saddam will acquire nuclear weapons fairly soon."[28] Two months later, George Bush claimed, "The evidence indicates that Iraq is reconstituting its nuclear weapons program."[29] Just days before the beginning of the war, Cheney took that claim even further on *Meet the Press*: "We believe Saddam Hussein has, in fact, reconstituted nuclear weapons."[30] But as David Kay concluded in October 2003 after leading the search for WMD in Iraq, "We have not uncovered evidence that Iraq undertook significant post-1998 steps to actually build nuclear weapons or produce fissile material."[31] In a later, postwar appearance on *Meet the Press*, Cheney confessed, "I did misspeak."[32]

The administration's claims regarding the imminence of the Iraqi threat were not only wrong; they directly contradicted the consensus judgment of the best analysis in the U.S. intelligence community. While the administration subsequently attempted to argue that it never actually said "imminent," its words certainly conveyed this message. In September 2002, Secretary of Defense Rumsfeld testified to the House Armed Services Committee, "Some have argued that the nuclear threat from Iraq is not imminent—that Saddam is at least five to seven years away from having nuclear weapons. I would not be so certain."[33] National security adviser Condoleezza Rice implied imminence when she said, "We don't want the smoking gun to be a mushroom cloud."[34] And President Bush himself systematically employed synonyms: "a threat of unique urgency," "a real and dangerous threat," and "a grave and gathering danger." As he put it in a September 2002 White House press briefing, "Each passing day could be the one on which the

Iraq regime gives anthrax or V X or someday a nuclear weapon to a terrorist ally."[35]

The U.S. intelligence community flatly disagreed. The classified National Intelligence Estimate (NIE) on Iraq in October 2002 stated unequivocally: in the absence of a U.S. attack, the likelihood of Saddam attacking us with chemical and biological weapons in the future was "low." On the other hand, if Saddam became convinced that we were about to topple his regime, intelligence analysts concluded, the likelihood he would attack us with chemical or biological weapons was "high."[36] In sum: to prevent an attack whose likelihood was low, the U.S. was taking action that made the likelihood of that attack high. Almost a year after the war began, CIA director Tenet reminded critics that U.S. intelligence "never said Iraq was an imminent threat." In fact, the NIE on Iraq presented a measured picture of the country's nuclear program. "If left unchecked," the NIE reported, "Iraq probably will have a nuclear weapon during this decade." It concluded: "Without [acquiring fissile] material from abroad, Iraq probably would not be able to make a weapon until 2007 to 2009."[37]

The administration's exaggerations about Iraq have seriously eroded foreign governments' and citizens' trust in the competence of American intelligence agencies, and corroded the credibility of the U.S. president. By exaggerating fears of nuclear weapons in the case of Iraq, and then being exposed, the administration has encouraged many people, abroad and at home, to discount the real and growing threat of nuclear proliferation and nuclear terrorism. A willingness to pull the trigger does Americans no good if the shooter does not know where to aim.

While the administration has correctly identified the threat of nuclear terrorism, it has not formulated a comprehensive strategy to address it. Without such a strategy, Americans will be no safer from a nuclear terrorist attack next year or the year following than they were on September 10, 2001.

Waging war on nuclear terrorism will require strategic focus in mobilizing a concert of the great powers based on a shared assessment of the threat, a vision of a world beyond nuclear terror, and a joint effort to persuade international publics of the urgency and legitimacy of the actions required to defeat this common danger. The move beyond the current war on terrorism to a serious war on nuclear terrorism would be ambitious. But the stretch involved would be no greater than the distance already traveled since September 11.

7

WHERE WE NEED TO BE:
A WORLD OF THREE NO'S

At the dawn of a new century, we find ourselves in a new
arms race. Terrorists are racing to get weapons of mass
destruction; we ought to be racing to stop them.

Former senator SAM NUNN

FOR ALL THE dangers enumerated in the earlier chapters of this book, a simple fact remains: nuclear terrorism is, in fact, preventable. Only a fission chain reaction releases the vast blast of energy that is the hallmark of a nuclear bomb. No fissile material, no nuclear explosion, no nuclear terrorism. It is that simple.

All that the United States and its allies have to do to prevent nuclear terrorism is to prevent terrorists from acquiring highly enriched uranium or weapons-grade plutonium. This "all," of course, will require a huge undertaking. But large as it is, this is a finite challenge, subject to a finite solution. The world's stockpiles of nuclear weapons and weapons-usable materials are vast but not unlimited. Technologies for locking up superdangerous or valuable items are well developed. The United States does not lose gold from Fort Knox, nor does Russia lose treasures from the Kremlin Armory. Producing additional fissile material requires large, complex, expensive, and visible facilities, leaving such enterprises vulnerable to interruption by a watchful, determined international community. Keeping nuclear weapons and materials out of the hands of the world's most dangerous people is thus a challenge to international will and determination, not to our technical capabilities.

The centerpiece of a strategy to prevent nuclear terrorism must be to deny terrorists access to nuclear weapons or materials. To do this, we must shape a new international security order according to a doctrine of "Three No's":

- No Loose Nukes
- No New Nascent Nukes
- No New Nuclear Weapons States

The first strand of this strategy—"No Loose Nukes"—begins with the recognition that insecure nuclear weapons or materials anywhere pose a grave threat to all nations everywhere. The international community can thus rightly insist that all weapons and materials—wherever they are—be protected to a standard sufficient to ensure the safety of citizens around the world. Russia, which holds the largest stockpile of actual and potential nuclear weapons, has been the principal focus of concern for the past decade, but in recent years a new, urgent test of this principle has come from Pakistan, where the developer of its nuclear establishment has been exposed as the kingpin in black-market sales of nuclear weapons technology.

Application of the second principle—"No New Nascent Nukes"—would prevent the construction of any national production facilities for enriching uranium or reprocessing plutonium. The head of the International Atomic Energy Agency, Mohamed ElBaradei, now recognizes that the existing system under the Nuclear Nonproliferation Treaty (NPT) erred in allowing nonnuclear states to build uranium enrichment and plutonium production plants. In his words, "This is a different ball game, and we have to change the rules."[1] Closing this loophole will require deft diplomacy, imaginative inducements, and demonstrable readiness to employ sanctions, including use of military capabilities, to establish a new bright line. Iran is currently testing this line. The international community's response will demonstrate the feasibility—or, alternatively, forfeit the possibility—of a world in which this principle holds.

The third element of this strategy draws a line under the current eight nuclear powers—the United States, Russia, Great Britain, France, China, India, Pakistan, and Israel—and declares unambiguously, "No more." North Korea poses a decisive challenge for the "No New Nuclear Weapons States" policy. Unless its current plans are aborted, North Korea will soon have something like eight nuclear weapons and facilities for producing a dozen more each year. If North Korea becomes a nuclear weapons state, South Korea and Japan will almost certainly go nuclear in the decade thereafter, making Northeast Asia a far more dangerous place than it is today. More important, if North Korea successfully completes its nuclear weapons production line, it might well sell weapons to others, including terrorists. In that future, the prospects for preventing nuclear terrorism would plummet.

Some critics disparage the call for a world of Three No's as little more than a nuclear version of "I have a dream." They maintain that the nuclear genie is out of the bottle, that nuclear proliferation is therefore unstoppable, and nuclear terrorism inevitable. They say that no matter how much we try to stop terrorists from attacking us with nuclear weapons, there is no such thing as enough.

It is realistic to recognize that the actions required are ambitious. But realism does not require fatalism or defeatism. In fact, most of the world is already signed up to the third no, could live with the second no, and supports the first. The Three No's framework stretches beyond current realities, but not further than we have stretched before. For courage as well as clues, it is instructive to recall the prevailing expectations of the early 1960s, when President John F. Kennedy predicted that "by 1970 there may be ten nuclear powers instead of four, and by 1975, fifteen or twenty."[2] Had those nations with the technical capacity to build nuclear weapons gone ahead and created their own arsenals, Kennedy's prediction would have been correct. But his warning helped awaken the world to the unacceptable dangers of unconstrained nuclear proliferation. The United States and other nations refused to accept these projections, instead negotiating international constraints, providing security guarantees, offering incentives, and posing credible threats. As a result, today 183 nations, including scores that have the technical capacity to build arsenals, have renounced nuclear weapons and have committed themselves, in the NPT, to eschew the nuclear option. Forty years after Kennedy's prediction, there are only eight nuclear weapons states, not twenty. Today's leaders can achieve similar success in combating nuclear terrorism.

NO LOOSE NUKES

The first goal in the plan to prevent nuclear terrorism must be to ensure that there is no place in the world where terrorists can acquire nuclear weapons or the materials from which such weapons can be made. To this end, every nuclear nation must be persuaded to lock down all weapons and fissile material to a new "gold standard"—and to do so on the fastest feasible timetable. Material that cannot reasonably be secured to this standard, particularly at research reactors in developing and transitional countries, must be removed.

The danger of "loose nukes" came into focus in 1991 amid signs of the Soviet Union's impending collapse. As fate had it, I was in Moscow in August 1991 when a group of conservatives in the Soviet security establishment attempted to overthrow President Mikhail Gorbachev. Tanks commanded by the coup makers ringed the Kremlin; Gorbachev, then on vacation in the southern part of the country, was placed under house arrest. With a longtime Russian friend, Andrei Kokoshin, later the national security adviser to Russian president Boris Yeltsin, I inspected the tank battalion and other military units at the Kremlin and elsewhere in Moscow. As we walked and talked, it became clear to both of us that while the coup would fail, the Soviet superpower was soon to be no more.

On the plane back to the United States, I composed a private memorandum to the chairman of the Joint Chiefs of Staff, Colin Powell, with whom I had worked in the Reagan administration. Entitled "Sounding the Alarm," that memo stated: "Soviet disunion could create additional nuclear states, provoke struggles for control of Soviet nuclear weapons, and lead to a loss of control of strategic or non-strategic nuclear weapons."[3] In the weeks that followed, President George H. W. Bush undertook what was later called the "unilateral-reciprocal" initiative, announcing that the United States would unilaterally remove all tactical nuclear weapons from its operational forces and challenging the Soviet Union to do likewise. (Tactical nuclear weapons are those with smaller yields and shorter ranges, designed primarily for battlefield use.) Gorbachev responded positively, withdrawing all tactical nuclear weapons from the outer reaches of the Soviet empire.

In the next twelve months, more than 22,000 tactical nuclear weapons were removed from the fourteen newly independent states that had formerly been part of the Soviet Union and returned to storage facilities in central Russia.[4] To facilitate this process, Senators Sam Nunn and Richard Lugar, without hearings or legislative action by any committee of the Senate, managed to attach to the Defense Authorization Bill a special rider authorizing $400 million of funds appropriated to the Department of Defense for securing Soviet (soon Russian) nuclear warheads. The Nunn-Lugar program continues to this day, and has been a major factor causing both governments to focus on the danger of loose nukes and facilitating actions to address the threat.

As the Clinton administration came to office, in January 1993, the focus of concern shifted from tactical nuclear weapons to the strategic nuclear arsenals left in Ukraine, Kazakhstan, and Belarus. (Strategic nuclear weapons are those aimed at an adversary's nuclear weapons, cities, military command-and-control infrastructure, and political leadership; they tend to be larger in yield and delivered by missiles launched from great distances.) With the breakup of the Soviet Union, the third largest nuclear arsenal was now in newly independent Ukraine; the eighth, in Kazakhstan; the ninth, in Belarus. More than four thousand nuclear warheads, most of them mounted on intercontinental ballistic missiles and aimed at targets in the United States, stood on alert, at risk of an unauthorized or accidental firing, and under ambiguous ownership and control. I was then serving as assistant secretary of defense with responsibility for strategy and plans toward the former Soviet Union. My colleagues and I analyzed an array of scenarios. A typical "what-if" involved Ukrainian efforts to wrest operational control of nuclear-armed ICBMs, which would provoke commando raids by Russian Special Forces, triggering unauthorized launches that delivered hundreds of nuclear warheads to American cities. Our challenge was to develop and execute strategies that would prevent such eventualities from playing out in real life.

Could the newly independent former Soviet states, having been dominated by Russia for centuries, be persuaded to give up the nuclear weapons within their borders, which appeared their best guarantor of independent survival and security? Fatalists dismissed the proposal to eliminate these arsenals as a fool's errand. Nonetheless, as a result of a bold strategy that defined a bright line of zero nuclear weapons in these states, intense U.S.–Russian cooperation, and careful orchestration of the full array of carrots and sticks, Ukraine, Kazakhstan, and Belarus each agreed in 1994 to eliminate all nuclear weapons on their soil. Before the end of 1996, every one of the nuclear weapons in these states had been deactivated and returned to Russia, where they are being dismantled and the nuclear material in the warheads reprocessed to produce fuel for civilian reactors.

If the good news is that all nuclear weapons were removed from the states that were previously part of the Soviet Union, the bad news is that the weapons were returned to Russia during a period of chaos and criminalization. As mentioned in chapter 3, Secretary of Defense Dick Cheney expressed the view in 1991 that if 99 percent of the arsenal of the former Soviet Union was safely recovered, that would constitute extraordinary performance. In fact, not a single former Soviet nuclear weapon has been found in another country or in an international arms bazaar. This incredible result is testimony to the determined efforts of the Russian government, including in particular the nuclear guardians in its Ministry of Defense and Ministry of Atomic Energy, supported by technical and economic assistance from the United States following from the Nunn–Lugar legislation and subsequent acts of Congress.

After an initial burst of energy, the Cooperative Threat Reduction Program soon bogged down in bureaucratic "business as usual." Cold War habits of thought began to reemerge. Summit announcements that the Russian and American militaries would now cooperate intimately in securing the jewels of the Russian military establishment ran against the grain of history, not to mention fifty years of explicit confrontation. Russian suspicions about espionage by the U.S. government, American complaints of diversion of funds by the Russians, resistance to anything "not invented here," and deeply ingrained attitudes and practices created obstacles that could be overcome only by high-level interventions. Congress could not resist adding cumbersome conditions to appropriations, playing pork-barrel politics, and subjecting the program to armies of lawyers intent on denying flexibility to the implementors. Thus at the end of the Clinton administration, in a celebrated "Report Card" on U.S. nonproliferation programs with Russia, an official task force chaired by Howard Baker and Lloyd Cutler concluded that the "existing scope, pace, and operation of the programs leave an unacceptable risk of failure and the potential for catastrophic consequences."[5] The Baker–Cutler Report Card called for a reinvention of this enterprise to finish the job of securing all weapons and material on a fast track with full funding, which they estimated would be $30 billion.[6]

The administration of George W. Bush entered office in 2001 skeptical of the Nunn–Lugar program. After months of delay and initial cuts in the program's budget, the administration responded to sharp criticism from Republican senator Lugar and others, and restored the funding to the levels that had prevailed during the Clinton administration. Management of the program, however, was left to new officials with no enthusiasm for it. Episodic initiatives, heroic efforts by isolated individuals, and occasional presidential declarations aside, the program has sunk deeper into the bureaucracies on both sides. At the end of the Bush administration's term in 2005, after thirteen years of effort since the fall of the Soviet Union, the nuclear security balance sheet will show that the job of securing Russia's nuclear weapons and material remains only half done, leaving 44,000 potential nuclear weapons' worth of HEU and plutonium vulnerable to theft.[7] To be sure, the job is physically and politically arduous. But to proceed at the current pace would be to give terrorists another thirteen years to shop.[8]

The contrast between the Bush administration's declarations and its behavior was underlined vividly in a sharp exchange between members of the Senate Foreign Relations Committee and Secretary of State Colin Powell in February 2004. A day after a fine speech by Bush highlighting the dangers of nuclear terrorism and calling for a bold response, Senators Lugar, Biden, and others chastised Powell for the disconnect between the president's words and the government's actions. Senator Lugar described a dispute with Russia over liability provisions that had "delayed destruction of 30 tons of plutonium," leaving these four thousand potential nuclear weapons vulnerable. With his characteristic understatement, Lugar concluded: "The public has a general impression, and the president certainly gave impetus to this yesterday, that a good number of these programs are moving. And I have an impression they are not."[9]

Powell felt blindsided, obviously unaware of the issue Lugar had raised. He responded with a general endorsement—he called Nunn–Lugar "a tremendous program"[10]—but was unable to provide any specifics about the delay in eliminating plutonium. Senator Biden refused to give him a pass: "The single most important nonproliferation tool available to us is here now. It's Nunn–Lugar. . . . It has not been funded fully. When it's been funded, there have been roadblocks thrown up. . . . I believe the president supports this . . . but he is whipsawed by ideological idiocy."[11] Returning to the State Department, Powell directed his subordinates to give him a memo explaining how, two years after the United States and the other G8 nations had committed to international support for projects like the destruction of plutonium, these programs were still being held up by technicalities.[12]

What is needed urgently now is to reexamine this challenge through the lens of 9/11. Having seen with our own eyes the attacks on the World Trade Center and the Pentagon, we do not need to wait for a nuclear 9/11 to envision what any president and every member of Congress, indeed every citizen, will demand on the morning after. Preventing the next act of nuclear terrorism will instantly become the absolute priority for the president and Congress. The actions that will be demanded then are the ones that should be taken now. Steadfast determination to prevent nuclear terrorism will run over disagreements over liability, objections about difficulty and expense, and business-as-usual delays, as if they were minor speed bumps.

The president must engage Russian president Vladimir Putin and persuade him to make preventing nuclear terrorism an imperative for Russia as well. While Putin has joined Bush in a number of statements declaring nuclear terrorism a significant danger, Russia has many priorities, and this one has not been at the top of the list in a country that has spent much of the last decade rebuilding its political, economic, and security institutions. The president must help Putin feel in his bones the threat of a nuclear terrorist attack on Russia. Making the Russian leader vividly aware of the situation should not be too difficult, in light of the repeated terrorist attacks by Chechen separatists on Moscow. Indeed, in this effort, the president can quote Putin's own words from the 2000 Millennium Summit at the United Nations, a call to block "the ways for spreading nuclear weapons" by "excluding use of enriched uranium and pure plutonium in world atomic energy production."[13]

Putin understands that Russia is currently poor and weak, and that its best hope for the modernization project to which he is committed requires integration with the Western markets and institutions to which the United States is the gatekeeper. Putin and his colleagues in Russia's national security establishment continue to search for a concept that will help them locate the new Russia in an emerging security order. The opportunity to stand shoulder to shoulder with an American president in leading an effort that implicitly recognizes Russia's continuing claim to superpower status in at least one realm should be irresistible.

In attempting to engage Putin as a full partner in this common cause, the president should start by reflecting on what would happen the day after a nuclear terrorist attack. How will the two presidents explain their acceptance of practices that left nuclear weapons less secure than gold in Fort Knox or the Kremlin Armory? If a state deliberately sold a nuclear weapon to terrorists who used it to attack the United States or Russia, how would either respond? For having harbored and protected Al Qaeda prior to the attack on the World Trade Center, Bush declared war on the Taliban rulers of Afghanistan and announced that any other regime that followed the Taliban's example would be treated likewise. What about a government that supplied a nuclear weapon to terrorists through distraction or neglect? If a weapon was stolen from Russia, or Pakistan, or the United States, who would be accountable? To whom? With what consequences? In the confrontation with the Soviet Union over missiles in Cuba in 1962, President Kennedy stated explicitly that "it shall be the policy of this Nation to regard any nuclear missile launched from Cuba against any nation in the Western Hemisphere as an attack by the Soviet Union on the United States, requiring a full retaliatory response upon the Soviet Union."[14] Should some analogous principle of nuclear accountability be developed?

A mutual commitment by the two presidents to do everything technically and physically possible to minimize theft of nuclear weapons and materials, and to demonstrate to the other that each has done that, would send a lightning bolt through both bureaucracies. A first step would be to develop a specific plan of action and sequence of performance-measurable milestones for securing all nuclear weapons, weapons-usable material, and know-how on the fastest possible timetable. This process would be overseen by a joint U.S.–Russian task force led by high-level appointees (Howard Baker or Sam Nunn would be appropriate American examples) reporting back to the two presidents on a weekly basis.

One major product of this effort would be the establishment of a new gold standard. The United States and Russia must devise a process by which each nation's methods of securing its own weapons and materials are sufficiently transparent to give others confidence that its stockpiles cannot be used by terrorists. This standard would reach the highest level of security by which other items of value and danger are protected. It would require states to build or strengthen their control systems, from personnel who have access to nuclear facilities, to electronic portal monitors that sound alarms if material is removed without authorization, to no-person zones surrounding the compound with heavy surveillance. It would also demand independent audits and tests of security systems led by retired nuclear guardians such as General Yevgeny Maslin (former commander of the Twelfth Main Directorate of the Russian Defense Ministry), General Eugene Habiger (former commander in chief of United States Strategic Command), and Siegfried Hecker (former director of Los Alamos National Laboratory). Final certification would be sent to cabinet-level officials and ultimately the president of each nation.

Once the United States and Russia have demonstrably addressed nuclear risks in their own societies, the two presidents must engage the leaders of other nuclear weapons states and secure their personal commitment to this enterprise.[15] These heads of government need to undertake an obligation to secure all weapons and materials in their territories to the new gold standard—and to be certified by another member of the nuclear club as having done so. Where technical or financial assistance is required in meeting these standards, the United States would be forthcoming in providing help. The two presidents must use all their powers of persuasion and refuse to accept no for an answer.

But what if a nuclear weapons state declines to go along with this plan? In early 2004, the world was stunned by revelations that A. Q. Khan, the developer of Pakistan's nuclear weapons program, surreptitiously ran a veritable "Wal-Mart of private-sector proliferation," in the words of Mohamed ElBaradei.[16] Securing nuclear weapons and materials from raids by terrorists or theft by corrupt employees is demanding. But securing money from theft by the head of the bank requires a different order of reporting, accounting, review, and redundancy. Clearly, ensuring that Pakistan's weapons and fissile material are secured to the gold standard will be the most difficult case.

Turning Pakistan's current shame over its exposure as the headquarters of the world's nuclear black market into an opportunity to end such practices will require subtlety. But one begins with a leader, Pakistani president Pervez Musharraf, who since 9/11 has cast his lot unambiguously with the United States and has committed himself to building a modern, moderate Muslim state—or to die trying. Revelations of past sins, repentance, and real reform offer Musharraf a chance not only to absolve his country but to make Pakistan a leader in the campaign for nuclear responsibility. By embracing the new gold standard that will protect Pakistan's nuclear weapons and materials against previous failures, Musharraf could join Presidents Bush and Putin as a nuclear statesman.

Most of what must be done to secure Pakistan's nuclear weapons and materials to the new standard will have to be done by the Pakistanis themselves as an organic extension of current practices. Musharraf is rightly proud of the core ethic and practices that have preserved Pakistan's army from corruption and made theft of its weapons a capital crime. In fact, one of the more enduring legacies of the Musharraf administration may be the Nuclear Command Authority (NCA), which he established in December 2003. Designed to bring greater centralized control over the Khan Research Laboratories and the Pakistani Atomic Energy Commission, the NCA is headed by Musharraf and vice-chaired by Pakistan's prime minister, and is divided into two units led by two three-star generals responsible for nuclear weapons and nuclear scientific personnel.[17] Following the revelations about Khan, some may say this measure is too little, too late, but it has nonetheless achieved an unprecedented degree of transparency and accountability for Pakistan's nuclear complex. Furthermore, Pakistan's efforts to root out Al Qaeda and Taliban figures in the country's North-West Frontier Province, revitalized after the two assassination attempts against Musharraf in December 2003, have shown what can be done once a leader has grasped the scope of the danger.

But the delicacy and sensitivity of this effort cannot be exaggerated. Pakistan's nuclear arsenal is designed, deployed, and managed first and foremost to deter its focal enemy, India. Pakistan fears that if India could locate its nuclear arsenal, it might preemptively destroy all of Pakistan's nuclear weapons. Similar fears have been harbored by every nuclear power in the early stages of its program. No reasonable country would divulge information that would leave its arsenal vulnerable to preemption. And while Pakistan is now a crucial ally of the United States in the war against Al Qaeda, if the United States was to supply "permissive action links" that require an electronic code from Musharraf for use of weapons, could Musharraf be confident that American officials had not retained some undisclosed ability to disable Pakistan's weapons? Many Pakistanis harbor an ingrained mistrust of the West, which will require that the United States adopt a firm but patient stance. This process can be facilitated by technical and financial assistance, as well as ongoing diplomatic initiatives to ease tensions on the subcontinent. But pushing for too much too soon could destabilize Musharraf and even lead to his overthrow by someone more sympathetic to bin Laden than to the United States.

Fortunately, China may be able to help. For many years, China has acted as an ally, mentor, and supplier of arms to Pakistan, and the two countries are united by their common antagonism toward India, following the adage, "The enemy of my enemy is my friend." A triangular process—in which China embraced the U.S.–Russian gold standard for its own arsenal and was certified by the United States as having done so, and China and the United States then each reviewed the security procedures for half of Pakistan's nuclear weapons and materials—might be acceptable. Musharraf and his colleagues would not have to fear that either the United States or China had the full picture of Pakistan's arsenal.[18] Private conversations and exchanges among nuclear weapons experts from Pakistan, China, and the United States, overseen by individuals who would report directly to the president of each country, could move step by step toward adequate security.

Finally, as proposed by my colleague Matthew Bunn at the Kennedy School of Government, a "global clean-out campaign" is needed to extract all nuclear material that cannot be secured to the gold standard from research reactors in developing or transitional countries. In chapter 3, we discussed the joint U.S.–Russian initiative in August 2002 that extracted three potential nuclear weapons from Vinca, Yugoslavia, facilitated by funds from a private foundation, the Nuclear Threat Initiative. In the aftermath of that success, the U.S. and Russian governments identified twenty-four Soviet-supplied research reactors of concern and agreed to work together to remove bomb-usable HEU from these facilities. Since then, material has been removed from Bulgaria, Romania, and Libya. But at the current rate, this project will not be completed until 2020.

In March 2004, Joel Brinkley and William Broad of the *New York Times* exposed the U.S. government's baffling lack of urgency in addressing the problem of American HEU at research reactors the United States had provided to forty-three countries under President Eisenhower's Atoms for Peace program.[19] Enough HEU for over a thousand nuclear weapons remains at these research reactors today. A review by the Department of Energy's inspector general points with special concern to HEU sitting at reactors in Iran, Pakistan, Israel, and South Africa in sufficient quantities for at least one bomb.[20] Imagine Iran using American HEU, supplied to the shah before the 1979 Islamic revolution, to make its first nuclear bomb. Evidently the irony has been lost on the secretary of energy and the president. It is worth recalling that after Iraq invaded Kuwait in 1990 and the United States was preparing to launch Operation Desert Storm, Saddam initiated a crash program to build a nuclear bomb, using HEU supplied by France and Russia for Iraq's two research reactors at Tuwaitha.[21]

As Brinkley and Broad explain, the lack of success in recovering HEU from these facilities is related to the fact that the United States is charging these countries $5,000 per kilogram to take these potential nuclear weapons back! Moreover, the individuals who are leading the effort work seven layers down in the Department of Energy's Environmental Management Program, whose mandate is cleanup, not national security. In fact, that unit has repeatedly been spotlighted by internal audits as among the least effective offices in a department that is regularly judged one of the least effective in Washington.

Where it is technically possible, research reactors should be modified to run on low-enriched uranium (LEU), which cannot be used in nuclear weapons, instead of HEU. Reactors that cannot be converted to LEU must be closed. In contrast to the years of struggle required to remove HEU from the Serbian reactor at Vinca, the American and Russian presidents should demand removal of all insecure material on the fastest possible timetable, and in any case within one year. Under the direction of the U.S. secretary of state and the Russian foreign minister, with support from the secretary of energy and the Russian minister of industry and energy, each nation should mobilize whatever resources are needed to get the job done, including technical and financial assistance, and demonstrate readiness to withhold whatever benefits target countries currently enjoy in their relations with the United States and Russia. For the secretaries and ministers, removing potential nuclear weapons from vulnerable sites in Uzbekistan, Belarus, Ghana, and Iran should be a first-order issue, pursued with the same focus and determination as the war on terrorism.

Each case will present unique obstacles and conditions for buying out the fissile material and closing down the site. Research done at these institutions is rarely cutting-edge science, but the reactor provides employment for the staff and prestige for the scientists. These people will undoubtedly resist giving up their livelihoods, and their governments will support them. In cases where medical isotopes or other items of commercial value are produced, alternative supplies can be provided. Officials overseeing this global clean-out must have the flexibility to improvise solutions: spending money for environmental cleanup, compensating unemployed staff, providing new research opportunities for scientists, and giving financial or other incentives to the governments of the affected countries. Most important, countries that comply should not be required to pay for our taking and transporting weapons-usable material.

The thought that it could take until 2020 to clean out the twenty-odd sites mentioned above is unacceptable. The successes in Yugoslavia, Bulgaria, and Romania show that the bureaucratic process and international diplomacy associated with these removals takes months to years, while the removal itself takes days to weeks. The presidents should personally cut this red tape and direct their ministers of foreign affairs and energy to complete the job in one year, or explain why they are unable to do so.

Senator Richard Lugar, the U.S. government's leading advocate for combating loose nukes, has proposed what he calls the "Lugar Doctrine." This doctrine would compile two lists—one enumerating states that harbor terrorist cells, and another cataloging states that possess unsecured weapons or materials of mass destruction—and then cross those states off each list one by one. In the senator's words, "We must demand that all such weapons and materials be made secure from proliferation, using the funds of that country supplemented by international funds if required. Our campaign would not end until all nations on both lists complied with these standards."[22]

NO NEW NASCENT NUKES

The second of the Three No's is "No New Nascent Nukes," which means no new national capabilities to enrich uranium or reprocess plutonium. Within the current framework of the NPT, nonnuclear states can legally develop facilities for enriching uranium to produce fuel for civilian nuclear reactors, and they may reprocess these reactors' spent fuel to extract plutonium. But the same facilities that can produce low-enriched uranium or plutonium for reactor fuel can also be used to produce highly enriched uranium or bomb-usable plutonium—the critical ingredients for nuclear weapons. As ElBaradei has noted, the current nonproliferation regime in which "each country now has the so-called sovereign right to develop plutonium and highly enriched uranium"[23] makes further proliferation virtually inevitable.

A policy of no new nascent nukes would, in effect, revise Article IV of the NPT in the light of what we now understand. The approach proposed is not only consistent with the spirit of Article IV, it also fulfills its essential purpose: allowing all signatories to the NPT to fully exploit the benefits of civilian nuclear technologies.[24] Making this de facto revision attractive to most, and inescapable for others, will require two further elements: a carrot guaranteeing a supply of reactor fuel to nonnuclear weapons states at less than half the national production cost and disposal of spent fuel (in effect, exposing any national decision to produce uranium or plutonium as economically irrational) and a stick to enforce adherence to the new strictures, especially by recalcitrant states. Enforcement should start with political isolation and economic sanctions but also include the readiness to use covert and overt military force if necessary.

In the 1950s, President Eisenhower launched his Atoms for Peace program, offering states access to civilian nuclear reactors and technologies in return for a commitment to forgo nuclear weapons. Eisenhower's bargain was later codified in the 1970 NPT, which prohibits nuclear weapons states (defined as the five acknowledged nuclear powers at the time—the United States, the Soviet Union, Britain, France, and China) from transferring nuclear weapons or associated technology to nonnuclear states, and obligates them to provide technologies for civilian nuclear activities. Nonnuclear states agreed not to seek weapons and to accept what were called "safeguards" on their civilian nuclear materials. But these safeguards do not guard or secure nuclear materials or plants. Instead, IAEA officials serve as accountants for these nuclear reactors to alert other nations if nuclear material is lost or stolen.

For over three decades, the NPT has served as the foundation of an arms control and nonproliferation regime that has grown and adapted much like a living organism. As flaws in the treaty have become evident, the international community has tightened existing constraints. For example, after the first Gulf War, the world was shocked by how close Saddam Hussein had come to acquiring a nuclear weapon. The IAEA in particular was concerned that existing safeguards and inspections were not up to the task of discovering illicit nuclear weapons development. In response, officials from the nuclear watchdog group drafted the Additional Protocol, which permits on-demand intrusive inspections of not only *declared* but also *suspected* nuclear sites. This authority increased the chances that inspectors would detect, for instance, a covert reactor big enough to make a bomb's worth of plutonium a year.

Yet loopholes remain. Article IV of the NPT guarantees "the inalienable right of all the Parties to the Treaty to develop research, production and use of nuclear energy for peaceful purposes." Conceived as an effective means of preventing proliferation, this constraint has instead left an escape clause that allows nations to legally build the infrastructure for a nuclear weapons program before withdrawing from the NPT and going the last mile to make nuclear bombs, test those bombs, and declare themselves nuclear weapons states. To amend the NPT will likely prove too difficult, since that would require action by all 188 member states. Instead, we need to orchestrate a consensus around the proposition that there will be no new national enrichment or reprocessing.

Today, nuclear weapons states and multinational consortiums supply uranium fuel for reactors around the world.[25] Other members of the NPT that operate nuclear power plants or research reactors buy fuel. Nuclear waste is currently held in temporary storage by the states operating power plants. The proposed strategy would prevent any new nations from producing their own fissile material by offering them a bargain that is so financially attractive that only a state with ulterior motives could turn it down. If that happened, nuclear aspirations would be evident and coercive measures brought to bear.

The deal is simple: if nonnuclear states agree to forgo enrichment or reprocessing capacity, the nuclear states would not only continue to meet the legitimate interests of the nonnuclear ones in civilian nuclear power and technologies but would guarantee to sell them nuclear fuel and dispose of their nuclear waste at less than half the national production cost. On economic grounds, this would be an offer no finance ministers could refuse, since their countries would be assured fuel and relieved of the responsibility for waste without the billion dollar–plus price tag. Suppliers could provide cross-guarantees or even create a nuclear fuel bank to ensure an uninterrupted source of fuel service and technologies. All transactions and operations of nuclear facilities would be subject to intrusive international inspections and thorough accounting to ensure against diversion. Moreover, the current enrichment of uranium and reprocessing of plutonium by the nuclear weapons states would become subject to international inspection and held to new security standards.

In seeking to address this challenge, ElBaradei has called for the "internationalization" of all fissile materials production, prohibiting any state from operating enrichment or reprocessing facilities.[26] Though international management of enrichment and reprocessing is not practical (given the managerial capacities of international organizations) or feasible (given the national security concerns of nuclear weapons states), his proposal focuses on the right problem and points in the right direction. Promotion and management of peaceful, proliferation-proof nuclear energy demands international oversight that is acceptable to all parties. As nuclear reactors spread across the globe, security and monitoring of nuclear fuel and waste must be stringent enough to prevent and detect any diversions for illicit weapons work. Persuading all states to adopt the Additional Protocol, enabling more intrusive IAEA inspections on demand, is a further element in this package. That effort can be assisted, as George W. Bush has proposed, by limiting the "import of equipment for their civilian nuclear programs"[27] to states that sign the Additional Protocol.

If complete fuel-cycle services are made available to all nonnuclear weapons states that want nuclear power, countries that choose not to participate and set out instead to build their own fissile production capabilities will find themselves at the fringes of the international community. Once the nuclear weapons states and the majority of the rest of the world have drawn the line against further proliferation, then diplomatic isolation, economic sanctions, and even military force may be required in persuading holdouts that it is in their interest to adhere to the augmented NPT regime. As the new regime takes hold, the UN Security Council should ground this principle in international law.

The extensive proliferation network run by Pakistan's A. Q. Khan has demonstrated the need for a web of constraints on both the local and the global levels to shut down black-market operations as well. Secretary Powell's March 2004 statement that the Khan operation "is a Pakistani internal matter" was as false as it was diplomatic.[28] The problem is not just that Khan spread nuclear-related materials so widely but that he was able to procure enrichment technology in the first place by stealing it from the European nuclear consortium Urenco, showing that nuclear vulnerability extended to supplier states. Domestically, all countries must improve police work, strengthen export controls, and criminalize acts of nuclear proliferation in a manner that fits the scale of the crime. Too frequently, exporters of nuclear-related technology, from Germany to Malaysia, have been treated with a slap on the wrist.

On the global level, the Bush administration's Proliferation Security Initiative—under which a posse of sixteen nations[29] interdict suspected shipments of weapons of mass destruction and missiles—should be expanded so that more states can participate in efforts to interdict those who bypass local export laws. Interpol should step up its international policing efforts. Proliferation should be criminalized internationally, making it not a technical trade violation but an international crime like piracy. To this end, the UN Security Council should pass the resolution proposed by the Bush administration in March 2004 requiring member states to "adopt and enforce appropriate effective laws" to stop "any non-state actor" from being able to "manufacture, acquire, possess, develop, transport or use nuclear, chemical or biological weapons and their means of delivery."[30] If adopted under chapter 7 of the UN Charter, this resolution would permit the use of military force to enforce compliance and send the message that peace will not stand for those who proliferate.

Iran is today the leading example of a country that is simultaneously exploiting the current nonproliferation regime and sneaking around it. A nonnuclear weapons signatory to the NPT, Iran has, since the mid-1990s, been building major enrichment and reprocessing plants that can quickly be adapted to produce bomb fuel. At the same time, it has been a leading customer for Pakistan's black-market sales of nuclear infrastructure, materials, and designs. Iranian officials adamantly deny any interest in nuclear weapons. "This industry is strictly for peaceful use," argues Iranian foreign minister Kamal Kharrazi. "No one can deprive us of this natural, legal and legitimate right."[31] Iran's behavior, however, makes sense only as part of a weapons program.

Iran's civilian nuclear energy program was halted after the Islamic revolution in 1979 but resumed large-scale activity in 1992, when Russia signed an $800 million contract to complete a nuclear reactor in the city of Bushehr and to lease fuel for the reactor after it became operational. Bushehr is the first of what Iran hopes will be a series of reactors for producing electricity. For a country rich in fossil fuels that can generate electricity at a significantly cheaper cost, investment by Iran in nuclear power raised questions from the outset.[32]

Distrust over Iran's stated nuclear intentions intensified in February 2003, when the IAEA uncovered a pilot centrifuge plant in Natanz, as well as a heavy-water reactor fuel plant in Arak, and neither had been disclosed by Iran as required by its NPT obligations. In light of these discoveries, the IAEA demanded an explanation. To avoid having allegations of noncompliance with the NPT brought before the UN Security Council, Iran agreed to provide a "correct and complete" accounting to the IAEA of eighteen years of secret nuclear activity, accept the Additional Protocol to the NPT, and temporarily suspend uranium enrichment.

Before the ink was dry on Iran's pledges, questions arose over interpretation. First, Iran disputed the IAEA's claim that its commitment to suspend uranium enrichment would include halting construction of enrichment facilities. When the country finally agreed to stop construction in February 2004, Kharrazi defiantly stated, "We suspended uranium enrichment voluntarily and temporarily. Later, when our relations with the IAEA return to normal, we will definitely resume enrichment."[33] Meanwhile, investigations into A. Q. Khan's black-market network exposed Iran's purchase of sophisticated Pakistani centrifuge designs and technology, proving that yet again the Islamic Republic had failed to come clean. Subsequent IAEA fact-finding missions found hard evidence of traces of HEU in several Iranian facilities—including bomb-grade material enriched to 36 percent in one case and 90 percent in another, for which Tehran had no plausible explanation.[34] In March 2004, Iranian defense minister Ali Shamkhani admitted that the military was involved in Iran's nuclear program, having built nuclear centrifuges for civilian use.[35] The question of why the military would be involved in the construction of components for a civilian energy program remained unanswered. Iran continued to deny that it was pursuing a nuclear weapon and insisted that it had nothing to hide.

Iran is a serial confessor, successively owning up to the facts when its accusers have unambiguous evidence, while hiding what has yet to be found. Through a combination of legal and illegal actions, it now stands at the threshold of a nuclear weapon. Iran's drive for nuclear weapons has thus far been checked by a combination of obstacles created by Russia, the United States, Europe, and the IAEA, but it has not been entirely blocked. Russia has slowed completion of the nuclear reactor at Bushehr and has withheld supplies of fuel, pending an agreement to return the fuel; the United States has applied unilateral sanctions, named Iran a member of the "axis of evil," and hinted at forceful regime change; Europe has partially restrained investment and warned of further sanctions; and the IAEA has insisted on full disclosure of Iran's nuclear programs and inspections on demand, threatening to find Iran in violation of its

NPT obligations and refer the case to the UN Security Council for enforcement. In this multidimensional chess game, Iran has moved strategically and pragmatically in response to each of its opponents, seizing openings to move its nuclear program ahead wherever and whenever they arise.

A new approach is needed to convince the Islamic Republic that the costs of pursuing a nuclear infrastructure will exceed any potential benefits. In short, the United States and the other nuclear powers should offer Iran a grand bargain. In exchange for a commitment to freeze the country's development of enrichment and reprocessing facilities and ultimately dismantle them, Iran would receive the following: (1) the opportunity to pursue civilian nuclear power through a fuel-cycle agreement with Russia, at less than half the cost of producing fuel domestically; (2) American and international acceptance of the completion of the nuclear power plant at Bushehr and even additional reactors, provided that the fuel is delivered by and returned to Russia; (3) economic benefits from increased trade and investment resulting from a relaxation of U.S. unilateral sanctions and eventual entrance into the World Trade Organization; and (4) an American agreement not to use force to change the Iranian regime and to discuss Iran's legitimate security concerns.

According to a *Financial Times* report in March 2004, Iran offered its own version of this bargain through a Swiss intermediary following the war in Iraq, but the ideologically divided Bush administration could not even muster a response.[36] The administration's hard-liners apparently believe that the Iranian regime is on the verge of being overthrown and that negotiations are therefore pointless. It is worth recalling that many in the U.S. government believed the same thing about Saddam Hussein in the years following the 1991 Gulf War, only to marvel at his staying power. A *Financial Times* editorial rightly concluded, "The Bush administration does not appear even to be keeping its eye on the prize: a nonnuclear Iran whose security concerns are recognized in return for pursuing detente with its neighbors, and the world."[37]

All the parties that have worked to restrain Iran's nuclear program stand to gain from such a deal. Russia would enjoy economic benefits through the sale of reactors and fuel services, and first-mover advantages in the spent-fuel storage business; the Europeans, led by Britain, France, and Germany, could take the lead in trade and investment in Iran without American commercial retaliation; the United States would achieve its goal of a nonnuclear Iran without having to use force; the IAEA would accomplish its nonproliferation objectives; and, most important, the world would benefit from a peaceful, nonnuclear Iran, and an illustrative case that made "no new nascent nukes" a new bright line.

U.S. negotiators must persuade Iran that its effort to acquire a nuclear arsenal will only compound its deepening economic malaise and increase the threat of attack. If it refused to accept the deal, Iran would find itself economically isolated, unable to bring its vast natural resources to market and barred from inclusion in high-tech and other global industries. Worse, its nuclear facilities could be destroyed by American precision-guided missiles, like Saddam's palaces next door.[38]

In fact, Israel might conduct such an attack. Prime Minister Ariel Sharon told the *Times* of London in November 2002 that he would push Iran to the top of the "to-do list" after the war in Iraq.[39] A year later, Israel's defense minister, Shaul Mofaz, drew a line in the sand, declaring an Iranian nuclear bomb "intolerable" and warning that "only a few months are left for Israel and the world to take action and prevent Iran from getting the nuclear bomb."[40] Israel has recently been flexing its military muscles in ways not lost on Iranian intelligence. And Iran can have no doubt about Israel's willingness to pull the trigger, having witnessed the Israeli Air Force's destruction of Saddam's nuclear reactor at Osirak in 1981. As European negotiators explain to Iranian leaders that acceptance of their demands is Iran's best hope to hold off American military action, U.S. officials can explain that meeting America's requirements is the only way to forestall Israeli action. Iran's conservative leaders have shown themselves to be pragmatic in calculating and choosing their best option, even when it is not the preferred option. They are not likely to conclude that economic isolation and American or Israeli bombs serve their regime's best interests.

NO NEW NUCLEAR WEAPONS STATES

The third principle of the Three No's—"No New Nuclear Weapons States"—draws a bright line under today's eight nuclear powers and states unambiguously: no more. Successful implementation of both "No Loose Nukes" and "No New Nascent Nukes" will mean no new nuclear states. In fact, the overwhelming majority of nations on earth have signed up to the NPT regime that declares: no more. As the debate begins over international acceptance and complete implementation of the new principles, a single outlier is racing toward the nuclear finish line. Stopping North Korea from breaking and entering into the nuclear club must become a supreme priority.

During the Cold War, the rival superpowers served as enforcers, preventing nuclear proliferation within their spheres of control. The United States scotched South Korean and Taiwanese aspirations; the Soviet Union dissuaded North Korea. When the Soviet Union disappeared in December 1991, leaving superpower nuclear arsenals in Ukraine, Kazakhstan, and Belarus, intense U.S.–Russian cooperation zeroed these out. By contrast, when the United States and Russia failed to devise a common strategy on the subcontinent in the 1990s, Pakistan and India conducted nuclear weapons tests and declared themselves new entrants into the nuclear club. Similar distraction now risks allowing North Korea to do the same.

North Korea remains today, as former secretary of defense William Perry called it just before the second war against Iraq, "the most dangerous spot on earth."[41] In late 2002, after Pyongyang admitted to a secret uranium enrichment program, withdrew from the NPT, and expelled IAEA inspectors from the country, it returned to reprocessing plutonium, which it had forsworn as part of the 1994 Agreed Framework with the United States. U.S. intelligence agencies determined that, over the succeeding months, the North Korean regime removed eight thousand plutonium rods from its Yongbyon reactor—enough for five or six bombs, in addition to the one or two that North Korea is thought to have produced in the early 1990s during the first Bush administration.[42] U.S. air sensors along the North Korean border detected krypton-85, a telltale by-product of reprocessing. North Korea also reactivated the 5-megawatt reactor at Yongbyon, previously frozen under the 1994 agreement, and is constructing two 50-megawatt and 200-megawatt reactors as well as a secret uranium enrichment facility. On its current course, North Korea will soon be a nuclear weapons state with a serial production line capable of producing, by conservative estimates, eight to thirteen weapons a year, or fifty to seventy by the end of the decade.[43]

Were North Korea to be accepted as the ninth nuclear weapons state, this would unleash a proliferation chain reaction, with South Korea and Japan building their own nuclear weapons by the end of the decade. Taiwan would seriously consider following suit, despite the fact that this would risk war with China. Most unthinkable of all, nothing could prevent the world's leading supplier of missiles from becoming a Nukes R' Us for terrorists and other proliferators. In such a scenario, historians would justifiably condemn this generation's leaders for gross negligence in allowing a transformation in the international security order no great power would wittingly accept.

The Third No would begin with an unambiguous bright line: no nuclear North Korea. It would focus solely on this objective and subordinate all others, specifically regime change, to this goal. The first step would be to freeze North Korean nuclear weapons activity in its current state, thereby preventing a nuclear weapons production line. The next step would be to dismantle North Korea's fissile material production facilities, remove the fissile material, and ultimately eliminate the two, six, or eight weapons the country may now have.

President Bush has no strategy for North Korea. In one line, his policy has been: neither carrot nor stick. The divide between the "engagers" at the State Department and the "hard-liners" at the Pentagon and the vice president's office has been so wide that the combatants have resolved not to talk about it. The hard-liners' policy can be summed up in two words: "No blackmail." As Vice President Cheney reportedly said at a State Department meeting on North Korea, "We don't negotiate with evil; we defeat it."[44] The hard-liners are thus adamantly opposed to offering any carrot to Pyongyang, including its request for bilateral negotiations, but have been equally unwilling to describe what kind of stick they would use instead. The *Nelson Report,* an insiders' e-mail newsletter that provides the daily scoop on developments in both Washington and North Korea, describes this position as "a three-year stall by the administration in seriously engaging the [North Koreans], for fear that the U.S. will have to end up paying for what it wants . . . 'blackmail' payments to an odious regime which Bush clearly wants to replace."[45]

The engagers' camp, led by Secretary of State Colin Powell, understands that carrots must be offered as well as sticks. As the *Nelson Report* puts it, progress on North Korea requires that "for the first quid, there must be some kind of quo."[46] In April 2003, Powell succeeded in winning the president's authorization for six-party talks involving the United States, North Korea, China, South Korea, Japan, and Russia, while the Pentagon was distracted by the Iraq war. But the hard-liners soon returned to undetermine Powell's plan. David E. Sanger of the *New York Times* reported that "just days before President Bush approved the opening of negotiations with North Korea over its nuclear program, Defense Secretary Donald H. Rumsfeld circulated to key members of the administration a Pentagon memorandum proposing a radically different approach:

the United States, the memo argued, should team up with China to press for the ouster of North Korea's leadership."[47] Ultimately, the administration did agree to continue the multilateral dialogue with Pyongyang, but held out little hope for a resolution to the crisis. As one American official admitted prior to subsequent talks in February 2004: "The motto is 'Do no harm.' This is a placeholder to get us through the [presidential] election."[48]

As the Bush administration has fiddled, debating whether or not to talk to North Korea and, if so, in what arena and about what, Pyongyang has proceeded to reprocess more plutonium for more nuclear weapons every day. The administration's only consistent position has been to reiterate that there is "no crisis" on the Korean peninsula. As Powell told CNN's Wolf Blitzer in late December 2003, after North Korea announced plans to reactivate the nuclear reactor at Yongbyon, "It is not a crisis, but it is a matter of great concern."[49] This mantra, evidently chosen to avoid distraction from Iraq, has served American interests poorly as Pyongyang has continued creating new facts on the ground.

To overcome this dangerous paralysis, the Bush administration must first face up to the urgency of the threat. The United States needs to drop current objections and accept North Korea's proposal for direct, bilateral negotiations. North Korea is correct when it claims that only the United States can address its security concerns and only direct talks will resolve the countries' differences. As an unnamed American official told the *Washington Post*: "Basically, [the North Koreans] have said they don't give a damn about the other people. What they want is an agreement with us."[50] U.S. negotiators' sole condition should be that North Korea immediately freeze all nuclear activity for the duration of the talks.

Bush's next step would be to send a high-level envoy—Condoleezza Rice or Colin Powell—to Pyongyang for candid private discussions with North Korean president Kim Jong Il offering a combination of irresistible carrots and intolerable sticks. The president's representative would explain that North Korea faces a stark choice between two futures, neither of which includes nuclear weapons. In the first, it freezes its nuclear program and agrees to Bush's demand for "complete, verifiable, and irreversible dismantlement of all of North Korea's nuclear weapons programs"; receives a package of economic and diplomatic benefits in return; and survives with a security assurance that the United States will not seek to change its regime by force. In the second, the United States destroys North Korea's known nuclear facilities in a precision-bombing campaign, leaving Kim Jong Il with a choice between acceding to a nonnuclear future or initiating a second Korean War that will surely mean suicide for the North Korean regime.

To encourage Pyongyang to choose peaceful dismantlement, the United States should offer an array of carrots now, and excite Kim Jong Il's imagination about greater possibilities in the future.[51] Washington would offer to drop the threat of regime change and agree to an explicit bilateral nonaggression pledge, to be expanded later into a multilateral security assurance also signed by China, South Korea, Japan, and Russia. It would be prepared to rapidly expand its own food aid program to North Korea—whose citizens have long suffered from an inadequate supply—and open the door for Japan and South Korea to resume fuel oil shipments and other economic assistance, which they are eager to provide. This would give the North Koreans the economic help they have been craving while inoculating the Bush administration against blackmail charges. In the context of the line the administration has taken since 2001, this readiness to deal would likely appear to the North Koreans too good to pass up.

American negotiators would describe other benefits the North Korean regime could receive as it verifiably meets the demands for a freeze of fissile material production at Yongbyon, the two unfinished reactors, and the secret uranium enrichment site. The international community could finance a proposed natural gas pipeline, stretching from Sakhalin, in Russia, to Seoul, which would also provide energy to North Korea; resume construction of two light-water reactors offered in the 1994 Agreed Framework but suspended during the latest diplomatic crisis; provide financial aid for reconstruction of North Korea's electrical transmission grid, hydroelectric facilities, and transportation infrastructure; offer a North Korean version of the Nunn–Lugar program to secure and remove nuclear material from the country; and hold out the prospect of lifting trade sanctions and normalizing relations.

To persuade North Korea that peaceful denuclearization is its best choice, the United States must be able to threaten to eliminate North Korea's nuclear programs militarily. A number of informed and thoughtful Americans believe that the United States now has no realistic military option. Even some who favored a military solution in 2001 and 2002 argue today that since North Korea's withdrawal from the NPT and removal of the eight thousand fuel rods from Yongbyon, the targets are too dispersed and disguised. A final assessment depends on the latest facts, most of which are classified. But unless the United States can find a way to cause Kim Jong Il to fear a unilateral military attack, no negotiated settlement is likely to prove possible.

Since Kim Jong Il is known to be a great fan of movies, the president's emissary should give him a special video with extensive footage of American precision-guided munitions destroying particular offices, floors of buildings, even rooms in Saddam's palaces. Further footage should show new American technologies at work in Afghanistan, such as thermobaric bombs that suck the oxygen out of underground caves. While Kim's best hope is that the United States may not have identified the location of all his nuclear assets, he should be persuaded that we have. No viewer of the video should have any doubt that U.S. military forces can utilize submarines and bombers dispatched from American ports to strike any point on North Korean territory. North Korean military planners have long depended on their threat to destroy Seoul with more than five thousand artillery pieces dug into their hills thirty-five miles away, several hundred Scud missiles, combined with the threat of North

Korea's million-man army marching south in a bloody second Korean war. But, as former CIA chief James Woolsey points out, most if not all of these artillery pieces coud be destroyed at the start of hostilities.[52] The president's emissary must demonstrate to Kim Jong Il that after the United States destroys his known and suspected nuclear facilities, he will face a further fateful choice. On the one hand, he can launch a second Korean war that will mean the certain destruction of his regime. On the other, he can accept the consequences of a precise limited strike on specific military targets. U.S. planners must provide a persuasive picture of what will happen if Kim launches a second Korean war, showing that while his forces will be able to damage Seoul, its population will have been evacuated before the attack, dramatically limiting casualties. Its vaunted, but aging, artillery tubes will fire at most only once. Moreover, no North Korean soldiers will succeed in reaching Seoul, because American bombers will create a mile-wide kill zone through which nothing living will pass. While a North Korean attack might cause tens of thousands of deaths in the South, and perhaps thousands among American troops stationed there, Kim and his regime would certainly not survive.

The president's emissary would underscore the fact that the United States is neither calling for, nor threatening to start, a second Korean war. Just the opposite: the United States would offer the regime survival, economic support from its neighbors, and eventual integration into the international community as a verifiably nonnuclear state. But in the absence of a credible military threat, Kim is not likely to choose peaceful denuclearization.

A SUCCESS STORY IN THE MAKING?

For decades, Colonel Muammar el-Qaddafi topped the list of the world's state sponsors of terrorism. Thus, he startled the world when he officially renounced Libya's WMD programs in December

2003. If such a reversal of nuclear and terrorist ambitions could happen there, it could happen anywhere.

Consider Qaddafi's record. In April 1986, Libyan agents bombed La Belle Club discotheque in West Berlin, a popular gathering place for American soldiers, killing two servicemen and wounding more than two hundred people, among them forty-one Americans. Ten days later, President Ronald Reagan authorized precision strikes against multiple targets in Libya, including Qaddafi's official residence at Bab el-Azziziya. The strikes killed Qaddafi's fifteen-month-old daughter and came within inches of killing the leader himself. In December 1988, Libyan operatives responded, with an even deadlier bombing of Pan Am Flight 103 over Lockerbie, Scotland, killing all 259 people on board, mostly Americans, and eleven bystanders on the ground.

Qaddafi also provided sanctuary for a range of violent Palestinian groups, such as Abu Nidal's Fatah Revolutionary Council, and allowed them to organize and plot attacks against Western targets, much as Al Qaeda did from Afghanistan. He funneled Libya's petrodollars into brutal "liberation movements" around the world, including leftist guerrillas in Angola and Mozambique, the IRA in Northern Ireland, the Basque separatist group ETA in Spain, and the Moro Islamic Liberation Front in the Philippines. Terrorist training camps mushroomed in the Libyan desert—Japanese Red Army "soldiers," Yemeni socialists, and West Germany's Baader-Meinhof Gang. World-class despots, like Idi Amin of Uganda, were greeted with open arms in the Libyan capital, Tripoli.[53]

Why did a certified terrorist whom President Reagan labeled the "mad dog of the Middle East" undergo such a dramatic conversion? One answer is the war in Iraq. The defeat of the world's strongest Arab army—in three weeks, with only 115 battle deaths—did not go unnoticed in Tripoli. Qaddafi was transfixed by the video footage of Saddam's humiliating capture on December 13, 2003, replaying the images over and over.[54] After 9/11, hard-liners from the Bush foreign policy team, many of whom had cut their teeth in the Reagan administration, publicly threatened the Libyan regime in speeches with titles like "Beyond the Axis of Evil."[55] On the eve of the Iraq war, Qaddafi told the French daily *Le Figaro*, "When Bush has finished with Iraq, we'll quickly have a clear idea of where he's going. It won't take long to find out if Iran, Saudi Arabia or Libya will be targets as well."[56]

But the change of heart was driven by more than just fear of American military power. As the *Financial Times* has pointed out, Qaddafi was in the "confessional box" well before the 9/11 attacks.[57] In the late 1990s, Libya began severing ties with terrorist groups and took steps to redress the victims of, and escape the continuing punishment for, the Lockerbie bombing. In the spring of 1999, the regime turned over two Lockerbie suspects for prosecution in the Netherlands, later accepting responsibility for the bombing, and agreed to pay up to $2.7 billion to the victims' families. Qaddafi was one of the first Arab leaders to denounce the 9/11 attacks, urging Muslim charities to send aid to America. He even turned over his file on Al Qaeda to U.S. intelligence officials.

Unquestionably, two decades of sanctions hurt. Reagan imposed an embargo on Libyan oil in 1982, and more comprehensive sanctions followed the Berlin discotheque bombing in 1986. After the Lockerbie attack, the UN Security Council applied global sanctions on trade with Libya and barred travel and military sales to the country, effectively cutting it off from the rest of the world. Qaddafi was increasingly marginalized among fellow Arab leaders. Foreign investment stopped. The economy stagnated. Oil production fell by more than half, from a high of 3.3 million barrels a day in 1970 to 1.4 million in 2003. Unemployment reached 30 percent. Unrest grew as educated but jobless youths yearned for opportunity. Muslim extremist groups, never supportive of Qaddafi's "infidel regime," gained prominence. Qaddafi survived two failed coups and three attempts on his life.[58]

In this context, an increasingly pragmatic Libyan government began a search for alternatives. In June 2003, Qaddafi appointed a new prime minister, Shukri Ghanem, who holds a Ph.D. from the Fletcher School of Law and Diplomacy at Tufts University. Ghanem announced plans for economic modernization that required significant foreign investment. Qaddafi's own son, a doctoral student at the London School of Economics whom Qaddafi is grooming to succeed him, declared, "Now, finally, we are catching up with the times," prompting the *Wall Street Journal* to dub him "the public face of a Westernizing Libya."[59] According to Prime Minister Ghanem, Libyans see relations with the United States as "the elixir of life." "America has everything," said one university student, "and we want it."[60]

The United States responded to Libya's newfound openness by offering a series of quid pro quos. In demanding concessions from Libya over the Lockerbie case in 2001, American and British negotiators emphasized that Libya could expect UN sanctions to be lifted if they met their demands. Two years later, in a brilliant display of phased negotiations, a U.S.–British team offered another deal: eventual elimination of all sanctions, including those imposed by the United States, in exchange for full renunciation and dismantlement of Libya's WMD programs. Having tasted the benefits of life without the UN trade embargo, Libya was eager to escape U.S. sanctions as well and move toward a full normalization of relations with the West. Notably absent from these discussions was any explicit threat of regime change. As one former National Security Council official put it, "One reason the Bush administration was able to take a more constructive course with Libya was that . . . the neoconservatives at the Pentagon and in the shop of Under Secretary of State John Bolton were left out of the loop."[61]

Of course, the carrots of foreign investment and ties with the West were not enough to prompt Libya's renunciation of WMD. In fact, when UN sanctions were lifted following Libya's decision to turn over the Lockerbie suspects, freer trade enabled the regime to accelerate its nuclear acquisition project with Pakistan and various foreign agents. The military stick was indispensable in convincing

Qaddafi and his cronies that, in Bush's words, "nuclear weapons do not bring influence or prestige. They bring isolation and otherwise unwelcome consequences."[62] Still, it was equally important to convey to Libya that there were opportunities for rehabilitation for the penitent and that regime change was not inevitable.

Libya is now the Bush administration's number one nonproliferation success story. Officials rightly point to this story as an object lesson for other rogue states that want to return to the community of nations. As one top official said with regard to North Korea, "The objective is like Libya . . . a commitment to dismantle the whole thing."[63] But the Libyan case should also serve as a model for American policy makers, showing how a finely tuned application of sticks and carrots can lead an erratic sponsor of terrorism with a thirst for weapons of mass destruction on the road to readmittance to the society of civilized nations. The best hope for achieving the results we need in Iran and North Korea is for the U.S. government to apply the formula that worked for Libya.

        we are today to the Three No's will be a long, hard slog. Strong rhetoric but intermittent attention will not convince Pakistan to secure its nuclear stocks against Al Qaeda and against black marketeers within its nuclear establishment; nor will it persuade Iran to forgo an enrichment and reprocessing capability, or roll back North Korea's nuclear weapons program. Nonetheless, the overwhelming majority of nations are aligned in this effort. A handful of recalcitrants currently threatens to collapse the global nuclear order. The Three No's offer organizing principles for this essential project, which is within reach of the civilized world—if we stretch.

8

GETTING FROM HERE TO THERE:
A ROAD MAP OF SEVEN YESES

There is a consensus among nations that proliferation
cannot be tolerated. Yet this consensus means little unless
it is translated into action.

PRESIDENT GEORGE W. BUSH

TRANSFORMING THE PREDICAMENT we face today into a world of Three
No's will require major changes in the agenda and daily actions of the
United States and other governments. As dramatically as we moved
beyond prosecuting terrorists before 9/11 to the war on terrorism
thereafter, we must now move to a war on nuclear terrorism. While
the centerpiece of this effort should be to realize the Three No's in
Russia and Pakistan, Iran and North Korea, full-scale war on nuclear
terrorism will require many related initiatives. Here we summarize
the most important of these under the rubric of Seven Yeses:

- Making the prevention of nuclear terrorism an absolute national
  priority
- Fighting a strategically focused war on terrorism
- Conducting a humble foreign policy
- Building a global alliance against nuclear terrorism
- Creating the intelligence capabilities required for success in
  the war on nuclear terrorism

- Dealing with dirty bombs
- Constructing a multilayered defense

MAKING THE PREVENTION OF NUCLEAR TERRORISM AN ABSOLUTE NATIONAL PRIORITY

As the saying goes, priority is measured not by what you say but by what you do. President Bush's speechwriters can point to dozens of ringing declarations calling on Americans and the world to act against what the president calls the "ultimate nightmare." Unfortunately, these words have not been matched by deeds. Consider four key fronts in a real war on nuclear terrorism.

First, while money is not the most important thing, it nonetheless provides the wherewithal for necessary actions. The distinguished task force headed by Howard Baker and Lloyd Cutler in 2000 called for tripling U.S. expenditures on the Nunn–Lugar Cooperative Threat Reduction Program to secure nuclear weapons and materials in the former Soviet Union. Instead, in its first budget, the Bush administration cut funds for the program. While later budgets restored funding to the previous level of $1 billion, the administration's 2005 budget submission again calls for cutting funds in the year ahead.[1]

Contrast this with Bush's call in September 2003 for $87 billion in "supplemental spending" for the war in Iraq. If the war on nuclear terrorism is an absolute national priority, the president should tell his commanders in this war to do whatever it takes to finish the job without funding constraints. Total war on nuclear terrorism could cost $5 billion a year, or perhaps even $10 billion. In a current budget that devotes more than $500 billion to defense and the war in Iraq, a penny of every dollar for what Bush calls "our highest priority" would not be excessive.

Second, the president should appoint an individual of stature who reports directly to him as his commander in a real war on nuclear terrorism. In the aftermath of 9/11, President Bush called on Tom Ridge to resign the governorship of Pennsylvania, join the White House staff, and serve as the nation's commander in an effort to secure the homeland. Subsequently, Congress created the Department of Homeland Security, and the president appointed Ridge as its secretary. Today, if the president asked, at a cabinet meeting, who is responsible for preventing nuclear terrorism, six or eight hands in the room might go up, or none. In conceiving, organizing, and orchestrating the elements of the government to focus on an absolute priority, someone must have lead responsibility and be held accountable.

Third, the president must make prevention of nuclear terrorism a priority for himself personally, as well as for the secretary of defense, the secretary of state, the secretary of the Treasury, the director of central intelligence, the secretary of homeland security, the attorney general, the director of the FBI, and many other key officials. They must consider every day what they and the members of their departments should do in this war. They should demand daily or weekly reports from their subordinates on what has been accomplished, where they have encountered roadblocks, and what is required from whom in order to achieve measurable milestones in an operational plan.

Fourth, in his meetings and phone calls with foreign leaders the president must convince them to embrace this priority. He must use America's considerable leverage to persuade other nations to take actions necessary for success in the war on nuclear terrorism. For example, while the United States has many priorities for Pakistan, including democratization, drugs, human rights, and progress in resolving the dispute with India over Kashmir, the Pakistani government's role—witting and unwitting—in A. Q. Khan's nuclear black-marketeering is unacceptable. The Pakistani government's systems for securing its nuclear weapons and materials (as well as technologies and designs) must be strengthened on the fastest possible timetable to reach the gold standard. Given Musharraf's personal vulnerability to assassination by people within his own government, including the military and intelligence services, and his uncertain hold on power, he can easily be overwhelmed by demands from America and other countries. President Bush must therefore decide what matters most, communicate that message unambiguously, and assure that the agencies of his government who have other priorities stay on message.

FIGHTING A STRATEGICALLY FOCUSED WAR ON TERRORISM

The German philosopher Friedrich Nietzsche observed that "the most common form of human stupidity is forgetting what one is trying to do." In the war on terrorism, the U.S. government has had great difficulty staying strategically focused. After a strong start, the diversion of attention and resources to war in Iraq sucked much of the drive out of the war on terrorism and blurred the targets.

In October 2003, two years after the declaration of the war on terrorism, Secretary of Defense Donald Rumsfeld attempted to stand back from the fray and examine the big picture. In a provocative Top Secret, two-page memo to his six closest associates, Rumsfeld poses the central question: "Are we winning or losing the Global War on Terror?"[2] Rumsfeld leaves his answer unstated, noting that "we lack the metrics to know if we are winning or losing." But as the memo asks more specific questions and offers Rumsfeld's own hunches about answers, it becomes clear that we are not winning:

- "Is it possible to change the Department of Defense fast enough to successfully fight the Global War on Terror?" Rumsfeld's answer: No. He suggests that perhaps a new institution should be created for this purpose.
- "Are we capturing, killing, deterring, and dissuading more terrorists every day than the *madrassas* and the radical clerics are

recruiting, training, and deploying against us?" He suspects not, answering that "we are having mixed results with Al Qaeda; a great many remain at large."

- "Does the U.S. need to fashion a broad, integrated plan to stop the next generation of terrorists?" He answers yes, but notes, "The U.S. is putting relatively little effort into a long-range plan; the cost-benefit ratio is against us! Our cost is billions against the terrorists' cost of millions."

For courage and clarity in asking the tough questions, Rumsfeld deserves to be commended. But the fact that the secretary of defense was asking about the emperor's clothes more than two years after the war on terrorism had been declared is not reassuring. Several months after Rumsfeld's memo, a careful study published by the Army War College responded to several of his questions less tentatively, concluding: "The Global War on Terrorism as it has been so far defined and conducted is strategically unfocused; promises much more than it can deliver; and threatens to dissipate scarce U.S. military and other means over too many ends."[3]

In February 2004, CIA director George Tenet and FBI director Robert Mueller presented to the Senate Intelligence Committee the annual threat assessment, "The Worldwide Threat 2004." Just a little more than a year earlier, Tenet had reported that "the threat environment we find ourselves in today is as bad as it was last summer, the summer before 9/11."[4] Aware of the dangers of stating anything so pointedly in an election year, Tenet avoided an equivalent bottom line on today's threat in his 2004 report. Itemizing a number of ways in which "the Al Qaeda leadership structure we charted after September 11 is seriously damaged," he nonetheless warned that "the group remains as committed as ever to attacking the American homeland." He continued: "I am not suggesting Al Qaeda is defeated. It is not. We are still at war." Tenet highlighted Al Qaeda's vigorous, ongoing quest for nuclear weapons, alerting Congress that "in addition to Al Qaeda, more than two dozen other terrorist groups are pursuing chemical, biological, radiological, and nuclear materials." And about the larger war on terrorism, he offers the chilling conclusion that "the steady growth of Osama bin Laden's anti-U.S. sentiment through the wider Sunni extremist movement and the broad dissemination of Al Qaeda's destructive expertise ensure that a serious threat will remain for the foreseeable future—with or without Al Qaeda in the picture."[5]

Mueller agreed with Tenet's assessment, but offered a bleaker bottom line: "It is a changed threat, in my mind, to the United States, no less of a threat than we had perhaps a year ago, perhaps a more significant threat." Focusing specifically on dangers to the American homeland, he warned about "strong indications that Al Qaeda will revisit missed targets until they succeed, as they did with the World Trade Center. And the list of missed targets now includes both the White House as well as the Capitol."[6]

A strategically focused war on terrorism would zero in on three key objectives. First, it would spare no effort in the military, economic, and diplomatic campaign to defeat and destroy Al Qaeda's leadership. It would seek to capture or kill the individual masterminds who organize the killing of the largest number of Americans. At the top of this list stand Osama bin Laden, Ayman al-Zawahiri (his second in command), and Mullah Muhammad Omar (the former Taliban leader of Afghanistan). But in pursuing terrorists worldwide, it would be mindful of Rumsfeld's caution about producing more new terrorists than we eliminate. Second, in combating what President Bush rightly calls the "world's most destructive technologies," it would go to the source with a determined campaign to lock down all weapons and materials and clean out any that cannot be rapidly secured to a standard that gives American citizens confidence that terrorists cannot steal them.

Third, this war would recognize America's dependence on high levels of voluntary cooperation by other states, especially their intelligence agencies and law enforcement communities. In the war on terrorism, the long pole in the tent is fine-grained, local intelligence, the same kinds of tips from the same kinds of sources that lead to drug busts and other law enforcement successes. In March 2002, Pakistani police officers working with the FBI launched a series of predawn raids that captured twenty-six suspected Al Qaeda and Taliban fugitives from their homes in the cities of Faisalabad and Lahore, in eastern Pakistan. The operation proved a successful union of the FBI's technical capacity to track suspects and the Pakistanis' up-to-the-minute human intelligence to pinpoint their exact location at the time of the raid.[7] Though tangential to the war on terrorism, the capture of Saddam was made possible by Kurdish officials and other local sources who fed information to U.S. forces on the dictator's whereabouts.[8] The United States would thus nurture deeper relationships with key allies and partners, with greater sensitivity to their citizens' concerns.

CONDUCTING A HUMBLE FOREIGN POLICY

The most memorable foreign policy line from the 2000 campaign came from candidate George W. Bush, who called for the United States to conduct a "humble foreign policy." He said, "If we are an arrogant nation, they will resent us, but if we are a humble nation, but strong, they will welcome us."[9] Unfortunately, either the president forgot his advice or he did not mean it. Vice President Cheney and other members of the administration evidently never heard it, or never agreed. As a consequence, in an era when America's share of world power has never been greater, its international standing has fallen to the lowest point in modern history.

The presumption of America's reliable benevolence served as the bedrock for six decades of Republican and Democratic administrations' leadership of the world. That belief has been damaged, perhaps beyond repair. In the aftermath of World War II, America emerged as the world's leading nation, not just as a reflection of its power but also because the leaders and citizens of other countries believed in America's basic goodwill and good sense. Winston Churchill effectively summarized this presumption: "The best hope of the world lies in the strength, will, and good judgment of the U.S."[10] Churchill was acutely aware that the United States had no monopoly on wisdom or power but, as he put it, "The United States can always be counted on to do the right thing, after it's exhausted every other alternative."[11]

After the war was won, leaders we now revere as "wise men"— Harry S. Truman, George C. Marshall, Arthur H. Vandenberg— understood that without American leadership in building an international security order, the conditions that had claimed twenty-five million lives in World War I and fifty million in World War II could lead to a third world war, from which there might be few survivors. They also saw that a durable peace would require new institutions that engaged the other great powers, and indeed the world, in shared undertakings. The United Nations, the North Atlantic Treaty Organization, the U.S.–Japanese Security Treaty, and, in the economic sphere, the International Monetary Fund, the General Agreement on Tariffs and Trade, and the World Bank provided structures within which to address issues of common concern. Critics who call this American imperialism complain that these institutions were made in America. So they were, and so they were designed. However, they served not narrow, short-term American interests but an enlightened self-interest in creating a world in which America, its allies, and the rest of the world could enjoy peace and prosperity. These efforts succeeded, resulting in a long peace, victory in the Cold War, and the greatest expansion of global wealth in history.

The greatest casualty of the war in Iraq has been the erosion of this trust. As *Newsweek* columnist Fareed Zakaria observed in its aftermath, "Having traveled around the world and met with senior government officials in dozens of countries over the past year, I can report that with the exception of Britain and Israel, every country the administration has dealt with feels humiliated by it."[12] Former ambassador Ed Djerejian's congressional task force on public diplomacy concluded, in October 2003, that "the bottom has indeed fallen out of support for the United States."[13] Even deeply sympathetic European thinkers such as Robert Cooper, a senior British diplomat and former national security adviser to Tony Blair, are uncomfortable with an America unbound. Having expressed support for many of the key tenets of the Bush administration's foreign policy, including preemptive war, Cooper nevertheless argues, "The idea of a single country exercising unrestrained and unrestrainable power is not welcome."[14]

Why does the erosion of this trust in America matter? First, like the great conflicts of the past, the war on terrorism is a battle of alliances. Whether it be the cooperation of Thai police in capturing the Indonesian Al Qaeda ringleader Hambali, or Pakistani operations against Taliban and Al Qaeda remnants on the Pakistan–Afghanistan border, international cooperation and coordination has been indispensable to progress in the war on terrorism. This is even more true of a war on nuclear terrorism. Convincing other countries to support the actions required to enforce the Three No's means persuading them of the specific proliferation risks posed by Iran, North Korea, Pakistan, and others. Making that case after the massive intelligence failure and evident political hyperbole about threats posed by Iraq will be much harder. As Arthur Schlesinger, Jr. has noted, "It is doubtful that President Bush could once again rally a 'coalition of the willing' in a preventive war against Iran or North Korea."[15]

Second, the longer-term war on terrorism, including nuclear terrorism, is a battle for hearts and minds. In democracies, citizens' views matter because they elect governments. The support of foreign leaders does us little good if voters turn them out of office. In March 2004, Spaniards clearly interpreted the Madrid terrorist bombings as a sign that their participation in the war against Iraq had made Spain a target. The strongly pro-American prime minister Jose Maria Aznar was replaced by a new leader who asserted that the decision to go to war in Iraq was "based on lies" and characterized the occupation as a "fiasco."[16]

Successful prosecution of terrorists like Mounir el-Motassadeq—the only conspirator in the 9/11 attack to have been convicted as of this writing—depends on judges, prosecutors, and police in other countries. This point was demonstrated dramatically in March 2004 when Klaus Tolksdorf, the presiding judge on a German appeals court, threw out Motassadeq's conviction and sent the case back to the lower court that had sentenced him to fifteen years in prison. A spokesperson for the U.S. Justice Department said, "We will continue to cooperate with Germany in the fight against our common foe, the terrorists." But the German judge clearly spoke to America, as well as to his fellow citizens, when he explained, "We cannot abandon the rule of law. That would be the beginning of a fatal development and ultimately a victory for the terrorists." As Judge Tolksdorf concluded: "The fight against terrorism cannot be a wild, unjust war."[17]

In the words of General John Abizaid, the head of U.S. Central Command, the war on terrorism is "a battle of ideas as much as it is a military battle."[18] When most of the world views the United States as unconstrained and unconstrainable; when half of the German population believes that the U.S. government is as great a threat to world peace as North Korea; when three times as many Pakistanis trust Osama bin Laden "to do the right thing regarding world affairs" than they do President Bush—the longer-term war on terrorism is clearly in trouble.

Humility in foreign policy does not require passivity or even deference. Rather, it demands thinking strategically about what the United States needs most from other nations and groups to preserve our security, not reacting emotionally to real or perceived diplomatic insults. More than two hundred years ago, James Madison offered a compelling rationale for the "decent respect for the opinions of mankind" in *Federalist* 63:

An attention to the judgment of other nations is important to every government for two reasons: The one is, that independently of the merits of any particular plan or measure, it is desirable on various accounts, that it should appear to other nations as the off-spring as a wise and honorable policy: The second is, that in doubtful cases, particularly when the national councils may be warped by some strong passion, or momentary interest, the presumed or known opinion of the impartial world, may be the best guide that can be followed.[19]

American leaders are the trustees of the nation's unique place in the world—a position of primacy that inescapably discombobulates and even threatens others, including our friends, but at the same time provides an opportunity to build a world safe for America and our values. Precisely because the United States is so powerful on all dimensions relative to all competitors, style matters. Asking, listening, taking account of the views of others, especially when they disagree, does not require giving them a veto on matters of vital national interest. But as the alpha male of the pack displays judgment as well as strength to maintain his position, the American unipower must show itself to be thoughtful as well as forceful. As Henry Kissinger puts it, "In the heyday of their pre-eminence, the Roman and British empires managed to transform their power into consensus and their governing principles into widely accepted norms. The United States has not yet achieved such a position."[20]

In crafting this humble foreign policy, America's leaders should follow the example of cadets at West Point, who, in their first weeks at the academy, are required to memorize, and to recite on command, Major General John Schofield's definition of discipline:

The discipline which makes the soldiers of a free country reliable in battle is not to be gained by harsh or tyrannical treatment. On the contrary, such treatment is far more likely to destroy than to make an army. It is possible to impart instruction and give commands in such a manner and such a tone of voice to inspire in the soldier no feeling but an intense desire to obey, while the opposite manner and tone of voice cannot fail to excite strong resentment and a desire to disobey. The one mode or the other of dealing with subordinates springs from a corresponding spirit in the breast of the commander. He who feels the respect which is due to others cannot fail to inspire in them regard for himself, while he who feels, and hence manifests, disrespect toward others, especially his inferiors, cannot fail to inspire hatred against himself.[21]

BUILDING A GLOBAL ALLIANCE AGAINST NUCLEAR TERRORISM

The United States cannot undertake or sustain the war on nuclear terrorism unilaterally. Fortunately, it need not try. Today, all the great powers share vital national interests in the proposed campaign. Each has sufficient reason to fear nuclear weapons in the hands of terrorists, whether they are Al Qaeda, Chechens, or Chinese Uighur separatists. Each nation's best hope to achieve conditions essential for its security requires cooperation with the others. The great powers are therefore ripe for mobilization for a global concert—indeed, a grand alliance against nuclear terrorism. The mission of this alliance should be to minimize the risk by taking every action physically, technically, and diplomatically possible to prevent nuclear weapons or materials from being acquired by terrorists.

Existing alliances are ill suited to address this global security threat. NATO covers one area, the U.S.–Japanese Security Treaty another. The nuclear nonproliferation regime consists of a patchwork of treaties like the NPT; informal agreements like the Nuclear Suppliers Group and the Proliferation Security Initiative; nuclear-free zones in Latin America, Southeast Asia, and the Australia–Pacific region; and assorted bilateral pacts. Meeting the threat of nuclear terrorism will require a global response.

Construction of this new alliance should begin with Russia and the United States. Americans and Russians have a special obligation to address this problem, since they created it—and since they still own 95 percent of all nuclear weapons and materials. As they demonstrate a new seriousness about this threat, the United States and Russia will be able, jointly, to engage China. After a long period during which it regarded nuclear development as an internal affair, China has recently taken a stand against the proliferation of nuclear weapons, and now affirms principles consistent with the Three No's. Moreover, despite the sensitivities involved, the United States and China have been sharing technologies for securing and accounting for nuclear materials.[22]

While signing up the other nuclear weapons states and the non-nuclear great powers will be an arduous task, America and its allies have the economic and diplomatic heft to move even the more reluctant states to our side of the ledger on high-priority issues. With international partners adding their leverage to America's diplomatic repertoire, bringing Pakistan into the global alliance should be no more difficult than convincing Musharraf to cooperate with the war on terrorism. To avoid a public opinion backlash, Musharraf could keep his distance from the United States by inviting China or another alliance nation to handle sensitive verification and inspection tasks. Meanwhile, India has a powerful incentive to welcome the alliance, since New Delhi would be the most likely target for any unsecured Pakistani nuclear device. With international donors footing most of the bill, compliance would cost the two countries relatively little while increasing the transparency and security of each other's nuclear arsenal. Cooperating with the alliance would legitimize both Pakistan and India as nuclear weapons states and open the door to sources of development aid.

Initially, members of the alliance would join in five common undertakings. First, they would embrace the gold standard for all nuclear weapons and materials on their own territory and the program to speed the clean-out of all potential nuclear weapons at research reactors or other facilities that cannot be secured. The leader of each country would pledge to hold personally accountable the entire chain of command in his or her government to achieve this result quickly. Understanding that each nation bears the responsibility for the security of its nuclear materials, the members should nonetheless offer any needed technical and financial assistance. To that end, the G8's Global Partnership against the Spread of Weapons and Materials of Mass Destruction, created in 2002, in which the seven other members pledged to match U.S. expenditures of $1 billion a year for threat reduction programs, should be expanded, on a dollar-for-dollar basis, to match U.S. increases in its funding.

Second, the alliance would shape a consensus in support of, or at least acquiescing to, enforcement of the Three No's, beginning with North Korea, Iran, and Pakistan. During the Cold War, when the United States and the Soviet Union cooperated, nuclear aspirants were stymied. Only when one of the nuclear powers cooperated with an aspirant, or when the superpowers were competing or distracted, did other nuclear weapons states realize their ambitions. India and Pakistan offer vivid case studies. The failure, particularly on the part of the United States and Russia, to restrain these two nations resulted in their testing weapons openly and declaring themselves nuclear weapons states in 1998. Subsequent Russian–American–Chinese cooperation in nudging India and Pakistan back from the brink suggests what can be accomplished.

Third, the new alliance should develop a robust nonproliferation regime to shut down the sale and export of nuclear technologies, materials, and know-how. Joint examination of the frightening facts about A. Q. Khan's remarkable global black market should stimulate inventive, determined prevention. The first response must be the criminalization of all proliferation activities, and passage of the

UN resolution called for by both President Bush and Mohamed ElBaradei. Nuclear trafficking should become an international crime worse than piracy. Individual offenders should be locked up; businesses that aid and abet such activity should be shut down. Building on the work of the Nuclear Suppliers Group, members of the alliance would strengthen controls over the export of all technologies that can be of use to proliferators. Nuclear technologies that can be used to produce fissile material would not be sold to states not already possessing those capabilities, and sales of dual-use items (which have both nuclear and nonnuclear uses) would be scrutinized by all authorities in the alliance. Intelligence sharing and cooperative police action would enforce the new rules; track the actions of black marketeers and rogue scientists illicitly selling their knowledge; and freeze the financial assets of possible proliferators, many of whom developed multinational financial networks to cover their tracks during the years of Khan's empire.

Fourth, the alliance should adapt lessons learned in U.S.–Russian, U.S.–Chinese, and other cooperative ventures in the campaign against the Taliban and Al Qaeda—especially the importance of intelligence sharing and affirmative counterproliferation, including disruption and preemption to prevent acquisition of materials and know-how by nuclear wannabes. In addition to intelligence sharing, joint training for preemption against terrorists, criminal groups, or rogue states attempting to acquire WMD would provide an enforcement mechanism for alliance commitments.

Finally, the alliance should be not just a signed document but a living institution committed to its mission. Like the G8, the leaders of the key member states should meet annually; their ministers, quarterly. But unlike the G8, and more like NATO, the alliance should have a secretariat that coordinates working groups on specific topics, develops work plans, and tracks performance in meeting established milestones. In the process, the members should develop shared assessments of threats and identify actions the states can take, individually and collectively, to address the threats. Moreover, they should identify activities beyond the agenda that advance the mission of the alliance, including topics that will be uncomfortable for some of the members, such as the Comprehensive Test Ban Treaty or the appropriateness of new programs in the established nuclear states.

Objections will surely be raised about the unfairness of a regime in which some states are allowed to possess nuclear weapons while others are not. But that distinction is already embedded in the NPT, to which all nonnuclear weapons states except North Korea are signatories. Although the treaty nominally commits nuclear weapons states to eventually eliminate their own weapons, it never set a timetable, and no one expects that to happen anytime soon.

The United States and its allies have the power to define and enforce global constraints on nuclear weapons. By doing so they can preserve all nations from the nightmare of a world in which nuclear terrorists destroy civilization as we know it. To make this order acceptable, however, they must marginalize the role of nuclear weapons and nuclear threats in international affairs. Still short of the "Fourth No" that some believe this program logically requires—namely, "No Nuclear Weapons"—the nuclear states visible rejection of nuclear weapons as viable foreign policy tools would go a long way toward creating such a world. In that spirit, the United States and Russia should accelerate current programs to reduce their arsenals, and the Bush administration should drop its plans to conduct research into new types of nuclear weapons. After a 2002 Nuclear Posture Review advocating the integration of nuclear weapons into conventional strike options, the administration sought and Congress finally authorized $21 million for the study and development of new "bunker busters," "mini-nukes," and preparation for nuclear testing. In its budget proposal for 2005, the administration asked for an additional $485 million for these programs over the next five years. These decisions should be reversed.

As Senator Dianne Feinstein of California has pointed out, "Our own nuclear posture could provoke the very nuclear-proliferation activities that we are seeking to prevent."[23]

CREATING THE INTELLIGENCE CAPABILITIES REQUIRED FOR SUCCESS IN THE WAR ON NUCLEAR TERRORISM

In David Kay's one-word summary, American intelligence about large stockpiles of Iraqi weapons of mass destruction was "wrong." Analyzing the reasons for this striking failure, the former chief of U.S. weapons inspections concludes that the CIA has essentially lost any serious capability for clandestine operations: either collection or covert action.[24] In 1991, when Kay led a team of inspectors in Iraq after the Gulf War, he had been surprised to find that the CIA had no secret agents there. When UN inspectors left the country in 1998, again, the United States had no secret agents in Iraq.[25] As a result, the CIA relied on Iraqi émigrés and defectors, most of whom turned out to be unreliable or even deliberately misleading; foreign intelligence services, which also depended on the same émigré reports; and its own analysts' projections and speculations.

Unfortunately, the American intelligence community's poor performance in assessing Iraqi WMD was not unique. Both the joint Senate-House intelligence committees' review of 9/11 and the National Commission on Terrorist Attacks upon the United States have documented patterns of action—and more often inaction—that strain credulity. After Al Qaeda had attacked the United States repeatedly, including bombing two U.S. embassies in 1998, how many CIA agents did the United States have in Afghanistan tracking bin Laden? The 9/11 Commission's report answers: zero. In its summary: "Going into the year 2000, the CIA had never laid American eyes on bin Laden in Afghanistan."[26] In 1998, CIA director

George Tenet declared that "we are at war" with Al Qaeda. But a top official at the FBI's Counterterrorism Division confessed during the joint congressional intelligence inquiry that he "was not specifically aware of that declaration of war."[27]

President Clinton's national security adviser, Sandy Berger, told the 9/11 commissioners that Clinton gave unambiguous instructions to the CIA to kill bin Laden.[28] But CIA officials, from the director to those at the operational levels, testified that the message they heard from the Clinton administration was that "the only acceptable context for killing bin Laden was a credible capture operation."[29] CIA agents attempted to enlist Northern Alliance leader Ahmed Shah Massoud in this effort. After hearing the CIA's carefully worded instructions about what he could and could not do to apprehend bin Laden, Massoud told the briefer: "You Americans are crazy. You guys never change."[30]

Asked by the Senate Intelligence Committee why the CIA never picked up Marwan al-Shehhi, the pilot who crashed American Airlines Flight 175 into the south tower of the World Trade Center, despite the fact that two years earlier German intelligence had passed on to CIA his first name and phone number, CIA director Tenet replied: "The Germans gave us a name, Marwan—that's it—and a phone number. They didn't give us a first and last name until after 9/11."[31] Excuse me, *New York Times* columnist Maureen Dowd quipped: "As one guy I know put it, 'I've tracked down women across the country with a lot less information than that.'"[32]

North Korea remains a black hole. The United States has apparently been unable to locate Pyongyang's clandestine HEU facility, or even to confirm its existence. Donald Gregg, a former CIA station chief and U.S. ambassador to South Korea, calls North Korea "the longest-running intelligence failure in U.S. history."[33] There have been successes in other areas, such as the uncovering of the A. Q. Khan network and the voluntary termination of Libya's weapons program. But these achievements tell us as much about what we do not know as about what we do. After all, U.S. intelligence agencies failed to detect Khan's operation until it had spread across the globe, and American officials were shocked to find how much technology Libya had acquired unbeknownst to them.

Most consequential of all were American intelligence predictions about Iraq's stockpile of weapons of mass destruction. While President Bush has minimized this intelligence failure, being so wrong on such a major venture risks turning the United States into the boy who cried wolf. Unquestionably, this failure has compromised our ability to address other, more serious threats. As Steven Weisman and David E. Sanger of the *New York Times* reported in February 2004: "In recent months, China, citing the failure to find weapons in Iraq, has questioned the quality of American intelligence about the North Korean nuclear program and suggested that it should not be a focus of the negotiations."[34]

What kind of intelligence capabilities are required for a successful war on nuclear terrorism? The challenge is extreme, perhaps even excessive. But there are four steps the intelligence community must take to meet the threat.

First, American intelligence must move beyond its Cold War mindset. The United States continues to rely too heavily on high-tech solutions, such as spy satellites and eavesdropping technologies, spending many thousands of dollars on technology for every dollar devoted to recruiting agents inside countries like Iraq or infiltrating groups like Al Qaeda. The National Security Agency (NSA), which collects and interprets communications from around the world, employs thirty thousand electronic eavesdroppers, while the CIA's Directorate of Operations—its human spies—has only about four thousand employees.[35] The most sophisticated secret technologies cannot uncover small-scale insider theft, or even nuclear efforts camouflaged in highly visible civilian research programs. As Tenet has acknowledged, "The difference between producing low-enriched uranium and weapons-capable high-enriched uranium is only a matter of time and intent, not technology. It would be a significant challenge for intelligence to confidently assess whether this red line has been crossed."[36]

The United States must therefore develop more creative, diverse human sources of intelligence—individuals who live in foreign lands, speak local languages and dialects, can penetrate terrorist organizations, and can recruit citizens of other countries and members of groups like Al Qaeda. Existing human intelligence is largely unable to track terrorists in the Middle East or Central Asia because of a lack of linguistic and cultural training. In 1999, the NSA hired a total of fourteen analysts with foreign language proficiency.[37] According to an anonymous former senior operative from the CIA's Near East Division, "The CIA probably doesn't have a single truly qualified Arabic-speaking officer of Middle Eastern background who can play a believable Muslim fundamentalist."[38] Another case officer put it more bluntly: "Operations that include diarrhea as a way of life don't happen."[39]

Second, the United States must cultivate long-term strategic relationships with foreign intelligence agencies. As Brent Scowcroft, who served as national security adviser to Presidents Gerald R. Ford and George H. W. Bush and is chairman of George W. Bush's Foreign Intelligence Advisory Board, noted, "The cooperation of the intelligence services of every friend and ally we can muster will greatly magnify our strength."[40] Intelligence cooperation must include regional and local police forces who would first recognize the existence of a terrorist cell with nuclear ambitions, or a local wholesaler who uses the business as a front for shipping nuclear technologies.

Third, the American intelligence community must enhance its data-mining efforts to process, analyze, and disseminate open sources of intelligence. Open sources can include international media broadcasts, Internet chat rooms, financial markets, and court proceedings. An example of how such intelligence is translated into effective counterproliferation policies is demonstrated by the Wisconsin Project on Nuclear Arms Control, which—by scanning the public domain—has identified more than 3,500 firms involved in the global trafficking of nuclear and missile technologies. Its Risk Report database is sold as a bimonthly CD-ROM to the CIA, the Department of Defense, and export officials in Western and Eastern Europe to prevent the sale of sensitive technologies to businesses involved in proliferation.

Finally, and above all, intelligence assessments must be credible. When the president calls on allies and friends to prevent nuclear proliferation—or, worse, nuclear terrorism—leaders on the other end of the line must find the facts believable. That requires distinguishing sharply between what is known and what is not known. During the Cuban missile crisis in October 1962, President Kennedy sent former secretary of state Dean Acheson to ask Charles de Gaulle for his support. When Acheson offered to show the French president the satellite reconnaissance photos of Soviet missiles in Cuba, de Gaulle put his hand up and said, "Mr. Secretary, it's not necessary. I know the president, I trust him. I need not see it." As Zbigniew Brzezinski, who served as national security adviser to President Jimmy Carter, recently noted of de Gaulle's response, "Would any foreign leader today react the same way to an American emissary sent abroad to say that Country X is armed with weapons of mass destruction that threaten the United States? It is unlikely."[41]

DEALING WITH DIRTY BOMBS

The good news about dirty bombs and attacks on nuclear reactors is that they present far less catastrophic threats than true nuclear terrorism. The bad news, however, is that radioactive materials are so widely available in the industrial economies that even a determined effort to deny terrorists access to such material is bound to fail. While nuclear power plants can be hardened, they are what the

U.S. military calls a "fixed target." All fixed targets are vulnerable to attack if terrorists can muster sufficient force or corrupt an insider. After all, the World Trade Center towers and the Pentagon were fixed targets, too.

What, then, is to be done? First, we must have more stringent accounting and control of the radioactive isotopes with the greatest potential to produce mass disruption if dispersed by terrorists. That list includes cesium, used in cancer treatment; cobalt, utilized to irradiate food to kill bacteria; and americium, used in the mining industry to search for oil sources.[42] Initially on a national basis, but in time globally, standards for securing and transporting these materials must be developed for the industries and academic institutions that use them. The Department of Energy's Off-Site Source Recovery Project must be funded to reach its target of securing eighteen thousand unwanted, privately held radioactive sources long before today's estimated completion date of 2010.[43] While helping the private sector meet the new standards, the federal government must pass and enforce tougher laws to penalize those who fail to comply.

Second, we must improve our ability to detect radioactive materials at airports and harbors, on highways, and at other potential target sites. Routine checks of scrap-metal yards and landfills with simple Geiger counters would be sufficient to protect against accidental disposal of dangerous radiation sources.[44] Detecting a shielded radiation source or dirty bomb, however, will require new technologies that allow finer discrimination between dangerous materials and natural background radiation. Such improved equipment, needed for a multilayered defense against nuclear terrorism, will be even more effective against dirty bombs, since the most dangerous dirty-bomb ingredients are far more visible to sensors than is the core of a nuclear weapon.

Protecting nuclear power plants poses different challenges. Improved airline security, tightened screening of workers, and enhanced security against truck bombs are useful steps that are already under way. The Nuclear Regulatory Commission has redesigned the hypothetical threat against which each U.S. nuclear power plant must defend itself, presenting the industry with a higher standard. Now individual plants must be monitored and held accountable for implementing new security measures.

We also need to improve our ability to respond in the event of an attack. As a first step, emergency personnel should be trained to diagnose radiation exposure, protect themselves, and treat the victims. The federal government must also sponsor research into faster and more effective ways to clean up areas contaminated by radioactive debris. In March 2002, Henry Kelly, the president of the Federation of American Scientists, advised the Senate Foreign Relations Committee that "the ability to decontaminate large urban areas might mean the difference from being able to continue inhabiting a city and having to abandon it."[45] Better decontamination techniques would help limit the public's exposure to lingering radiation, reduce the economic impact of the event, and make such attacks less attractive to terrorists.

Perhaps the most important thing that the government can do, however, is to be prepared to educate and communicate with the public. A dirty-bomb report submitted in 1999 to the Air Command and Staff College concluded that "panic might produce casualties and damage far in excess of the actual device itself."[46] The government's response to an attack can have an enormous impact on the public's reaction. New York City mayor Rudolph Giuliani's confident, candid, and reassuring appearances following the 9/11 attacks were instrumental in holding the city together and preventing panic. To coordinate communications following an attack, federal, state, and local authorities must designate a single credible authority to provide timely information.[47] By preparing educational materials, including videos, in advance for distribution to television and radio stations, authorities can provide the media with a consistent, instructive message for a frightened public.[48]

CONSTRUCTING A MULTILAYERED DEFENSE

The only way to eliminate the threat of nuclear terrorism is to lock down the weapons and materials at the source. As former senator Sam Nunn has said, "Acquiring weapons and materials is the hardest step for terrorists to take, and the easiest for us to stop. By contrast, every subsequent step in the process is easier for the terrorists to take, and harder for us to stop."[49] However, recognizing that even the best efforts to secure weapons and fissile material may not achieve 100 percent success, and that some nuclear material may already be loose, we cannot rely exclusively on any single line of defense.

If a headline in tomorrow's *New York Times* were to read "Russian Officials Cannot Account for Five Nuclear Weapons Following Midnight Raid," what steps would we wish we had taken to give ourselves a better chance of preventing a nuclear terrorist attack? As discussed in chapters 4 and 5, terrorists who conducted such a raid would still face several hurdles: smuggling the weapon or fissile material out of the country, transporting it to a safe haven, preparing it for use, smuggling it into the United States, and avoiding detection long enough to detonate it at the target. Each of these hurdles offers opportunities to make ourselves measurably safer.

The United States must convince all nations to strengthen their domestic laws against trafficking in nuclear materials and technology. Denying terrorists sanctuaries where they can train and plan is essential, because it forces them to prepare their nuclear weapon while hiding from authorities. But the law must also come down hard on nuclear traffickers when they are caught. Of course, the prospect of long prison sentences is unlikely to deter fanatics like the 9/11 hijackers, but it could discourage some intermediaries. Most of the individuals convicted of smuggling nuclear materials before September 2001 received sentences of five years or less in prison. A German exporter convicted of treason for sending advanced plans for uranium enrichment centrifuges to Iraq in 1989 spent just one year in jail.[50]

The United States must also lead a global initiative to strengthen international export and border controls. In the early 1990s, concerns about nuclear proliferation prompted the United States to help governments in the former Soviet bloc monitor their borders for nuclear smuggling. From 1992 to 2001, six federal agencies were given $140 million to purchase radiation monitors, install and maintain equipment, and train border officials in approximately thirty countries. By 2002, Department of Energy officials reported that the radiation portal monitors they provided to Russia had detected 275 cases involving radioactive material.[51] In at least one case, customs officials in Bulgaria, a country that received U.S. training in interdicting nuclear smuggling, seized weapons-usable material that had been hidden inside the trunk of a car.[52]

But seen through the prism of 9/11, these efforts seem woefully inadequate. The agencies responsible for these programs in the ten years before 9/11 actually failed to spend $53.9 million of the $140 million that Congress gave them—over a third of their total budgets.[53] Radiation detection equipment provided by the State Department sat in the U.S. embassy in Lithuania for two years because of a disagreement about providing a power supply line costing $12,600.[54] After 9/11, federal spending on interdicting nuclear smuggling increased, reaching a peak of more than $221 million in 2003. In 2004, however, funding levels slipped to $127 million, and the president's budget request for 2005 held spending constant at that level.[55] For international border controls to form a true second line of defense, the United States needs to expand these programs to include other regions where nuclear smuggling is most likely to occur, such as Central Asia and the Middle East.

The United States must also focus its own border control efforts on nuclear terrorism. As discussed in chapter 5, U.S. borders present, at best, "Swiss cheese" barriers to nuclear smuggling. There are steps that the government must take to shrink some of the most egregious holes. Air cargo, most of which is never subject to security screening, should be held to the same security standards as cargo arriving in the United States via land or sea. And all shipments entering the United States need to be scanned for radiation using the best available technology. Although Congress appropriated funding to install radiation portal detectors at every major U.S. seaport in 2003, in January 2004 only the seaport in Hampton Roads, Virginia, had the technology fully installed, and Customs and Border Protection authorities were just announcing plans to deploy the systems around the country.[56] The Department of Homeland Security has yet even to request funds for radiation portal detectors for the country's southern border.[57] Since these portal detectors offer a nonintrusive way to scan trucks, rail cars, and cargo containers for radioactive materials, the United States should be hurrying to install them at every major point of entry. Researching next-generation scanning and radiation detection technology needs to be a high priority as well, since only better technology can resolve the tension between our need for security and our need for unimpeded movement of legitimate travelers and goods.

For perspective, it is useful to note that the layer of defense on which the nation is currently spending more money than on all the others is missile defense, where the latest budget request has topped $10 billion. Against the threat of nuclear terrorism, this initiative is virtually irrelevant, since terrorists are not likely to acquire a weapon that is small enough to be delivered by missile, and even less so the missile itself. This allocation of funds suggests that the Bush administration and Congress do not fully grasp the nature of the nuclear terror threat.

NOTHING OF THE preceding discussion is meant to suggest that implementing the Seven Yeses is going to be easy. It is not. It will take time, and money, and the courage of our convictions to stay focused on the single goal of preventing a nuclear terrorist attack. But the fact remains that such a program, while ambitious, is without question within the capabilities of the U.S. government, if our political leaders are willing to give this effort the priority it deserves. Like the Cold War, the war on nuclear terrorism will probably be a "long, twilight struggle," but that does not mean it is unwinnable. After all, the United States won the Cold War, and it did so by keeping its attention focused not only on confronting the Soviet Union militarily and diplomatically but also by taking steps to ensure that such confrontations never escalated to the point where nuclear weapons would be used. That effort took thought, fortitude, and focus, qualities that are within our reach today.

The time has come for us to confront the fact that no one is going to save us from nuclear terrorism but ourselves. The choice is ours, to grab this beast by the horns, or to be impaled on its horns. We do not have the luxury of hoping this beast will simply go away.

CONCLUSION

Are these the shadows of the things that Will be, or are
they shadows of things that May be only?

CHARLES DICKENS,
A Christmas Carol

THE SPIRIT OF Christmas Future answers Scrooge that while the past
is fixed, the future is contingent on his actions. On the current
course, Tiny Tim will not live to celebrate his twelfth birthday, the
light will go out of Bob Cratchit's life, and Scrooge will join his former partner, Jacob Marley, in the chains and flames of hell. But "if
the course be departed from, the ends will change."

On the current course, nuclear terrorism is inevitable. Indeed, if
the United States and other governments keep doing what they are
doing today, a nuclear terrorist attack on America is more likely
than not in the decade ahead. With a ten-kiloton nuclear weapon
stolen from the former Soviet arsenal and delivered to an American
city in a cargo container, Al Qaeda can make 9/11 a footnote. And if
not Al Qaeda, one of its affiliates can step up, using a weapon built
of HEU from Pakistan or North Korea or from a research reactor in
Uzbekistan.

No one who has studied the facts doubts that another catastrophic
terrorist attack is coming. Wayne Downing, a retired Army general
who served as President Bush's counterterrorism chief following

the September 11 attacks, told the *Washington Post,* "These guys continue to go back after targets they have tried to get before. That's why I expect they're going to go back to Washington and . . . New York."[1] An anonymous official who works next door to the White House put it more bluntly: "They are going to kill the White House. I have really begun to ask myself whether I want to continue to get up every day and come to work on this block."[2] Some intelligence analysts suspect that Muammar el-Qaddafi's motive in confessing and opening Libya completely to American intelligence and international weapons inspectors is his belief that a WMD terrorist attack on America is in the offing and he wanted to get himself off the retaliation list.

Detonated in Times Square, a ten-kiloton weapon could kill one million New Yorkers. And why should bin Laden or other terrorists stop with one? Four nuclear explosions, in New York, Washington, Chicago, and Los Angeles, could achieve Al Qaeda's gruesome goal of killing four million Americans.

The good news about nuclear terrorism is that this ultimate catastrophe is, in fact, preventable. The bottleneck for terrorists is acquiring nuclear weapons or the fissile material from which they could make nuclear weapons. Advanced societies have technologies for preventing theft of items that they are determined to secure. Making highly enriched uranium or plutonium from scratch requires lengthy, expensive, and visible efforts that a vigilant international community can interrupt. This specter challenges our determination, not our technical capabilities.

In Dickens's tale, Scrooge becomes a new man, pledging solemnly to "honor Christmas in my heart, and try to keep it all the year. I will live in the Past, Present, and the Future. The Spirits of all Three shall strive within me. I will not shut out the lessons they teach."

If the president, members of Congress, and even citizens saw our future on the current path as vividly as Scrooge saw his, what could we do?

PERSONAL PRESIDENTIAL PRIORITY

A president who takes the threat of nuclear terror seriously would assemble the members of the core national security team and work with them to develop a comprehensive strategy, an operational plan, and a specific timetable for achieving measurable objectives over the next one hundred days, the next year, and beyond. Key pillars in what might become a ten-point program have been discussed in earlier chapters:

- ***Absolute national priority*** for himself and his administration.
- A ***gold standard*** for nuclear weapons and materials to make them as secure as gold in Fort Knox.
- A ***global alliance against nuclear terrorism*** starting with a concert of great powers that share vital interests in this objective.
- ***Global clean-out*** of all fissile material that cannot be secured to the gold standard.
- ***Stopping new national production of fissile material***—beginning with Iran.
- ***Shutting down nuclear black markets***—focusing first on Pakistan.
- ***Blocking the emergence of nuclear weapons states***—starting with North Korea.
- Engaging the global alliance in a ***comprehensive review of the nonproliferation regime*** to fill gaps and strengthen weaknesses.
- ***Revising nuclear weapons states' postures and pronouncements*** to marginalize nuclear weapons from any role in international politics.
- ***Prosecuting the war on terrorism*** to eliminate masterminds and groups that would conduct nuclear terrorist attacks.

This is not a project like sending a man to the moon, where the president can make a decision, persuade Congress to appropriate the money, and leave implementation to the government. Even with the best possible security team, the issue will initially require an hour of the president's time every day—tracking progress, breaking logjams, calling foreign leaders whose governments are backsliding, and holding individuals accountable. After the first hundred days, demands on the president's time will diminish. But until the job is done—and it could take as long as four years to get all the pieces in place—he must continue to follow up each and every week. Given the scores of high-priority demands on any president's time, it is understandable that neither George W. Bush nor his predecessor Bill Clinton made such an effort. But if Americans become the victims of a nuclear terrorist attack, how will the president explain why he spent those minutes engaged in other pursuits?

CONGRESSIONAL PRIORITY

Members of Congress can also become significant players on this issue. An earlier chapter told the story of Senators Sam Nunn and Richard Lugar, who in 1991 recognized an emerging threat that the administration was neglecting, and who attached an amendment to the Defense Authorization Bill for funds to assist in securing and eliminating former Soviet nuclear weapons. Through these efforts, they put this issue on the agenda for both the U.S. and Soviet governments. Subsequently, the Nunn–Lugar Cooperative Threat Reduction Program (now known as Nunn–Lugar–Domenici) has become the umbrella for a family of related initiatives that are heatedly debated in Congress each year. Dozens of members of the House and Senate have taken a personal interest in preserving and expanding the authority, funds, and flexibility for this activity and in pressing insufficiently motivated executive-branch managers to act with greater urgency.

New members of Congress can educate themselves about the problem. Members who are seen by their colleagues as knowledgeable on particular issues emerge as leaders. They can assign a member of their staff to track it, and they can zero in on a portion of the agenda, such as potential nuclear weapons left at research reactors in developing or transitional countries. They can make nuclear terrorism a high-visibility issue by taking a seat on one of the key committees (Foreign Relations, Armed Services, Intelligence, or Energy, and associated appropriations subcommittees) to press executive-branch officials on what they are doing, and not doing, to address the problem. They can also visit sites to observe the problem firsthand and report back with vivid illustrations, as Senators Howard Baker and Bob Graham, Representatives Curt Weldon and John Spratt, and many of their colleagues have done after inspecting nuclear facilities in Russia. They can utilize their research and regulatory resources—from personal staffs to the Congressional Research Service, Congressional Budget Office, and General Accounting Office—to keep the spotlight on government action or inaction. They can wield their power of the purse by withholding funds for White House priorities if the executive branch is not meeting the challenge. When required, they can become an irritant to the party leadership, even when it controls the White House.

Skeptics about the possibility that a single member of Congress can make a difference should read George Crile's book *Charlie Wilson's War*, published in 2003. A socially liberal, fervently anti-Communist representative from Texas, Wilson made it his personal cause to expel the Soviet Union from Afghanistan. Throughout the 1980s, he championed and oversaw the covert funding of mujahedeen forces fighting the Soviets there, increasing spending from $5 million in 1980 to $400 million (including $200 million that Wilson coaxed out of the Saudis) in 1992. President Mohammad Zia ul-Haq of Pakistan, who allowed the CIA to operate in and ship arms through his country, singled out Wilson as the individual who contributed the most to the defeat of the Russians in Afghanistan, asserting: "Charlie did it."[3]

CITIZENS' PRIORITY

What can private citizens do? For her work in pushing nations around the world to sign a treaty banning land mines, Jody Williams won the Nobel Peace Prize in 1997. When she began, the thought of banning a universally accepted weapon was dismissed as a utopian fantasy. Besides, she occupied no position of authority and had no special standing on a matter that required decisions by presidents and national legislatures. Nonetheless, with seven colleagues and a fax machine, Williams carried out an unprecedented lobbying and publicity campaign, eventually attracting the support of more than one thousand organizations in over sixty countries, as well as the support of a wide range of celebrities, from Princess Diana to Nelson Mandela to General Norman Schwarzkopf. In less than a decade, that citizens' initiative convinced 150 nations to renounce land mines, destroy current stocks, and prohibit future manufacture of this weapon.

Few citizens have the time or chutzpah to undertake such a campaign. Nonetheless, there are many other things they can do to help prevent nuclear terrorism. They can start by reading and paying attention to the almost daily news reports that touch on this topic. Members of organizations that take stands on political issues (such as churches, synagogues, mosques, labor unions, and business associations) can put the prevention of nuclear terrorism on their agendas. Armed with knowledge and perhaps the support of a local interest group, citizens can press this issue with their political candidates.

Especially during campaign seasons, citizens can talk directly to candidates. At fund-raisers, citizens can find an opportunity to put a serious question to a nominee seeking to become their representative or senator. Even in larger groups, in most states, an individual determined to do so can find a way to talk directly to his or her representative. If the citizen is prepared to work on the candidate's campaign, from canvassing and holding visibility signs to getting out the vote, his or her chances of talking to the candidate and encouraging that candidate to take an interest in a policy issue that matters increase significantly. If one has connections to individuals in news organizations covering the campaign or organizing debates, or if one is fortunate enough to ask a question, my suggestion is that one asks: What is the most important issue that is not likely to be debated in this campaign?

For perspective in answering that question, it is worth recalling the most important issue never raised in the presidential campaign of 2000. Less than a year after Americans voted in November, Al Qaeda orchestrated a megaterrorist attack on the World Trade Center and the Pentagon. Yet in none of the presidential debates, none of the debates among candidates for nomination to the presidency, and none of the Senate or House campaigns that I have been able to identify was the issue of terrorism even raised.

If one goes further back, to 1996, Senator Lugar attempted to raise this issue in his campaign for the Republican nomination for president—without effect. One of his television ads in New Hampshire briefly told the story of terrorists who steal three nuclear warheads and threaten to detonate them in the United States. The ad ends with a child asking her mother at bedtime: "Mommy, won't the bomb wake everybody up?"

AFTERWORD

IN THE FIRST presidential debate of the 2004 presidential campaign, the moderator asked the two candidates: "What is the single most serious threat to the national security of the United States?" In a rare instance of agreement, Senator John Kerry and President George W. Bush both answered that it was nuclear terrorism. As the president said: "I agree with my opponent that the biggest threat facing the country is weapons of mass destruction in the hands of a terrorist network."

About this debate, the *Philadelphia Inquirer* observed, "The two most disagreeable men in America (at least with each other) agreed on something terribly important when they met last month for their first debate. John Kerry and President Bush both asserted that the single greatest danger facing the United States is nuclear terrorism. Their synchronized skating on the issue excited even the unexcitable moderator Jim Lehrer so much that he even paused to confirm it."[1]

In the final weeks of the campaign, Vice President Dick Cheney made nuclear terrorism a centerpiece of his stump speech, arguing that "the biggest threat we face now as a nation is the possibility of

terrorists ending up in the middle of one of our cities with deadlier
weapons than have ever been used against us . . . nuclear weapons
able to threaten the lives of hundreds of thousands of Americans."
According to Cheney, "That's the ultimate threat. For us to have a
strategy that's capable of defeating that threat, you've got to *get
your mind around that concept*" (emphasis added).[2]

My goal in writing *Nuclear Terrorism* was to help American pol-
icymakers and thinking citizens get our minds around this concept.
Psychologically, the devastation that would be caused by a nuclear
bomb exploding in an American city remains almost inconceivable.
Physically, however, it is possible to describe in excruciating detail
just what an explosion would look like, feel like, and do. This book's
companion Web site, www.nuclearterrorism.org, allows the reader
to enter his or her own zip code and see the consequences of a ten-
kiloton nuclear bomb (the same size as the one that Dragonfire
warned was in New York City in October 2001) detonating in one's
own neighborhood.

A single nuclear bomb in a single American city would be a nation-
altering event. After the explosion of a second terrorist nuclear bomb,
many urban dwellers would reconsider their decision to live in large
cities. Nuclear terrorism is not only an existential threat to the idea
of America it is also a threat to civilization as we know it. A nuclear
terrorist attack is the face of nuclear danger today—the post–Cold
War successor to the specter of global nuclear war that hung over previous generations. As readers of this book know, this threat is at once
"inevitable" and "preventable." But in the year since this book was first
published, evidence supporting the proposition about the likelihood,
indeed inevitability, of a nuclear terrorist attack absent a major departure for current policy and practice has mounted.

- The *9/11 Commission Report* found that "Al Qaeda has tried to
  acquire or make weapons of mass destruction for at least ten
  years. There is no doubt the United States would be a prime
  target." It also provides additional detail about occasions when

Osama bin Laden's Al Qaeda operatives were scammed in their attempts to buy nuclear weapons–usable material.[3]

- Michael Scheuer, the former head of the CIA's bin Laden task force and the author of the book *Imperial Hubris* (under the pseudonym "Anonymous"), revealed that the CIA had tracked "the careful, professional manner in which Al Qaeda was seeking to acquire nuclear weapons" since 1996.[4] Scheuer also details how in May 2003 bin Laden obtained a fatwa from a Saudi cleric, Shaykh Nasir bin Hamid al-Fahd, providing a religious justification to use nuclear weapons against the United States. Entitled "A Treatise on the Legal Status of Using Weapons of Mass Destruction Against Infidels," it asserts that "if a bomb that killed 10 million of them and burned as much of their land as they have burned Muslims' land were dropped on them, it would be permissible."[5]

- The story of Abdul Qadeer Khan's global nuclear black marketeering continues to advance, with important new details coming to light monthly. Recent revelations include sales to Libya of blueprints for an advanced Chinese nuclear warhead thirty-four inches in diameter and thus small enough to be deliverable by missile,[6] and delivery to North Korea and Iran of advanced high-speed centrifuges needed to enrich uranium, and the blueprints and equipment required to build more.[7] It is now known that his network sold entire centrifuge facilities that could be shipped whole, manufactured from parts produced in Europe and put together in Malaysia.[8] Intelligence officials—and a cadre of dedicated reporters—have also been retracing trips made by the father of Pakistan's nuclear bomb to see where else he may have done what business. He was a well-traveled man, having made stops in Afghanistan, Egypt, Iran, Ivory Coast, Kazakhstan, Kenya, Mali, Mauritania, Morocco, Niger, Nigeria, North Korea, Saudi Arabia, Senegal, Sudan, Syria, Tunisia, and the United Arab Emirates.[9]

- From September 1–3, 2004, in Beslan, Russia, Chechen guerilla forces demonstrated yet again their organizational capacity to seize facilities inside Russia, as well as their readiness to kill ruthlessly—this time capturing and killing schoolchildren. On the first day of the hostage crisis, President Putin dispatched additional troops to guard Russia's undersecured nuclear facilities. Whatever the security at these facilities was the day before the school seizure, Putin understood that it was inadequate the day after. Immediately following the hostage taking, Putin proclaimed, "We are dealing with the direct intervention of international terror against Russia, with total and full-scale war."[10] But despite Putin's initial response to Beslan, the follow-up lags. While repeatedly warning about the threat of international terrorism and "the use of weapons of mass destruction that terrorists may obtain,"[11] Presidents Putin and Bush have yet to make preventing nuclear terrorism the highest security priority of their two governments.

- Matthew Bunn, a senior research associate at the Kennedy School of Government, publishes a frequently updated report titled "Anecdotes of Nuclear Insecurity."[12] This compilation of recent incidents demonstrates the continuing vulnerability of Russian nuclear facilities to theft. In October 2004, a force of forty-seven men identified as Dagestanis, armed with clubs and crowbars, seized control of a secret nonnuclear Russian military research and development facility in the town of Zelenograd. The intruders climbed into the facility on ladders, taking control of all of its secret documents and equipment. Local Russian forces retook the facility, and all forty-seven of the attackers were arrested.[13]

- The existence of previously undeclared nuclear experiments in South Korea (which included work on uranium enrichment and plutonium reprocessing) and Egypt came to light in 2004. While short of nuclear weapons programs, these experiments could serve as insurance policies for South Korea and Egypt against developments in North Korea and Iran.

· The seriousness of Iran's ambitions to acquire nuclear weapons is increasingly evident. In early 2005, estimates of when, on the current track, Iran would cross that goal line ranged from twelve to thirty-six months. It is now known that members of the A. Q. Khan network held more than a dozen meetings with Iranian nuclear scientists in the mid- to late 1990s.[14] IAEA inspectors, and national intelligence agencies, are actively searching for the still-undisclosed fruits of that collaboration. In his State of the Union speech, President Bush named Iran "the world's primary state sponsor of terror—pursuing nuclear weapons while depriving its people of the freedom they seek and deserve." Vice President Cheney put Iran "at the top of the list" of the world's "trouble spots,"[15] noting that "the Israelis might well decide to act first and let the rest of the world worry about cleaning up the diplomatic mess afterward."[16] Israeli Prime Minister Ariel Sharon announced that "Iran's nuclear missile program is today the greatest danger not just to Israel, but to the world."[17] Clearly, the United States and Israel are keeping the military option open. It has also been reported that the Pentagon is carrying out covert operations in Iran in an attempt to pinpoint the location of nuclear sites to target.[18]

· In February 2005 North Korea announced that it had "manu-factured nukes for self-defense to cope with the Bush adminis-tration's undisguised policy to isolate and stifle" the regime and that it will "bolster its nuclear weapons arsenal."[19] Pyongyang also declared that it would suspend participation in talks aimed at rolling back its nuclear capabilities "for an indefinite period."[20]

· Mohamed ElBaradei has begun sounding the alarm about the likelihood that trendlines will collapse—or even explode—the entire nonproliferation regime. ElBaradei has called for urgent action on a global agenda that parallels the doctrine of the Three No's, including: a five-year moratorium on building new capacity for uranium enrichment and plutonium separation, conversion of HEU reactors to use low-enriched uranium, establishing the "additional protocol" as an international norm, decisive action by the United Nations Security Council in the case of withdrawal from the Non-Proliferation Treaty, invoking Security Council Resolution 1540 to pursue and prosecute any illicit trading in nuclear material and technology, accelerated implementation on the part of the five nuclear weapons states that are party to the NPT of their "unequivocal commitment" to nuclear disarmament, and the necessity of resolving existing security problems worldwide that influence states' decisions about whether to seek nuclear weapons.[21]

Having survived another year without a nuclear terrorist attack, and indeed without any major terrorist attack on the United States, the great unanswered question remains: Why? Clearly the Bush administration has been doing some things right—undoubtedly more than its critics credit. On the other hand, Osama bin Laden has raised the bar, challenging the Al Qaeda movement to trump 9/11. The list of such attacks that meet that test is short. The U.S. interrogation of the mastermind of the 9/11 attack, Khalid Sheikh Mohammed, has yielded many insights into Al Qaeda's modus operandi and tradecraft. In planning that assault, a single cell worked for six years to prepare for the hijacking of the American jumbo jets that would attack the World Trade Center and the Pentagon. If a similar cell is now in its fifth or sixth year of preparation for a nuclear terrorist attack, we may not know until a mushroom cloud engulfs an American city.

The most important conceptual, policy-relevant advance in this book is the proposition that nuclear terrorism is in fact *preventable* by a feasible, affordable checklist of actions. Organizing a strategy for prevention under the doctrine of Three No's outlined in this book would allow policy makers and citizens to focus simultaneously on what is urgent and what is important.

No Loose Nukes. While much has been done, regrettably much remains undone. In Russia, the world's largest storehouse of weapons and materials, fewer potential nuclear bombs were secured in the two years after 9/11 than in the two years prior, according to the Department of Energy reports.[22] And even as Secretary of Energy Spencer Abraham took the lead in proposing a new Global Threat Reduction Initiative that in 2004 removed highly enriched uranium from Libya and Uzbekistan, material from which terrorists can make bombs remains vulnerable to theft at research reactors in twenty further risky transitional or developing countries. However, at their February 2005 summit meeting in Bratislava, Slovakia, Presidents Bush and Putin for the first time accepted personal responsibility for addressing the threat and for assuring that their governments secure loose nuclear material in their countries on an accelerated timetable. Advancing the previous schedule, they set 2008 as a target by which this danger should be substantially contained. They committed their governments to developing new emergency-response procedures for missing nuclear or "dirty bomb" materials and addressed the issue of risky research reactors in transitional and developing countries. They pledged that all U.S. and Russian research reactors provided to developing and transitional countries will be converted from highly-enriched uranium to low-enriched uranium fuel from which nuclear weapons cannot be made. They also created a "Senior Interagency Group," chaired by Secretary of Energy Sam Bodman and Rosatom Director Alexander Rumyantsev, to oversee the implementation of these efforts and report back to the presidents regularly, the first report due by July 1, 2005. This represents significant progress in confronting the danger of loose nuclear weapons. Closing the gap between their words, on the one hand, and the hundreds of specific actions required to protect both countries' citizens from a terrorist's nuclear bomb, on the other, will demand daily attention by both presidents.

No New Nascent Nukes. This principle is emerging as a potential new international norm. The fact is sinking in that if a state builds facilities for enriching uranium or reprocessing plutonium, it has passed the highest hurdle and crossed the last bright line before producing nuclear weapons. Mohamed ElBaradei's call for a five-year moratorium on any new national production of uranium or plutonium in order to give the international community time to develop a better system for providing fuel for peaceful nuclear reactors is an important start. In their negotiations with Iran, the nations of the European Union have focused on an extended voluntary moratorium on any new activity that would lead to Iranian national enrichment of uranium or reprocessing of plutonium. But unless and until the United States enters the game with an objective and a strategy that moves to a grand bargain along the lines proposed in chapter 7, the haggling between the Europeans and the Iranians will likely offer little more than temporary delay, or even cover, for secret Iranian efforts to complete a full-fledged uranium enrichment program.

No New Nuclear Weapons States. Unless interrupted by a sharp departure from what the United States, China, and Russia are currently doing, North Korea will soon complete the reprocessing of the eight thousand fuel rods that will provide it enough plutonium for six additional bombs. In the wake of its February 2005 announcement that it possesses nuclear weapons, North Korea may decide to conduct a nuclear weapons test or, like Israel, it may settle for nuclear-armed status without a demonstrable test. In either case, it will continue its accelerated efforts to repair and construct production lines that will produce materials for several additional bombs a year. On the current path, a state known informally as "Missiles R' Us" is destined to become "Nukes R' Us." While the strategy outlined in chapter 7 for persuading North Korea to freeze and stand down appears too bold for many critics, the alternative of diverting of eyes and hoping that this will somehow go away is reckless. On the current course, North Korea's development of nuclear weapons and a nuclear weapons production line promises to become the greatest failure in the nearly 230-year history of American foreign policy.

As the Bush administration establishes foreign policy priorities for its second term, where will this threat, declared by the president to be the "single greatest danger to American national security," rank operationally? We can only hope that the curious gap that existed between words and deeds on this issue in the first term closes rapidly. If this is the single greatest danger, the president should make the prevention of a nuclear terrorist attack on an American city an absolute priority. During the Cold War, presidents recognized that preventing a general nuclear war was a necessary condition for the pursuit of any other objective. In Ronald Regan's oft-quoted one-liner: "A nuclear war can never be won, and must therefore never be fought." That produced a categorical imperative to do everything technically feasible to prevent nuclear war. After five trillion dollars and four decades, America's Cold War strategy —pursued by Republican and Democratic presidents alike— produced victory in the Cold War. In combating nuclear terrorism, we need a similarly focused commitment married to a coherent strategy and urgent daily action.

In December 2004, the UN High-level Panel on Threats, Challenges, and Change issued its report on threats to the global community. Among a dozen global ills from AIDS and poverty to civil war and environmental degradation, the panel gave pride of place to the proliferation of nuclear weapons and the specific threat of nuclear terrorism. In sober but stark terms they warned that a continuation of current trends risked a "cascade of proliferation."[23] To avoid this dark future, the panel usefully recommended a number of actions, including an extended moratorium on constructing reprocessing and enrichment facilities and a guarantee from Security Council members to defend nonnuclear states if attacked by a nuclear-armed opponent. While useful, these steps alone are unlikely to affect the behavior of problem states, let alone dangerous nonstate actors. If we are to avoid the impending disaster about which the panel rightly warns, and the consequent cascade of nuclear bombs exploding in our cities, the United States will have to engage the major parties in a global campaign to prevent nuclear terrorism now.

FREQUENTLY ASKED QUESTIONS
ABOUT NUCLEAR TERRORISM

What is fission?
Fission is the process that occurs when an atom's nucleus splits, releasing a massive amount of energy.

What is fissile material?
Fissile material is matter that can sustain a fission chain reaction. The two fissile materials used in nuclear weapons are uranium-235 and plutonium-239.

Why is fissile material used in nuclear weapons?
Fissile material is the essential ingredient required to produce the self-sustaining chain reaction that causes a nuclear explosion.

What is weapons-grade fissile material?
"Weapons-grade" refers to purified fissile material that is most suitable for use in a nuclear weapon. A concentration of more than 90 percent is optimal for both uranium-235 and plutonium-239; at concentrations of less than 20 percent, production of a self-sustaining chain reaction is almost impossible.

How much fissile material is needed to make a nuclear weapon?
As little as thirty-five pounds of uranium-235 or nine pounds of plutonium-239 is required to make a working nuclear bomb.

Is it easier to use uranium or plutonium as the fissile material for a nuclear weapon?

Uranium-based bombs are easier to make and much less radioactive—and therefore safer to handle—than plutonium bombs. However, four times more uranium than plutonium is needed for a working weapon.

Why is producing fissile material the highest hurdle in making a nuclear weapon?

Making fissile material is expensive and time-consuming, requiring roughly $1 billion and a decade of intensive effort.

How many states have weapons-grade fissile material?

There are thirty-two states with approximately 3,200 tons of weapons-grade fissile material, enough to make more than 240,000 nuclear weapons. (For more information, see the Nuclear Threat Initiative [NTI], *Controlling Nuclear Warheads and Materials,* http://www.nti.org/e_research/cnwm/overview/cnwm_home.asp.)

Is weapons-grade fissile material still being produced today?

Yes. India and Pakistan openly produce such material, while Israel refuses oversight of its nuclear activities. North Korea and Iran are actively working to produce it. The United States stopped producing fissile material for nuclear weapons in 1992.

Have terrorists acquired fissile material?

No, not to the best of anyone's knowledge, although terrorists are trying. For example, according to the Justice Department, "from at least as early as 1992, Osama bin Laden . . . and others known and unknown made efforts to obtain the components of nuclear weapons." (For more information, see NTI, "The Demand for Black Market Fissile Material," http://www.nti.org/e_research/cnwm/threat/demand.asp.)

If a president judged it as important as the war on terrorism, how long would it take to lock down the world's supply of fissile material?

It would take several years to secure the world's supply of fissile material if it was made as high a priority as the war on terrorism. (For more information, see NTI, *Controlling Nuclear Warheads and Materials,* http://www.nti.org/e_research/cnwm/overview/cnwm_home.asp.)

If a president judged it as important as the war on terrorism, how much would it cost to secure the world's supply of fissile material?

The total cost would probably be between $30 billion and $50 billion. (For more information, see Howard Baker and Lloyd Cutler, "A Report Card on the Department of Energy's Nonproliferation Programs with Russia," http://www.ceip.org/files/projects/npp/pdf/DOERussiaTaskForceReport011001.pdf.)

How long would it take to build a nuclear weapon?

It would take a decade, even if the necessary technology, funding, equipment, and scientific expertise were available, because of the difficulties in producing fissile material. If a group started with fissile material obtained elsewhere, it could make an elementary nuclear weapon in less than one year.

Does having a nuclear reactor help in building a nuclear weapon?

Yes. Several states have used civilian nuclear reactors as a cover to make nuclear weapons. The spent-fuel waste produced by a civilian reactor contains plutonium that, if separated out, can be used to make a bomb.

What is uranium, and where is it found?

Uranium is a radioactive element that can be used in nuclear weapons. It is found in nature—in hard rock or sandstone—throughout the world.

What is yellowcake?

"Yellowcake" is uranium ore milled from mined rock that is smashed, chemically soaked, and filtered into a coarse powder. It is widely available—with global production at about 64,000 tons a year—and poorly tracked. For instance, in January 2004, two pounds of Iraqi yellowcake were found in a load of scrap metal being recycled in the Netherlands. However, it would take hundreds of tons of yellowcake and several years of enrichment to make enough weapons-grade fissile material for a bomb.

What is highly enriched uranium (HEU)?

HEU is a form of uranium in which the isotope uranium-235 has been increased from its average natural level of 0.7 percent of uranium ore to greater than 20 percent.

What is plutonium, and where is it found?

Plutonium is a man-made radioactive element that can be used in nuclear weapons. Only trace amounts of plutonium are found in nature. Almost all existing plutonium is a by-product of nuclear reactors.

Are there sizable supplies of uranium and plutonium?

Yes. The global supply of uranium ore will not be exhausted in the foreseeable future. Plutonium is a by-product of the fission process in nuclear reactors, and would thus run out only when uranium did.

How is weapons-grade uranium-235 extracted out of uranium ore?

Uranium-235 is slightly lighter in mass than the remaining uranium ore. Separation techniques capitalize on this difference. For example, one method—gaseous centrifuge enrichment—spins gaseous uranium hexafluoride in cylinders, so the lighter uranium-235 moves toward the inner wall, where is it collected. (For more information, see the Wisconsin Project, "Bomb Facts: How Nuclear Weapons Are Made," http://www.wisconsinproject.org.)

How is plutonium-239 extracted—that is, what is plutonium reprocessing?

Plutonium-239 is chemically separated from spent reactor fuel by removing spent-fuel rods from a nuclear reactor, chopping them up, and then dissolving them in nitric acid. The resulting liquid is further separated into plutonium, uranium, and radioactive waste. (For more information, see Federation of American Scientists, "Plutonium Production," http://www.fas.org/nuke/intro/nuke/plutonium.htm.)

How many states have sought nuclear weapons?

Approximately twenty-eight, including Britain, China, France, India, Israel, Pakistan, Russia, the United States, and North Korea, as well as Argentina, Australia, Belarus, Brazil, Canada, Egypt, Germany, Iraq, Italy, Japan, Kazakhstan, Libya, Romania, South Africa, South Korea, Sweden, Taiwan, Ukraine, and Yugoslavia.

How many states have nuclear weapons?

Eight: Britain, China, France, India, Israel, Pakistan, Russia, and the United States. North Korea may have two—or as many as eight—nuclear weapons.

How many states had nuclear weapons and then relinquished them?

Four: South Africa had six nuclear weapons by the 1980s and then, just prior to the transfer of power to the post-apartheid government, dismantled them; Ukraine, Kazakhstan, and Belarus together had more than four thousand nuclear weapons on their territories when the Soviet Union dissolved, and they agreed in 1994 to return them to Russia.

How many nuclear weapons are there in the world?
The Natural Resources Defense Council estimates that as of 2002, there were around twenty thousand nuclear weapons in the world. (For more information, see NRDC, "Table of Global Nuclear Weapons Stockpiles, 1945–2002," http://www.nrdc.org/nuclear/nudb/datab19.asp.)

What are the largest and smallest nuclear bombs ever produced?
The Soviets produced the largest-ever nuclear bomb, "Tsar Bomba," with an estimated yield of 100 megatons—or 6,500 times the yield of the bombs dropped on Hiroshima and Nagasaki. The United States produced the smallest confirmed nuclear weapon, the "Davy Crockett," with a yield of 0.25 kilotons and weighing only 50 pounds.

Why do states develop nuclear weapons?
Nuclear weapons have been developed for a combination of reasons: security, prestige, and domestic bureaucratic politics.

If all the resources needed to design a working nuclear bomb are readily available, isn't nuclear proliferation inevitable?
No. President Kennedy predicted that by 1970 there would be fifteen to twenty nuclear weapons states. Although there are over forty states capable of making a bomb, as of today, only eight have nuclear weapons. The record shows that nonproliferation works when it is given serious attention and resources.

What prevents states from seeking nuclear weapons?
States forgo nuclear weapons for a number of reasons: inadequate national resources, technological constraints, the international nuclear taboo, international treaties, domestic politics, international inducements, security assurances, aid, threats of sanctions and coercion, and the limited strategic utility of nuclear weapons.

Is the United States testing or producing additional nuclear weapons?

No. However, subcritical testing—using less fissile material than the critical mass needed for a self-sustaining nuclear fission reaction—has been performed. And the Bush administration has persuaded Congress to fund new nuclear weapons research.

How do states secure their nuclear weapons?

Optimally, states use a combination of barriers, guards, surveillance cameras, motion sensors, background checks on personnel, and locks built into the actual nuclear weapons. The United States and most nuclear powers employ all these protections. Unfortunately, because of Russia's enormous nuclear stockpile and lack of funds, its nuclear facilities have been left inadequately protected. (For more information, see NTI, *Controlling Nuclear Warheads and Materials*, http://www.nti.org/e_research/cnwm/overview/cnwm_home.asp.)

Has the United States ever accidentally lost a nuclear weapon?

Yes. Experts estimate that at least eleven have been lost. For example, in 1958 a damaged U.S. bomber was ordered to drop a nuclear weapon into the Atlantic before landing. It was never recovered and rests somewhere off the coast of Savannah, Georgia. (For more information, see the Center for Defense Information, http://www.cdi.org/Issues/NukeAccidents/accidents.htm.)

Has Russia ever accidentally lost a nuclear weapon?

Russia denies that any of its nuclear weapons have gone missing, although it admits that some fissile material has been lost or stolen. Moscow's assurance that "all nuclear weapons are in place" is wishful thinking, since at least four nuclear submarines with nuclear warheads sank and were never recovered by the Soviet Union.

Have terrorists ever stolen or built a nuclear weapon?

No, but they are trying to. In 1998, Osama bin Laden issued a statement titled "The Nuclear Bomb of Islam," declaring, "It is the duty of Muslims to prepare as much force as possible to terrorize the enemies of God."

Has any state ever sold a nuclear weapon to a terrorist?

No. Although the potential for such a sale exists, there is no documented case of a state selling a nuclear weapon to a terrorist.

Could terrorists acquire HEU or plutonium?

Yes. There have been dozens of documented thefts and sales of fissile material to potential terrorists who were subsequently captured. Russia's substantial amounts of poorly secured HEU and plutonium remain a prime target for theft. (For a regularly updated list of incidents of theft, see NTI, *Controlling Nuclear Warheads and Materials: Recent Updates,* http://www.nti.org/ e_research/cnwm/overview/cnwm_home.asp#updates.)

Could a nuclear power reactor be targeted by terrorists to cause a nuclear explosion?

There is no possibility of a nuclear explosion at a civilian reactor. However, a terrorist attack on a nuclear power plant could cause a massive release of radiation.

Could terrorists deliver a nuclear weapon, or the fissile material required to build one, into the United States undetected?

Yes. HEU and plutonium are easy to conceal and give off faint radiation signals, and thus could be smuggled into the United States almost as easily as illegal drugs.

What are weapons of mass destruction (WMD)?

In common parlance, WMD refers to nuclear, biological, and chemical weapons. In fact, it is a misnomer. Chemical weapons kill few; death from biological weapons can be contained by effective countermeasures. When a nuclear bomb explodes, mass destruction is unavoidable.

How would a nuclear explosion affect the surrounding area?

There are three major effects of a nuclear explosion: searing heat, overpressure from the blast, and long-term radiation. The intensity of the effects depends on the yield of the weapon and the distance from the blast. (For more information, see the Federation of American Scientists, "Nuclear Weapon Effects," http://www.fas.org/nuke/intro/nuke/effects.htm.)

What is a dirty bomb?

A dirty bomb uses conventional explosives such as dynamite to spread radioactive material. It is also known as a radiological dispersal device.

What is radioactivity?

Radioactivity is the process by which unstable elements become more stable by emitting particles and energy. This process is measured in "half-life," the time it takes half of a radioactive material to decay into a more stable element. The half-life of plutonium-239 is 24,000 years; that of uranium-235 is 704 million years.

What is radiation?

Radiation consists of the particles and energy released into its surrounding environment by a decaying unstable element. Sources of radiation include the sun, microwaves, X-ray machines, and fissile material.

What is radiation sickness?

Radiation sickness occurs when a person is exposed to large amounts of radiation, usually within a short period of time. Such exposure can cause nausea, vomiting, weakness, hair loss, hemorrhaging, and death.

Is a dirty bomb a weapon of mass destruction?

No. Instead, it is sometimes called a "weapon of mass disruption" because of the panic it would cause, as well as the costs of decontamination.

Is a dirty bomb a nuclear weapon?

No. A dirty bomb does not result in a nuclear explosion. It simply spreads radioactive material.

What radioactive materials could be used to make a dirty bomb?

Any type of radioactive material could be used to make a dirty bomb. Weapons-grade plutonium and spent nuclear reactor fuel would be the most deadly, but also the most difficult to acquire. Other potential sources, including americium, cesium, and strontium, are found in hospitals, at industrial and construction sites, and at food irradiation plants.

What is easier to build, a dirty bomb or a nuclear bomb?

A dirty bomb is easier to make. In its simplest form, it is no more than a stick of dynamite and some radioactive material in a shoe box.

Has a dirty bomb ever been used?

The only known dirty bomb–related incident occurred when Chechen rebels planted radioactive cesium packed with dynamite in a Moscow park. Fortunately, the authorities quickly located the material before it was dispersed.

What hazards does a dirty bomb pose?

A dirty bomb's greatest threat is the economic cost of decontamination. Deaths from the blast of the "bomb" part of the device would result directly from the stick of dynamite—or whatever other explosive material is used. The "radioactive" part of the device would not be likely to cause any immediate deaths but, depending on exposure and treatment, could increase the likelihood of cancer and other diseases decades later. (For more information, see Peter D. Zimmerman and Cheryl Loeb, "Dirty Bombs: The Threat Revisited," http://hps.org/documents/RDD_report.pdf.)

FOR MORE INFORMATION, VISIT THE FOLLOWING ONLINE RESOURCES

- The single best source is the Nuclear Threat Initiative: http://www.nti.org. At NTI, the best publication on nuclear terrorism is *Controlling Nuclear Warheads and Materials*: www.nti.org/cnwm. The NTI Web site invites interested individuals to get involved, presents a Safer World agenda, and identifies further ways citizens can make a difference (see below).
- The Belfer Center for Science and International Affairs (BCSIA):
  - http://bcsia.ksg.harvard.edu
  - Managing the Atom: http://bcsia.ksg.harvard.edu/atom
  - http://www.nuclearterrorism.org
- Carnegie Endowment for International Peace: http://www.ceip.org
- Center for Nonproliferation Studies: http://cns.miis.edu
- Council on Foreign Relations: http://www.terrorismanswers.com
- Federation of American Scientists: http://www.fas.org
- Institute for Science and International Security: http://www.isis-online.org
- National Resources Defense Council: http://www.nrdc.org
- Nuclear Weapon Archive: http://www.nuclearweaponarchive.org
- U.S. Nuclear Regulatory Commission: http://www.nrc.gov
- Wisconsin Project on Nuclear Arms Control: http://www.wisconsinproject.org

TO BECOME MORE DIRECTLY INVOLVED,
CHECK OUT THESE ACTIVIST GROUPS

- Nuclear Threat Initiative's Safer World Campaign: http://www.saferworld.org
- 20/20 Vision: http://www.2020vision.org
- Acronym Institute for Disarmament Diplomacy: http://www.acronym.org.uk
- Arms Control Association: http://www.armscontrol.org
- Business Executives for National Security: http://www.bens.org
- British American Security Information Council: http://www.basicint.org
- Campaign for Nuclear Disarmament: http://www.cnduk.org
- Coalition to Reduce Nuclear Dangers: http://www.crnd.org
- Council for a Livable World: http://www.clw.org
- Greenpeace Nuclear Campaign: http://archive.greenpeace.org/nuclear
- International Physicians for the Prevention of Nuclear War: http://www.ippnw.org
- Lawyers Alliance for World Security: http://www.lawscns.org
- Los Alamos Study Group: http://www.lasg.org
- Nautilus Institute for Security and Sustainable Development: http://www.nautilus.org
- Nuclear Threat Reduction Campaign: http://justice.policy.net/ntrc/index.vtml
- Physicians for Social Responsibility: http://www.psr.org
- Ploughshares Fund: http://www.ploughshares.org
- Pugwash: http://www.pugwash.org/
- Russian American Nuclear Security Advisory Council: http://www.ransac.org
- Union of Concerned Scientists: http://www.ucsusa.org

NOTES

INTRODUCTION

1. Massimo Calabresi and Romesh Ratnesar, "Can We Stop the Next Attack?" *Time,* 11 March 2002.
2. David Johnston and James Risen, "Traces of Terrorism: The Intelligence Reports; Series of Warnings," *New York Times,* 17 May 2002.
3. Jeffrey Kluger, "Osama's Nuclear Quest: How Long Will It Take Before al-Qaeda Gets Hold of the Most Dangerous of Weapons?" *Time,* 12 November 2001.
4. Bill Keller, "Nuclear Nightmares," *New York Times Magazine,* 26 May 2002; Mark Riebling and R. P. Eddy, "Jihad@Work," National Review Online, 24 October 2002.
5. Keller, "Nuclear Nightmares."
6. Tom Ridge, private discussion with author during visit to Belfer Center for Science and International Affairs, JFK School of Government, Harvard University, 11 February 2004.
7. "Hijacked Plane Targeted Nuke Complex 29 Years Ago," AP, 19 September 2001.
8. Greenpeace Nuclear Campaign, http://archive.greenpeace.org/comms/97/nuclear/reactor/chern11.html.
9. Gregory J. Van Tuyle, Tiffany L. Strub, Harold A. O'Brien, Caroline F. V. Mason, and Steven J. Gitomer, "Reducing RDD Concerns Related to Large Radiological Source Applications," Los Alamos National Laboratory, September 2003.
10. Personal correspondence.
11. "Two Years Later, the Fear Lingers," *Pew Research Center for the People and the Press,* 4 September 2003.
12. United States Department of Energy, Howard Baker and Lloyd Cutler, cochairs, Russia Task Force, "A Report Card on the Department of Energy's Nonproliferation Programs with Russia," 10 January 2001.

13. Howard H. Baker, Jr., cochair, Russia Task Force, "Department of Energy Nonproliferation Programs with Russia," Panel I of a Hearing of the Senate Foreign Relations Committee, 28 March 2001.

14. See Matthew Bunn, Anthony Wier, and John P. Holdren, *Controlling Nuclear Warheads and Materials: A Report Card* (Washington, D.C.: Nuclear Threat Initiative and the Project on Managing the Atom, Harvard University, March 2003).

15. Remarks made by former CIA director John Deutch at BCSIA Director's Seminar, 17 March 1998.

16. John Foster, "Nuclear Weapons," *Encyclopedia Americana,* vol. 20 (New York: Americana, 1973), pp. 520–22.

17. John Emshwiller, Michael Orey, Daniel Machalaba, and Rebecca Smith, "Nuclear Security Fears Mushroom," *Wall Street Journal,* 17 October 2001.

18. "'Why We Fight America': Al-Qa'ida Spokesman Explains September 11 and Declares Intentions to Kill 4 Million Americans with Weapons of Mass Destruction," *The Middle East Media Research Institute,* 12 June 2002. [Translated and excerpted from: Suleiman Abu Gheith, "In the Shadow of the Lances," *Center for Islamic Research and Studies,* www.alneda.com.]

19. Andy Serwer, "The Oracle of Everything," *Fortune,* 11 November 2002.

1: WHO COULD BE PLANNING A NUCLEAR TERRORIST ATTACK?

1. Georg Mascolo and Holger Stark, "Operation Holy Tuesday," *New York Times,* 27 October 2003.

2. Yosri Fouda, "Masterminds of a Massacre—9/11—One Year On," *Australian Sunday Times,* 9 September 2002, citing the author's interview with Khalid Sheikh Mohammed and Ramzi Binalshibh, April 2002.

3. Kamran Khan and Molly Moore, "2 Nuclear Experts Briefed bin Laden, Pakistanis Say," *Washington Post,* 12 December 2001.

4. Peter Baker, "Pakistani Scientist Who Met bin Laden Failed Polygraphs, Renewing Suspicions," *Washington Post,* 3 March 2002.

5. David Albright and Holly Higgins, "A Bomb for the Ummah," *Bulletin of the Atomic Scientists,* March/April 2003, pp. 49–55. Daniel Benjamin and Steven Simon, *The Age of Sacred Terror* (New York: Random House, 2002), pp. 203–4.

6. Gopalaswami Parthasarathy, "Pakistan Plays Nuclear Footsie; Does Anyone Care?" *Wall Street Journal,* 2 January 2004.

7. Israr Ahmad, "The Rationale of Islamic Jihad," http://www.the-quest.info/viewpoint/, accessed on January 2004.

8. Albright and Higgins, "A Bomb for the Ummah."

9. Bill Clinton, "Remarks by the President on the Patients' Bill of Rights," Office of the Press Secretary, 28 May 1998.

10. Baker, "Pakistani Scientist."
11. Khan and Moore, "2 Nuclear Experts."
12. Kamran Khan, "Pakistan Releases Nuclear Scientists for Ramadan's End," *Washington Post,* 16 December 2001.
13. Albright and Higgins, "A Bomb for the Ummah."
14. Daniel Pearl and Steve Levine, "Pakistan Has Ties to Group It Vowed to Curb: Military State's Elite Is Linked to Activities of Nuclear Scientist," *Wall Street Journal,* 24 December 2001.
15. George W. Bush, "Remarks by the President in the Rose Garden," 20 December 2001.
16. Dan Murphy, "'Activated' Asian Terror Web Busted," *Christian Science Monitor,* 23 January 2002.
17. George Tenet, "Unclassified Version of Director of Central Intelligence George J. Tenet's Testimony before the Joint Inquiry into Terrorist Attacks against the United States," 18 June 2002.
18. Donald Rumsfeld, Defense Department news briefing, 16 January 2002.
19. Alan Cullison and Andrew Higgins, "Files Found: A Computer in Kabul Yields a Chilling Array of Al Qaeda Memos," *Wall Street Journal,* 31 December 2001.
20. David Albright, "Al Qaeda's Nuclear Program: Through the Window of Seized Documents," Nautilus Institute Policy Forum Online, 6 November 2002.
21. Daniel Benjamin and Steven Simon, *The Age of Sacred Terror* (New York: Random House, 2002), p. 128.
22. National Intelligence Council, *Annual Report to Congress on the Safety and Security of Russian Nuclear Facilities and Military Force,* February 2002.
23. Bob Port and Greg B. Smith, "'Suitcase Bomb' Allegedly Sought: Bin Laden Eyes Russian Stockpile," *Seattle Times,* 3 October 2001.
24. Benjamin Weiser, "U.S. Says bin Laden Aide Tried to Get Nuclear Material," *New York Times,* 26 September 1998.
25. Anna Badkhen, "Al Qaeda Bluffing About Having Suitcase Nukes, Experts Say; Russians Claim Terrorists Couldn't Have Bought Them," *San Francisco Chronicle,* 23 March 2004.
26. Yoav Stern, "Report: Al-Qaida Has Obtained Tactical Nuclear Explosives," *Ha'aretz,* 8 February 2004.
27. Barton Gellman, "Fears Prompt U.S. to Beef Up Nuclear Terror Detection," *Washington Post,* 3 March 2002.
28. Colin Powell, news conference, 17 September 2001.
29. Eliza Manningham-Buller, speech at the City of London Police Headquarters, 16 October 2003; http://www.homeoffice.gov.uk/docs2/james_smart_lecture2003.html.
30. "Bali Death Toll Set at 202," *BBC News,* 19 February 2003.

31. Shawn Donnan, "Indonesian Police Name 16 Suspects of Bombing," *Financial Times*, 20 August 2003.
32. "Ammonium Nitrate Was Used; Moderates Demand Indonesia Move to Curb Extremists," *Boston Globe*, 22 October 2002.
33. Jane Perlez, "Group Linked to Al Qaeda Seen behind Jakarta Blast," *New York Times*, 7 August 2003.
34. Ellen Nakashima, "Inquiry Shows Indonesian's Ties to Al Qaeda," *Washington Post*, 29 March 2003.
35. For a detailed analysis of Chechen separatists' nuclear ambitions, see Simon Saradzhyan, "Russia: Grasping Reality of Nuclear Terror," BCSIA Discussion Paper 2003–02, Kennedy School of Government, Harvard University, March 2003, http://bcsia.ksg.harvard.edu/publication.cfm?program= ISP&ctype=paper&item_id=374.
36. BBC Monitoring Service, 5 February 2002.
37. ITAR-TASS, 31 October 2002.
38. Nabi Abdullaev, "Picture Emerges of How They Did It," *Moscow Times*, 6 November 2002.
39. CDI Terrorism Project, "In the Spotlight: The Special Purpose Islamic Regiment," 2 May 2003, http:www.cdi.org/terrorism/spir.cfm.
40. "Possible bin Laden Link to Murder of Engineers," *Financial Times*, 19 November 2001. See also Robert Bruce Ware, "West Missed bin Laden's Nuclear Wake-up Call from Chechnya," David Johnson's Russia List, 1 December 2001.
41. Saradzhyan, "Russia."
42. "Hezbollah's Time Is Coming in US Anti-terror War: Senior US Diplomat," *Agence France Presse*, 5 September 2002. "Hezbollah Turns Up the Volume," *CBS Evening News*, 17 April 2003.
43. "Hezbollah: 'A-Team of Terrorists,'" *60 Minutes*/CBSNews.com, 18 April 2003.
44. Jeffrey Goldberg, "In the Party of God: Are Terrorists in Lebanon Preparing for a Larger War?" *New Yorker*, 14 October 2002.
45. Augustus Richard Norton, "Hizballah: From Radicalism to Pragmatism," *Middle East Policies*, no. 4 (January 1998), pp. 147–58.
46. "An Open Letter: The Hizballah Program," http://www.ict.org.il/Articles/ Hiz_letter.htm.
47. Daniel J. Wakin, "Hezbollah Seen Making Subtle Changes after War in Iraq," *New York Times*, 11 May 2003.
48. George Tenet, testimony before the Senate Select Committee on Intelligence, 24 February 2004.
49. Goldberg "In the Party of God."
50. "Iran Vows to Retaliate If Israel Attacks," Associated Press, 24 December 2003.

51. Dana Priest and Douglas Farah, "Terror Alliance Has U.S. Worried," *Washington Post,* 30 June 2002.
52. Arnaud de Borchgrave, "Commentary: An Islamist Nuke?" UPI, 19 March 2003.
53. "Weapons of Mass Destruction: Trade between North Korea and Pakistan," CRS Report RL31900, 7 May 2003.
54. Jessica Stern, *Terror in the Name of God: Why Religious Militants Kill* (New York: HarperCollins, 2003).
55. "9 Arrests over Musharraf Kill Plot," Associated Press, 12 January 2004.
56. Staff of the Senate Government Affairs Permanent Subcommittee on Investigations, "Global Proliferation of Weapons of Mass Destruction: A Case Study on the Aum Shinrikyo," Sec. III, 31 October 1995, http://www.fas.org/irp/congress/1995_rpt/aum/index.html.
57. Ibid., Sec. IV.
58. Richard Falkenrath, Robert Newman, and Bradley Thayer, *America's Achilles' Heel* (Cambridge, Mass.: MIT Press, 1998).
59. Staff of the Senate Government Affairs Permanent Subcommittee on Investigations, "Global Proliferation of Weapons of Mass Destruction."
60. Ibid., Sec. VI.

2: WHAT NUCLEAR WEAPONS COULD TERRORISTS USE?

1. CBS, "The Perfect Terrorist Weapon," *60 Minutes,* host, Steve Kroft, 7 September 1997.
2. Dmitry Safonov, "Individualnaya Planirovka," *Izvestia,* 27 October 2001.
3. Barton Gellman, "Fears Prompt U.S. to Beef Up Nuclear Terror Detection," *Washington Post,* 3 March 2002.
4. The current nuclear inventory (warheads) is as follows: United States, 10,600; Russia, 8,600; China, 400; France, 350; United Kingdom, 200; Israel, 200; Pakistan, 50; India, 35. Natural Resources Defense Council, "Global Nuclear Stockpiles, 1945–2002," *The Bulletin of the Atomic Scientists,* November/December 2002, pp. 103–4. An accounting of military fissile material (248 tons of plutonium and 1,665 tons of HEU) is available from the Institute for Science and International Security, "Production and Status of Military Stocks of Fissile Material, end of 1999," summary table [http://www.isis-online.org/mapproject/supplements. html]. An accounting of civilian fissile material (approximately 196 tons) is available from David Albright, "Separated Civil Plutonium Inventories: Current and Future Directions," June 2000, table 1 [http://www.isis-online.org/publications/puwatch/civilpu.html].
5. I am indebted to my colleague John Holdren for this comparison.
6. Natural Resources Defense Council (NRDC), *Nuclear Weapons Databook,* vol. 1, p. 75.

7. Ibid., p. 60. To view a declassified training film for Navy SEALs, see http://www.pbs.org/wgbh/pages/frontline/shows/russia/suitcase/.

8. Stephen Schwartz, ed., *Atomic Audit: The Costs and Consequences of U.S. Nuclear Weapons since 1940* (Washington, D.C.: Brookings Institution Press, 1998).

9. NRDC, *Databook*, vol. 1, p. 33.

10. Ibid., vol. 1, pp. 54, 309

11. Ibid., vol. 1, p. 311.

12. Nikolai Sokov, "'Suitcase Nukes': Permanently Lost Luggage," Center for Nonproliferation Studies, Monterrey Institute of International Studies, 13 February 2004.

13. David Smigelski, "A Review of the Suitcase Nuclear Bomb Controversy," Russian American Nuclear Security Advisory Council, Policy Update, September 2003.

14. http://cns.miis.edu/pubs/week/020923.htm.

15. www.atomicmuseum.com/tour/np6.cfm.

16. NRDC, "Estimated Russian Stockpile," *Bulletin of the Atomic Scientists,* September 1995.

17. Schwartz, *Atomic Audit.*

18. "Testimony of Toshiko Saeki" and "Testimony of Yoshito Matsushige," Voice of Hibakusha, http://www.inicom.com/hibakusha/index.html; Fujie Urata Matsumoto, as quoted in Takashi Nagai, *We of Nagasaki: The Story of Survivors in an Atomic Wasteland* (New York: Duell, Sloan and Pearce, 1964), p. 42; William L. Laurence, "Atomic Bomb on Nagasaki," *New York Times,* 9 September 1945; Richard Rhodes, *The Making of the Atomic Bomb* (New York: Touchstone, 1986), pp. 713–33.

19. Rhodes, *The Making of the Atomic Bomb*, p. 728.

20. Ibid., p. 742.

21. Ibid., pp. 734, 740.

22. A. B. Pittcock et al., *Environmental Consequences of Nuclear War: Physical and Atmospheric Effects,* 2nd ed. (New York: John Wiley and Sons, 1989), p. 6.

23. Rhodes, *The Making of the Atomic Bomb*, p. 715.

24. Ibid., p. 716.

25. http://hyperphysics.phy-astr.gsu.edu/hbase/nucene/bomb2.html.

26. http://newnet.lanl.gov/mrem.htm.

27. Hotspot Health Physics Code, Lawrence Livermore National Laboratory.

28. http://users.rcn.com/jkimball.ma.ultranet/BiologyPages/C/Cancer Risk.html.

29. Office of Technology Assessment, *Environmental Monitoring for Nuclear Safeguards* (Washington, D.C.: Government Printing Office, 1995).

30. Institute for Energy and Environmental Research, http://www.ieer.org/comments/fallout/pr0202.html.

31. Y. E. Dubrova, "Nuclear Weapons Tests and Germline Mutation Rate," *Science*, vol. 295 (2002).

32. Institute for Energy and Environmental Research, http://www.ieer.org/comments/fallout/pr0202.html.

33. Nuclear Regulatory Commission, "Fact Sheet on the Accident at Three Mile Island," http://www.nrc.gov/reading-rm/doc-collections/fact-sheets/3mile-isle.html.

34. David Marples, "The Decade of Despair," *Bulletin of the Atomic Scientists,* May 1996. Felicity Barringer, "Chernobyl: Five Years Later the Danger Persists," *New York Times Magazine,* 14 April 1991.

35. Yuri M. Shcherbak, "Ten Years of the Chernobyl Era," *Scientific American,* April 1996.

36. Michael Grunwald and Peter Behr, "Are Nation's Nuclear Power Plants Secure?" *Washington Post,* 4 November 2001.

37. NUREG/CR-6451, "A Safety and Regulatory Assessment of Generic BWR and PWR Permanently Shutdown Nuclear Power Plants," prepared by Brookhaven National Laboratory for Nuclear Regulatory Commission, August 1997.

38. Edward J. Markey, "Markey, Lowey Question Security at Indian Point," *News from Ed Markey,* 14 January 2003.

39. "Schumer Urges NRC to Launch Safety Probe at Indian Point," press release, 10 December 2002.

40. For information regarding security regulations at nuclear reactors, see the Nuclear Regulatory Commission's Web site at: http://www.nrc.gov/what-we-do/safeguards.html. For further analysis of nuclear reactor security and terrorism, see the Nuclear Control Institute Web site: www.nci.org.

41. John Mintz and Susan Schmidt, "Dirty Bomb Was Major New Year's Worry," *Washington Post,* 7 January 2004.

42. Testimony of Dr. Henry Kelly, president of the Federation of American Scientists, before the Senate Committee on Foreign Relations, 6 March 2002; http://www.fas.org/ssp/docs/030602-kellytestimony.htm.

43. Peter Zimmerman and Cheryl Loeb, "Dirty Bombs: The Threat Revisited," *Defense Horizons,* January 2004.

44. Margaret Talbot, "Hysteria Hysteria," *New York Times Magazine,* 2 June 2002.

3: WHERE COULD TERRORISTS ACQUIRE A NUCLEAR BOMB?

1. Mohamed ElBaradei, interview during the World Economic Forum, Davos, 22 January 2004.
2. Douglas Frantz and Josh Meyer, "For Sale: Nuclear Expertise," *Los Angeles Times*, 22 February 2004.
3. George W. Bush, "Remarks by the President on Weapons of Mass Destruction Proliferation," National Defense University, 11 February 2004.
4. Ibid.
5. Frantz and Meyer, "For Sale."
6. David E. Sanger and William J. Broad, "From Rogue Nuclear Programs, Web of Trails Leads to Pakistan," *New York Times*, 4 January 2004.
7. John Lancaster and Kamran Khan, "Pakistani Scientist Apologizes; Nuclear Assistance Unauthorized, He Says," *Washington Post*, 5 February 2004.
8. See Nuclear Threat Initiative, http://www.nti.org/db/nisprofs/kazakst/weapons/nuclearw.htm.
9. See http://www.nti.org/e_research/profiles/Iraq/Missile/2970_2971.html.
10. For the text of his interview, go to the *Frontline* Web site: http://www.pbs.org/wgbh/pages/frontline/shows/nukes/interviews/smirnov.html.
11. Matthew Campbell, "Serbia's Uranium Cache Raises Nuclear Stakes," *Sunday Times* (London), 26 March 2000.
12. Philipp C. Bleek, "Project Vinca: Lessons for Securing Civil Nuclear Material Stockpiles," *Nonproliferation Review*, Fall–Winter 2003.
13. Ibid.
14. See http://www.sgpproject.org/NunnKazakhstan.pdf.
15. See http://www.nti.org/db/nisprofs/russia/weapons/tacnukes/97nums.htm.
16. Interview on *Meet the Press*, 15 December 1991.
17. Olivia Ward, "Chechens Buying Arms—from Russian Troops," *Toronto Star*, 21 April 1995.
18. See Matthew Bunn, Anthony Wier, and John P. Holdren, *Controlling Nuclear Warheads and Materials: A Report Card* (Washington, D.C.: Nuclear Threat Initiative and the Project on Managing the Atom, Harvard University, 2003).
19. See http://www.fas.org/irp/program/collect/jennifer.htm.
20. Joshua Handler and William Arkin, *Neptune Paper no. 4*, Greenpeace, April 1989.
21. See Matthew Bunn, Anthony Wier, and John P. Holdren, "Anecdotes of Insecurity," *Controlling Nuclear Warheads and Materials: A Report Card and Action Plan* (Washington: Nuclear Threat Initiative and the Project on Managing the Atom, Harvard University, 2003).
22. Oleg Bukharin and William Potter, "Potatoes Were Guarded Better," *Bulletin of the Atomic Scientists* (May–June 1995).

23. Graham T. Allison, Owen R. Cote, Richard A. Falkenrath, and Steven E. Miller, *Avoiding Nuclear Anarchy: Containing the Threat of Loose Russian Nuclear Weapons and Fissile Material* (Cambridge, Mass.: MIT Press, 1996).

24. Tom Parfitt, "The Nuclear Nightmare," *The Times* (London), 3 March 2004.

25. Barton Gellman, "Fears Prompt U.S. to Beef Up Nuclear Terror Detection," *Washington Post*, 3 March 2002. The CIA's report of this has been disputed by some experts.

26. Ibid.

27. Vladimir Bogdanov, "A Pass to Warheads Found on a Terrorist," *Rossiiskaya Gazeta*, 1 November 2002.

28. U.S. Department of Energy, "A Report Card on the Department of Energy's Nonproliferation Programs with Russia," Howard Baker and Lloyd Cutler, cochairs, Russia Task Force, 10 January 2001.

29. General Accounting Office, *Nuclear Nonproliferation: Security of Russia's Nuclear Material Improving; Further Enhancements Needed* (Washington: GAO, 2001).

30. Howard H. Baker, testimony before Senate Foreign Relations Committee, 28 March 2001.

31. "Russian Official Refuses to Rule Out Chance That Nuclear Materials Were Stolen," *TV6*, Moscow, 13 November 2001, translated by BBC Monitoring Service. See also Matthew Bunn, Anthony Wier, and John P. Holdren, "The Threat in Russia and the NIS," *Controlling Nuclear Warheads and Materials: A Report Card* (Washington, D.C.: Nuclear Threat Initiative and the Project on Managing the Atom, Harvard University, March 2003).

32. "International Agency Concerned by Russian Traffic in Nuclear Materials," ITAR-TASS, 2 April 2001.

33. Jon B. Wolfsthal, "Keeping a Nuke Peddler in Line," *Los Angeles Times*, 11 January 2004.

34. Patrick E. Tyler and David E. Sanger, "Pakistan Called Libyans' Source of Atom Design," *New York Times*, 6 January 2004.

35. See http://www.ceip.org/files/pdf/Deadly_Arsenals_Chap12.pdf; http://www.thebulletin.org/issues/nukenotes/jf02nukenote.html; and http://www.globalsecurity.org/wmd/library/report/2001/south_asia.pdf.

36. Cited in Sanger and Broad, "From Rogue Nuclear Programs." Indeed, the bomb designs found in Libya reportedly had Chinese writing on them.

37. Ibid.

38. Gaurav Kampani, "Nuclear Watch—Pakistan: The Sorry Affairs of the Islamic Republic," Center for Nonproliferation Studies, January 2004.

39. See Robin Wright, "Ship Incident May Have Swayed Libya; Centrifuges Intercepted in September," *Washington Post*, 1 January 2004.

40. Gopalaswami Parthasarathy, "Pakistan Plays Nuclear Footsie; Does Anyone Care?" *Wall Street Journal*, 2 January 2004.

41. Ibid.

42. Ibid.

43. Ibid.

44. William J. Broad, David Rohde, and David E. Sanger, "Inquiry Suggests Pakistanis Sold Nuclear Secrets," *New York Times,* 22 December 2003.

45. Bryan Bender and Farah Stockman, "Extremist Influence Growing in Pakistan, U.S. Officials Fear," *Boston Globe,* 11 January 2004.

46. Ibid.

47. David E. Sanger and Thom Shanker, "A Nuclear Headache: What If the Radicals Oust Musharraf?" *New York Times,* 30 December 2003.

48. Ibid.

49. For an excellent account of the seizure, see Joby Warrick, "N. Korea Shops Stealthily for Nuclear Arms Gear; Front Companies Step Up Efforts in European Market," *Washington Post,* 15 August 2003.

50. Ibid.

51. Ibid.

52. See Wisconsin Project on Nuclear Arms Control, "North Korea: Nuclear/Missile Chronology," *The Risk Report,* vol. 6, no. 6, November/December 2000.

53. Gary Samore, *North Korea's Weapons Programme: A Net Assessment,* International Institute for Strategic Studies, 21 January 2004.

54. James Brooke, "North Korea's Need for Electricity Fuels Its Nuclear Ambitions," *New York Times,* 23 February 2003.

55. Bill Gertz, "N. Korea Threatens to Export Nukes; Reprocessing Work Called Nearly Complete," *Washington Times,* 7 May 2003.

56. See Joshua Kurlantzick, "Traffic Pattern: Pyongyang's Diplomatic Mafia," *The New Republic,* 24 March 2003.

57. Jeffrey Fleishman, "Sting Unravels Stunning Mafia Plot," *Philadelphia Inquirer,* 12 January 1999.

58. Ibid.

59. For the best discussion of the research reactor problem, see Matthew Bunn, Anthony Wier, and John P. Holdren, "Converting Research Reactors," *Controlling Nuclear Warheads and Materials: A Report Card and Action Plan* (Washington, D.C.: Nuclear Threat Initiative and the Project on Managing the Atom, Harvard University, 2003), http://www. nti.org/e_research/cnwm/securing/convert.asp.

60. Susan B. Glasser, "Russia Takes Back Uranium from Romania," *Washington Post,* 22 September 2003.

61. Peter Baker, "U.S.–Russia Team Seizes Uranium at Bulgaria Plant," *Washington Post,* 24 December 2003.

62. For an account of the exercise, see John J. Fialka, "Debate Widens over Most Effective Way to Secure Energy Department's Los Alamos Nuclear Site," *Wall Street Journal,* 15 March 2000.

63. "U.S. Nuclear Weapons Complex: Security at Risk," Project on Government Oversight, October 2001.
64. Mark Hertsgaard, "Nuclear Insecurity," *Vanity Fair*, November 2003.
65. "U.S. Nuclear Weapons Complex."
66. Hertsgaard, "Nuclear Insecurity."
67. "U.S. Nuclear Weapons Complex."
68. Institute for Science and International Security, "Production and Status of Military Stocks of Fissile Material, End of 1999," summary table [http://www.isis-online.org/mapproject/supplements.html].
69. Senator Charles Grassley, "Our Nuclear Weapons Labs: In Harm's Way," House Subcommittee on National Security, Veterans Affairs, and International Relations Committee on Government Reform, 24 June 2003.
70. See Markey press statement: http://www.nci.org/NEW/NT/markey-statement.htm.
71. For these and other examples, see Grassley, "Our Nuclear Weapons Labs."

4: WHEN COULD TERRORISTS LAUNCH THE FIRST NUCLEAR ATTACK?

1. John Mintz, "U.S. Threat Level Rises to Orange; Attack Risk May Be Highest Since 9/11," *Washington Post*, 22 December 2003.
2. Michael O'Hanlon and Ivo Daalder, "Let's Cool Those Terrorism Alerts," *Newsday*, 23 May 2002.
3. John Aristotle Phillips and David Michaelis, *Mushroom: The Story of the A-Bomb Kid* (New York: William Morrow, 1978).
4. Ibid.
5. Joseph Sullivan, "Nations Beat Path to Door of Princeton Senior for His Atom Bomb Design," *New York Times*, 8 February 1977.
6. Peter Feaver, *Guarding the Guardians: Civilian Control of Nuclear Weapons in the United States* (Ithaca, N.Y.: Cornell University Press, 1992); and William J. Broad, "Guarding the Bomb: A Perfect Record, But Can It Last?," *New York Times*, 29 January 1991.
7. Steven Schwartz, ed., *Atomic Audit: The Costs and Consequences of U.S. Nuclear Weapons since 1940* (Washington, D.C.: Brookings Institution Press, 1998), p. 515.
8. Richard Norris and William Arkin, "U.S. Nuclear Weapons Safety and Control Features," *Bulletin of the Atomic Scientists*, October 1991; Broad, "Guarding the Bomb."
9. Donald Cotter, "Peacetime Operations: Safety and Security," in Ashton Carter, John Steinbruner, and Charles Zraket, eds., *Managing Nuclear Operations* (Washington, D.C.: Brookings Institution Press, 1987), p. 50.
10. Feaver, *Guarding the Guardians*, p. 184.

11. Peter Stein and Peter Feaver, "Assuring Control of Nuclear Weapons: The Evolution of Permissive Action Links," Occasional Paper 2 (CSIA and University Press of America, 1987); Broad, "Guarding the Bomb."

12. Bruce Blair, *The Logic of Accidental Nuclear War* (Washington, D.C.: Brookings Institution Press, 1993); Sara Fritz and John Broder, "Nuclear Russian Roulette," *Los Angeles Times*, 31 August 1991.

13. Bill Gertz, "Russian Renegades Pose Nuke Danger; CIA Says Arsenal Lacks Tight Controls," *Washington Times*, 22 October 1996.

14. Ibid.

15. Dan Caldwell and Peter D. Zimmerman, "Reducing the Risk of Nuclear War with Permissive Action Links," in *Technology and the Limitation of International Conflict*, Barry M. Blechman, ed. (Washington, D.C.: Johns Hopkins Foreign Policy Institute, 1989).

16. Owen Cote, "The Russian Nuclear Archipelago," in Graham T. Allison et al., eds., *Avoiding Nuclear Anarchy: Containing the Threat of Loose Russian Nuclear Weapons and Fissile Material* (Cambridge, Mass.: MIT Press, 1996), p. 180.

17. James Glanz, "Testing the Aging Stockpile in a Test Ban Era," *New York Times*, 28 November 2000; Los Alamos National Laboratory, "Nuclear Weapons," April 2002, http://www.lanl.gov/worldview/news/pdf/Nuclear_Weapons.pdf.

18. Allison et al., *Avoiding Nuclear Anarchy*, p. 34.

19. John Holdren and Matt Bunn, "Technical Background: A Tutorial on Nuclear Weapons and Nuclear-Explosive Materials—Part Three," NTI, 25 November 2002.

20. Bill Keller, "Nuclear Nightmares," *New York Times Magazine*, 26 May 2002.

21. David Albright, "Securing Pakistan's Nuclear Weapons Complex," Institute for Science and International Security, 25 October 2001; Ashley Tellis, *India's Emerging Nuclear Posture: Between Recessed Deterrent and Ready Arsenal* (Santa Monica, Calif.: RAND, 2001), pp. 433–34.

22. Dan Stober, "No Experience Necessary," *Bulletin of the Atomic Scientists*, March/April 2003.

23. Ibid.

24. Howard Morland, "The H-Bomb Secret," *The Progressive*, November 1979.

25. Stober, "No Experience Neccessary."

26. Joby Warrick and Peter Slevin, "Probe of Libya Finds Nuclear Black Market," *Washington Post*, 24 January 2004.

27. Seymour M. Hersh, "The Deal," *The New Yorker*, 8 March 2004.

28. Stober, "No Experience Necessary."

29. George Hesselberg, "Let's Just See If You Can Make a Bomb," *Beloit College Magazine*, fall 2003.

30. Oliver Burkeman, "How Two Students Build an A-Bomb," *The Guardian,* 24 June 2003.

31. Ibid.

32. Douglas Waller, "Nuclear Ninjas," *Time,* 8 January 1996.

33. Ibid.

34. Joseph Biden, remarks at the Paul C. Warnke Conference on the Past, Present, and Future of Arms Control, Washington, D.C., 28 January 2004.

35. Nuclear Weapons Archive, "Section 8.0, First Nuclear Weapons," nuclearweaponarchive.org/Nwfaq/Nfaq8.html.

36. For a more detailed description of nuclear bomb design, see Owen Cote, Jr., "A Primer on Fissile Materials and Nuclear Weapon Design," in Allison et al., *Avoiding Nuclear Anarchy,* p. 222. Also, five former U.S. weapons designers analyzed the issue of terrorists building a nuclear bomb in Carson Mark, Theodore Taylor, Eugene Eyster, William Maraman, Jacob Wechsle, "Can Terrorists Build Nuclear Weapons?" in Paul Leventhal and Yonah Alexander, *Preventing Nuclear Terrorism* (Lexington, Mass.: Lexington Books, 1987).

37. Other methods to enrich uranium include: electromagnetic isotope separation, gaseous diffusion, aerodynamic processes, atomic vapor laser isotope separation, molecular laser isotope separation, and thermal diffusion. For more information, see the Wisconsin Project on Nuclear Arms Control, "Bomb Facts: How Nuclear Weapons are Made," http://www.wisconsinproject.org/.

38. William J. Broad, "Slender and Elegant, It Fuels the Bomb," *New York Times,* 23 March 2004.

39. David E. Sanger and William J. Broad, "From Rogue Nuclear Programs, Web of Trails Leads to Pakistan," *New York Times,* 4 January 2004.

40. Igor Reichlin, Mark Maremont, Jonathan Kapstein, and Jonathan Levine, "Iraq's Silent Allies in Its Quest for a Bomb," *Business Week,* 14 January 1991, p. 50.

41. Wisconsin Project on Nuclear Arms Control, "Bomb Facts."

42. Ibid.

43. Wisconsin Project on Nuclear Arms Control, "Pakistan: Nuclear Helpers," http://www.wisconsinproject.org/.

44. David E. Sanger, "North Korea Hides New Nuclear Site," *New York Times,* 23 July 2003.

45. David E. Sanger, "In North Korea and Pakistan, Deep Roots of Nuclear Barter," *New York Times,* 24 November 2002.

46. David Albright, "Al Qaeda's Nuclear Program: Through the Window of Seized Documents," *Nautilus Institute for Security and Sustainable Development,* 6 November 2002.

47. Barton Gellman, "Fears Prompt U.S. to Beef Up Nuclear Terror Detection," *Washington Post,* 3 March 2002.

5: HOW COULD TERRORISTS DELIVER A NUCLEAR WEAPON TO
ITS TARGET?

1. *Primetime Thursday,* ABC News, 11 September 2003.
2. "Border Breach? Customs Fails to Detect Depleted Uranium—Again," ABC News, 10 September 2003; http://abcnews.go.com/sections/wnt/ Primetime/sept11_uranium030910.html (as of 01/16/04).
3. "Border Breach?"
4. Robert Walpole, CIA national intelligence officer for strategic and nuclear programs, in testimony before Senate, 11 March 2001.
5. See Stephen E. Flynn, "The Fragile State of Container Security," written testimony before the Senate Governmental Affairs Committee, 20 March 2003.
6. Three hundred or more metric tons of cocaine, 5,000 of marijuana annually, per the International Narcotics Control Strategy Report 2002; http://www.state.gov/documents/organization/18166.pdf.
7. Sarah Murray, "Importers Pay the Price of Heavy Security," *Financial Times,* 13 January 2004.
8. Customs commissioner Robert C. Bonner, speaking at the Center for Strategic and International Studies, 26 August 2002.
9. Murray, "Importers Pay the Price of Heavy Security."
10. Bruce Loveless, Daniel McClellan, Claudia Risner, and John Valentine, "Keeping Terrorists Out of the Box: Examining Policies to Counter Seaborne Container Terrorism," Kennedy School of Government, Harvard University, National Security Program, 19 June 2003.
11. Robert C. Bonner, in testimony before the Department of Homeland Security, Senate Committee on Commerce, Science, and Transportation, 9 September 2003.
12. Flynn, "The Fragile State of Container Security."
13. "Container Security: Current Efforts to Detect Nuclear Materials, New Initiatives, and Challenges," General Accounting Office, testimony before the House Subcommittee on National Security, Veterans Affairs, and International Relations, Committee on Government Reform, 18 November 2002.
14. "Customs Service: Acquisition and Deployment of Radiation Detection Equipment," General Accounting Office, testimony before the House Subcommittee on Oversight and Investigations, Committee on Energy and Commerce, 17 October 2002.
15. Ibid.
16. Leslie Miller, "Gaps Cited in Transportation Security," Associated Press, 10 September 2003.
17. Gary Hart and Warren B. Rudman, "America—Still Unprepared, Still in Danger," Council on Foreign Relations Independent Task Force Report, 2002.

18. Philip Shenon, "U.S. Widens Checks at Foreign Ports," *New York Times,* 12 June 2003.
19. Ibid.
20. See www.fedex.com.
21. Keith Johnson, Anthony Pasztor, and Scott Neuman, "Security Blind Spot: Air Cargo—While Passengers Are Screened, Freight Is Seldom Scrutinized," *Wall Street Journal,* 27 January 2004.
22. "UPS Says Air Cargo Secure; Pilots Call for More Security," Associated Press, 20 August 2002.
23. Dan Reed, "Air Cargo Stowaway Shows Security Lapse," *USA Today,* 10 September 2003.
24. "Fear of Flying," *Economist,* 10 January 2004.
25. Reed, "Air Cargo Stowaway Shows Security Lapse."
26. Bryan Bender, "Flying Freight-Class Reopens Debate," *Boston Globe,* 10 September 2003.
27. Blake Morrison, "Screeners Miss Even Obvious Items," *USA Today,* 1 July 2002.
28. James M. Loy and Robert G. Ross, "Global Trade: America's Achilles Heel," *Defense Horizons,* no. 7, Center for Technology and National Security Policy, National Defense University, February 2002.
29. Jim Bronskill, "Who's Keeping Track of Terrorists?" *Ottawa Citizen,* 29 January 2000.
30. Opening statement of Senator Charles Grassley of Iowa, Committee on Finance Oversight Hearing, "The U.S. Border: Safe or Sieve?" 30 January 2003.
31. White House, "Securing America's Borders Fact Sheet: Border Security," Office of the Press Secretary, 25 January 2002.
32. Kevin Sullivan, "'Billions' Worth of Drugs Entered U.S. by Tunnel," *Washington Post,* 1 March 2002.
33. Anna Cearley, "A Hole in Security?" *USA Today,* 7 May 2003.
34. Hart Seely, "Mohawk Reservation Poses Special Challenges for Border Patrol," Newhouse News Services, 2003.
35. Sarah Schweitzer, "Border Arrest Fuels Canada Ire over U.S. Security," *Boston Globe,* 26 November 2002.
36. "Extra Funding May Go to Maintaining U.S. Borders," Associated Press, 23 October 2001.
37. Kevin Johnson, "Drugs Invade via Indian Land," *USA Today,* 6 August 2003.
38. Jamie Dettmer, "Tighter Security in Store for Seaports," *Insight on the News,* 25 February 2002.
39. Tamar Jacoby, "Borderline," *New Republic,* 26 January 2004.
40. Andrew Schneider, "Elite U.S. Team Works to Keep Nuclear Bombs from Terrorists," *St. Louis Post-Dispatch,* 21 October 2001.

41. Jeffrey Richelson, "Defusing Nuclear Terror," *Bulletin of the Atomic Scientists,* March/April 2002.
42. "Combating Nuclear Terrorism," *New York Times Magazine,* 14 December 1980.
43. Schneider, "Elite U.S. Team Works to Keep Nuclear Bombs from Terrorists."
44. Richelson, "Defusing Nuclear Terror."
45. Christopher Lee, "Problems Hamper Officials' Search for 'Dirty Bombs,'" *Washington Post,* 14 March 2004.
46. "Top Worry New Year's Eve Was a Dirty Bomb," *Daily News* (New York), 8 January 2004.
47. David Kay, "Homeland Security and Nuclear Defense," panel presentation to the Lexington Institute, 27 February 2003.
48. Douglas Waller, "Nuclear Ninjas," *Time,* 8 January 1996.
49. Barton Gellman, "In U.S., Terrorism's Peril Undiminished," *Washington Post,* 24 December 2002.
50. Christopher Buettner and Martin Surks, "Police Detainment of a Patient Following Treatment with Radioactive Iodine," *Journal of the American Medical Association,* 4 December 2002.
51. Kay, "Homeland Security and Nuclear Defense."
52. Gellman, "In U.S. Terrorism's Peril Undiminished."
53. Kay, "Homeland Security and Nuclear Defense."

6: THROUGH THE PRISM OF 9/11

1. George W. Bush, address to a joint session of Congress, 20 September 2001.
2. Michael Howard, "Terrorism Has Always Fed Off Its Response," *The Times* (London), 14 September 2001. See also Michael Howard, "What's in a Name? How to Fight Terrorism," *Foreign Affairs,* January/February 2002.
3. "Excerpts from Report on Intelligence Actions and the Sept. 11 Attacks," *New York Times,* 25 July 2003.
4. Bush, address to Congress.
5. Ibid.
6. See http://www.un.int/usa/03_179.htm.
7. Bush, address to Congress.
8. Bob Woodward, *Bush at War* (New York: Simon and Schuster, 2002), pp. 243–44.
9. Bush has used some variation of this basic formulation in a number of speeches, press briefings, and publications. See, in particular, "National Security Strategy of the United States of America" (September 2002) and "National Strategy for Combating Weapons of Mass Destruction" (December 2002).

10. Glenn Kessler and Peter Slevin, "Cheney Is Fulcrum of Foreign Policy; in Interagency Fights, His Views Often Prevail," *Washington Post,* 13 October 2002.

11. Robert Kagan, "Democrats Sound Like Bush on Foreign Policy," *Wall Street Journal Europe,* 18 November 2003.

12. Press conference by President George Bush and Russian president Vladimir Putin, White House, 13 November 2001.

13. Fred Hiatt, "Staying on Offense; Bush's Focus Must Remain on Terrorism," *Washington Post,* 14 January 2002.

14. "U.S. Diplomat's Letter of Resignation," *New York Times,* 27 February 2003.

15. State of the Union address, 29 January 2002.

16. Ibid.

17. Paul Wolfowitz, interview with Sam Tanenhaus, *Vanity Fair,* July 2003.

18. Bryan Bender, "U.S. Shifting Focus, Agents from Kabul to Baghdad," *Boston Globe,* 18 August 2003.

19. Michael Hirsh, Mark Hosenball, and Sami Yousafzai, "Why Can't We Get Him?" *Newsweek,* 22 September 2003.

20. David E. Sanger and Eric Schmitt, "New U.S. Effort Steps Up Hunt for bin Laden," *New York Times,* 29 February 2004. As Senator Bob Graham put it, "Within six months of the first bombs falling on Afghanistan, this administration was diverting military and intelligence resources to its planned war in Iraq, which allowed Al Qaeda to regenerate." See Todd S. Purdum, "An Accuser's Insider Status Puts the White House on the Defensive," *New York Times,* 23 March 2004.

21. Colin Powell, *Meet the Press,* 29 December 2002.

22. European Commission, "Iraq and Peace in the World," November 2003.

23. German Marshall Fund, "Transatlantic Trends," June 2003.

24. Pew Research Center for the People and the Press, "Views of a Changing World 2003," June 2003.

25. Pew Research Center for the People and the Press, "A Year after Iraq War," March 2004.

26. Pew Research Center, "Views of a Changing World 2003."

27. "Clarke's Take on Terror," *60 Minutes,* 21 March 2004.

28. Dick Cheney, speech to Veterans of Foreign Wars, 26 August 2002.

29. George W. Bush, speech on Iraq, Cincinnati, Ohio, 7 October 2002.

30. Dick Cheney, *Meet the Press,* 16 March 2003.

31. Dana Priest and Walter Pincus, "Search in Iraq Finds No Banned Weapons; Tenet Assails Panel Leaders' Criticism of Prewar Data," *Washington Post,* 3 October 2003.

32. Dick Cheney, *Meet the Press,* 14 September 2003.

33. Donald Rumsfeld, testimony before House Armed Services Committee, 18 September 2002.

34. Condoleezza Rice, *Late Edition with Wolf Blitzer*, CNN, 8 September 2002.
35. George W. Bush, remarks in the Rose Garden, White House, 26 September 2002.
36. "C.I.A. Letter to Senate on Baghdad's Intentions," *New York Times*, 9 October 2002.
37. See http://www.fas.org/irp/cia/product/iraq-wmd.html.

7: WHERE WE NEED TO BE: A WORLD OF THREE NO'S

1. Joby Warrick, "U.S., Iran Are Urged to Talk over Nuclear Plans," *Washington Post*, 18 March 2004.
2. John F. Kennedy, news conference, Washington, 21 March 1963.
3. Graham Allison, "Sounding the Alarm," memo to Colin Powell, August 1991.
4. See http://www.nti.org/db/nisprofs/russia/weapons/tacnukes/97nums.htm.
5. Howard Baker and Lloyd Cutler, "A Report Card on the Department of Energy's Nonproliferation Programs with Russia," United States Department of Energy, 10 January 2001.
6. Ibid.
7. See Matthew Bunn, Anthony Wier, and John P. Holdren, *Controlling Nuclear Warheads and Materials: A Report Card and Action Plan* (Washington, D.C.: Nuclear Threat Initiative and the Project on Managing the Atom, Harvard University, 2003).
8. For the best update on current actions being taken to address this problem, as well as obstacles impeding such efforts, see Bunn, Wier, and Holdren, *Controlling Nuclear Warheads and Materials.*
9. Colin Powell, testimony before the Senate Foreign Relations Committee, chaired by Richard Lugar, 12 February 2004.
10. Ibid.
11. Ibid.
12. Author's interview with senior State Department official.
13. Vladimir Putin, address to the Millennium Summit, New York, 6 September 2000.
14. John F. Kennedy Library and Museum, "Radio and Television Report to the American People on the Soviet Arms Buildup in Cuba," White House, 22 October 1962.
15. The gold standard should reach beyond nuclear weapons states to include nonnuclear weapons states, such as Japan or Germany, with significant stockpiles of weapons-usable materials related to their civilian nuclear programs.

16. Mark Landler and David E. Sanger, "Pakistan Chief Says It Appears Scientists Sold Nuclear Data," *New York Times,* 24 January 2004.

17. Victoria Burnett, "Nuclear Concerns Bring a Stream of Visitors to Pakistan's Door," *Financial Times,* 6 March 2004.

18. I thank my colleague Martin Feldstein, professor of economics at Harvard University, for this idea.

19. Joel Brinkley and William J. Broad, "U.S. Lags in Recovering Fuel Suitable for Nuclear Arms," *New York Times,* 7 March 2004.

20. See http://www.ig.doe.gov/pdf/ig-0638.pdf.

21. Paul L. Leventhal and Edwin S. Lyman, "Who Says Iraq Isn't Making a Bomb?" *International Herald Tribune,* 2 November 1995.

22. Richard Lugar, speech to Nuclear Threat Initiative, Moscow, Russia, May 2002.

23. "ElBaradei Wants Tougher Non-proliferation Treaty," Reuters, 8 December 2003.

24. For a complementary view of this issue, see Ashton B. Carter, Arnold Kanter, William J. Perry, and Brent Scowcroft, "Good Nukes, Bad Nukes," *New York Times,* 22 December 2003.

25. For the most comprehensive, up-to-date study of the nuclear power industry, see John Deutch and Ernest Moniz, "The Future of Nuclear Power" (Cambridge: Massachusetts Institute of Technology, 2003). In addition to the nuclear weapons states, Japan has both an enriching and a reprocessing capacity; the Netherlands and Germany are partners with the UK in the uranium enriching consortium Urenco; and Australia has limited enrichment capability. The four largest commercial suppliers of enriched uranium are the Russian Federal Agency for Atomic Energy, USEC (USA), Eurodif (France), and Urenco (UK, Germany, Netherlands), with limited sales from CNNC (China). British Nuclear Fuels (BNFL) and the international consortium Cogema are the biggest reprocessors of plutonium. Belgium also has a substantial commercial plutonium fuel fabrication facility. In 2003, Brazil announced plans to begin enriching uranium for use in its nuclear power reactors, and to have the capacity to export excess stocks by 2014. Brazil, along with Argentina, had a nuclear weapons program that lasted from the mid-1970s until the early 1990s. They both renounced nuclear weapons and signed the NPT in 1997. See the International Atomic Energy Agency Web site for more information (www.iaea.org).

26. Mohamed ElBaradei, "Towards a Safer World," *The Economist,* 16 October 2003.

27. George W. Bush, "Remarks by the President on Weapons of Mass Destruction Proliferation," National Defense University, 11 February 2004.

28. David Rohde, "U.S. Will Celebrate Pakistan as a 'Major Non-NATO Ally,'" *New York Times,* 19 March 2004.

29. As of February 2004.

30. Colum Lynch, "U.S. Urges Curb on Arms Traffic," *Washington Post,* 25 March 2004.

31. Joby Warrick, "Iranian Nuclear Plans Found; U.N. Team's Discovery Raises Doubts about Tehran's Vow of Candor," *Washington Post,* 13 February 2004.

32. Gary Milhollin and Valerie Lincy, "Iran's Nuclear Card," Wisconsin Project on Nuclear Arms Control, February 2004.

33. Ali Akbar Dareini, "Iranians to Resume Enriching Uranium; Minister Discloses Military's Atomic Role," *Washington Post,* 11 March 2004.

34. William J. Broad, "Uranium Traveled to Iran Via Russia, Inspectors Find," *New York Times,* 28 February 2004.

35. Dareini, "Iranians to Resume Enriching Uranium."

36. Guy Dinmore, "Washington Hardliners Wary of Engaging Iran," *Financial Times,* 17 March 2004.

37. "Spurning Iran: U.S. Needs to Overcome Its History with the Islamic Republic," *Financial Times,* 17 March 2004.

38. See George Perkovich, "Dealing with Iran's Nuclear Challenge," *Carnegie Endowment for International Peace,* 28 April 2003.

39. Stephen Farrell and Robert Thomson, "Iran Is a Danger to the Middle East, to Israel, and to Europe," *Times* (London), 5 November 2002.

40. Mofaz during meetings with counterparts in Washington, November 2003, as reported by *Ma'ariv,* 16 November 2003.

41. William Perry, *The News with Brian Williams,* 5 March 2003. See also William J. Perry and Ashton B. Carter, "The Crisis Last Time," *New York Times,* 19 January 2003.

42. David E. Sanger, "Bush Envoy Briefs Panel after Talks on A-Bombs," *New York Times,* 3 March 2004. For CIA estimate of North Korean nuclear capability, see http://www.gwu.edu/~nsarchiv/NSAEBB/NSAEBB87/nk22.pdf.

43. Gary Samore, "North Korea's Weapons Programme: A Net Assessment," International Institute for Strategic Studies, January 2004.

44. "Libya's Welcome Move on Weapons," *The Age,* 23 December 2003.

45. "N. Korea . . . Outlook for 2004," *Nelson Report,* 18 December 2003.

46. Ibid.

47. David E. Sanger, "Administration Divided over North Korea," *New York Times,* 21 April 2003.

48. Glenn Kessler, "Hopes Lowered for U.S.–N. Korea Talks," *Washington Post,* 20 February 2004.

49. "Powell: North Korean Standoff 'Not a Crisis,'" CNN.com, 29 December 2003.

50. Mike Allen and Glenn Kessler, "Questions Linger on Plan for N. Korea," *Washington Post,* 21 October 2003.

51. R. James Woolsey and Thomas G. McInerney, "The Next Korean War," *Wall Street Journal,* 4 August 2003.

52. For an overview of how carrots led to the 1994 Agreed Framework, see Leon V. Sigal, *Disarming Strangers: Nuclear Diplomacy with North Korea* (Princeton, N.J.: Princeton University Press, 1998).

53. Scott Anderson, "The Makeover," *New York Times Magazine,* 19 January 2003.

54. "Beating Swords into Oil Shares," *The Economist,* 3 January 2004.

55. John R. Bolton, "Beyond the Axis of Evil: Additional Threats from Weapons of Mass Destruction," speech at the Heritage Foundation, 6 May 2002.

56. Patrick E. Tyler, "Libyan Stagnation a Big Factor in Qaddafi Surprise," *New York Times,* 7 January 2004.

57. "Sticks and Carrots to Get Disarmament," *Financial Times,* 22 December 2003.

58. Carla Anne Robbins, "Reaching Out: In Giving Up Arms, Libya Hopes to Gain New Economic Life—Gadhafi's Son and Others Expect Payback for Move; U.S. Denies Any 'Promises'—Dropping 'Leader's' Playbook," *Wall Street Journal,* 12 February 2004; Martin Indyk, "The Iraq War Did Not Force Gadaffi's Hand," *Financial Times,* 9 March 2004.

59. Ibid.

60. Ibid.

61. Flynt Leverett, "Why Libya Gave Up on the Bomb," *New York Times,* 23 January 2004.

62. Remarks by the president, White House, 19 December 2003.

63. Glenn Kessler, "U.S. Will Stand Firm on N. Korea," *Washington Post,* 16 February 2004.

8: GETTING FROM HERE TO THERE: A ROAD MAP OF SEVEN YESES

1. Nicholas D. Kristof, "A Nuclear 9/11," *New York Times,* 10 March 2004.

2. Donald Rumsfeld memo, 16 October 2003, published by *USA Today* as "Rumsfeld's War-on-Terror Memo," 22 October 2003.

3. Ibid.

4. Director of Central Intelligence George Tenet, testimony before the House and Senate Intelligence Committees, 17 October 2002.

5. Director of Central Intelligence George Tenet, testimony before the Senate Select Committee on Intelligence, 24 February 2004.

6. Director of the Federal Bureau of Investigation Robert Mueller, testimony before the Senate Select Committee on Intelligence, 24 February 2004.

7. Kamran Khan and Karl Vick, "FBI Joined Pakistan in Staging Raids," *Washington Post,* 30 March 2002.

8. James Drummond, "Kurdish Intelligence May Have Played Role in Finding Fugitive," *Financial Times,* 15 December 2003.

9. "The Second 2000 Gore–Bush Presidential Debate," 11 October 2000, transcript available from the Commission on Presidential Debates, http://www.debates.org/index.html.

10. Martin Gilbert, *Winston S. Churchill,* volume VIII, *Never Despair, 1945–1965* (Boston: Houghton Mifflin Co., 1988), p. 219.

11. David E. Sanger with Dexter Filkins, "U.S. Is Pessimistic Turks Will Accept Aid Deal on Iraq," *New York Times,* 20 February 2003.

12. Fareed Zakaria, "The Arrogant Empire," *Newsweek,* 10 December 2003.

13. "Changing Minds, Winning Peace: A New Strategic Direction for U.S. Public Diplomacy in the Arab and Muslim World," Report of the Advisory Group on Public Diplomacy for the Arab and Muslim World, 1 October 2003.

14. Robert Cooper, *The Breaking of Nations: Order and Chaos in the Twenty-first Century* (New York: Atlantic Monthly Press, 2004).

15. Arthur Schlesinger, "Eyeless in Iraq," *New York Review of Books,* 23 October 2003.

16. Rod Nordland, "Setting a Bad Example," *Newsweek,* 20 March 2004.

17. Desmond Butler, "German Judges Order a Retrial for 9/11 Figure," *New York Times,* 5 March 2004.

18. Thom Shanker, "U.S. Commander Surveys Challenges in Iraq Region," *New York Times,* 30 January 2004.

19. James Madison, *Federalist no. 63: The Senate Continued,* 1 March 1788.

20. Henry Kissinger, "Our Nearsighted World Vision," *Washington Post,* 10 January 2000.

21. John Schofield, in an address to the Corps of Cadets, 11 August 1879.

22. Hui Zhang, "Evaluating China's MPC&A System," conference paper presented at the Institute of Nuclear Materials Management 44th Annual Meeting, Phoenix, Arizona, 2003. Can be found at: http://bcsia.ksg.harvard.edu/BCSIA_content/documents/MPC&A.pdf.

23. Dianne Feinstein, "Policy May Lead to Danger, Not Safety," *Miami Herald,* 14 January 2004.

24. David Kay, speech at Kennedy School of Government, Harvard University, 22 March 2004.

25. Ibid.

26. National Commission on Terrorist Attacks Upon the United States, Staff Statement No. 7: "Intelligence Policy," March 2004. See http://www.9-11commission.gov/hearings/hearing8/staff_statement_7.pdf.

27. "Excerpts from Report on Intelligence Actions and the Sept. 11 Attacks," *New York Times,* 25 July 2003.

28. National Commission on Terrorist Attacks Upon the United States, "Intelligence Policy," pp. 8–9.

29. Craig R. Whitney, "In a War on Terror, Not All the Rules of War Apply," *New York Times,* 28 March 2004.

30. David Johnston and Todd S. Purdum, "Missed Chances in a Long Hunt for bin Laden," *New York Times,* 25 March 2004.

31. Director of Central Intelligence George Tenet, testimony before Senate Select Intelligence Committee, 24 February 2004.

32. Maureen Dowd, "Sorry, Right Number," *New York Times,* 29 February 2004.

33. Douglas Frantz, "N. Korea's Nuclear Success Is Doubted," *Los Angeles Times,* 9 December 2003.

34. Steven Weisman and David E. Sanger, "U.S. Urges North Korea to End Nuclear Work," *New York Times,* 20 February 2004.

35. "Time for a Rethink," *The Economist,* 20 April 2002.

36. Director of Central Intelligence George Tenet, "The Worldwide Threat 2004: Challenges in a Changing Global Context," testimony before the Senate Select Committee on Intelligence, 24 February 2004. With active on-site inspections, making a confident judgment about this issue is feasible.

37. Douglas Jehl, "Better at Languages, U.S. Spy Agencies Still Lag," *New York Times,* 4 March 2004.

38. Reuel Marc Gerecht, "The Counterterrorist Myth," *Atlantic Monthly,* July/August 2001.

39. Ibid.

40. Brent Scowcroft, "Build a Coalition," *Washington Post,* 16 October 2001.

41. Greg Miller and Maggie Farley, "Skepticism Greets U.S. Protestations over Iran," *Los Angeles Times,* 21 November 2003.

42. Henry Kelly, testimony before the Senate Foreign Relations Committee, 6 March 2002.

43. "Unsecured Radiation," *ScienCentral News,* 12 September 2003; http://www.sciencentral.com/articles/view.php3?language=english&type=article&article_id=218392057.

44. Michael A. Levi and Henry C. Kelly, "Weapons of Mass Disruption," *Scientific American,* November 2002.

45. Kelly, testimony, 6 March 2002.

46. Scott M. Michelson, USAF, and Darren D. Medlin, USAF, "Radiological Weapons of Terror," Air Command and Staff College, April 1999.

47. Levi and Kelly, "Weapons of Mass Disruption."

48. For more information on dirty bombs, see James Jay Carafano, "Dealing with Dirty Bombs: Plain Facts, Practical Solutions," *Heritage Foundation Backgrounder,* no. 1723, 27 January 2004, http://www.heritage.org/Research/HomelandDefense/bg1723.cfm.

49. Sam Nunn, "Preventing Catastrophic Terrorism," speech at International Institute for Strategic Studies, London, 20 January 2003.

50. Craig S. Smith, "Roots of Pakistan Atomic Scandal Traced to Europe," *New York Times,* 19 February 2004.

51. "Customs Service: Acquisition and Deployment of Radiation Detection Equipment," testimony of Gary L. Jones before the House Subcommittee on Oversight and Investigations, Committee on Energy and Commerce, 17 October 2002.

52. "Nuclear Nonproliferation: U.S. Efforts to Help Other Countries Combat Nuclear Smuggling Need Strengthened Coordination and Planning," GAO report 02-426, May 2002.

53. Ibid.

54. Ibid.

55. Budget figures available at http://www.nti.org/e_research/cnwm/interdicting/index.asp.

56. Peter Dujardin, "U.S. to Set Up New Radiation Detectors along Borders," *Newport News Daily Press,* 28 January 2004; "Radiation Portal Monitor Systems," Customs and Border Protection press release, January 2004.

57. Representative Jim Turner, House Select Committee on Homeland Security, hearing on the FY2005 Department of Homeland Security budget request, 12 February 2004.

CONCLUSION

1. Barton Gellman, "In U.S., Terrorism's Peril Undiminished," *Washington Post,* 24 December 2002.

2. Ibid.

3. George Crile, "Charlie Did It," *Financial Times,* 6 June 2003.

AFTERWORD

1. Carlin Romano, "Terrorism's Scariest Scenario: Nukes," *Philadelphia Inquirer,* 10 October 2004.

2. "Vice President and Mrs. Cheney's Remarks and Q&A in Carroll, Ohio," 19 October 2004, http://www.whitehouse.gov/news/releases/2004/10/20041020-2.html.

3. *The 9/11 Commission Report: Final Report of the National Commission on Terrorist Attacks Upon the United States* (New York: W. W. Norton & Company, 2004).

4. Anonymous, "How *Not* to Catch a Terrorist: A Ten-Step Program, from the Files of the U.S. Intelligence Community," *Atlantic Monthly,* December 2004.

5. John Ashcroft, remarks to House Judiciary Committee, 5 June 2003.

6. William Broad and David E. Sanger, "The Bomb Merchant: Chasing Dr. Khan's Network," *New York Times*, 26 December 2004.

7. Bill Powell, Tim McGirk, et al., "The Man Who Sold the Bomb," *Time*, 14 February 2005.

8. Ibid.

9. Broad and Sanger, "The Bomb Merchant."

10. Vladimir Putin, address to the nation, 4 September 2004, http://www.kremlin.ru.

11. Vladimir Putin, interview with the Greek media, *Rossiskaya Gazeta*, 6 December 2001.

12. See Matthew Bunn et al., http://www.nti.org/e_research/cnwm/threat/anecdote.asp.

13. Sergey Ptchikin, "Needles of Patriots: Attempts Made to Privatize Unique System for Protection Against Terrorists," *Rossiskaya Gazeta*, 21 December 2004, translated by Foreign Broadcast Information Service.

14. Powell et al., "The Man Who Sold the Bomb."

15. David E. Sanger, "Cheney Says Israel Might 'Act First' on Iran," *New York Times*, 21 January 2005.

16. "Bush Administration Keeping Wary Eye on Iran," *USA Today*, 21 January 2005.

17. William Safire, "Two Internal Splits," *New York Times*, 5 January 2005.

18. Seymour M. Hersh, "The Coming Wars," *New Yorker*, 24 January 2005.

19. James Brooke, "North Korea Says It Has Nuclear Weapons and Rejects Talks," *New York Times*, 10 February 2005.

20. Ibid.

21. Mohamed ElBaradei, "Seven Steps to Raise World Security," *Financial Times*, 2 February 2005.

22. Matthew Bunn and Anthony Wier, *Securing the Bomb: An Agenda for Action* (Cambridge, MA: Project on Managing the Atom, Harvard University, 2004).

23. *A More Secure World: Our Shared Responsibility*, report of the Secretary-General's High-level Panel on Threats, Challenges, and Change, United Nations, 2004.

ACKNOWLEDGMENTS

THIS BOOK CRYSTALLIZES thoughts that have been many years in the making. More than three decades ago I began analyzing nuclear danger in my study of the most dangerous moment in human history: the Cuban missile crisis of 1962. *Essence of Decision* explores that "eyeball-to-eyeball" confrontation in which not only rational but also "accidental" or "unauthorized" factors might have led to nuclear weapons exploding on American soil.

Subsequently, both in government and as a member of the community of national security analysts outside governments, I have benefited from the insights of more colleagues than I could ever acknowledge. As special adviser to Secretary of Defense Caspar Weinberger in the Reagan administration, a member of the Defense Policy Board for Secretaries Weinberger, Carlucci, Cheney, Aspin, Perry, and Cohen, and assistant secretary of defense under Secretaries Les Aspin and William Perry in the first term of the Clinton administration, I have been both part of the problem and an occasional contributor to solutions.

At Harvard's John F. Kennedy School of Government in the 1980s, with Al Carnesale and Joseph Nye, I codirected the Avoiding Nuclear War Project supported by the Carnegie Corporation. Dozens of scholars collaborated in research that produced *Hawks, Doves, and Owls: An Agenda for Avoiding Nuclear War* (1985), *Fateful Visions: Avoiding Nuclear Catastrophe* (1988), and *Windows of Opportunity: From Cold War to Peaceful Competition in U.S.–Soviet Relations* (1989).

The fate of the nuclear arsenal left behind by the Soviet Union has been a central research focus at the Belfer Center for Science and International Affairs (BCSIA) since 1991. Over the past decade, several hundred scholars have participated in this ongoing work, products of which include *Soviet Nuclear Fission: Control of the Nuclear Arsenal in a Disintegrating Soviet Union* (1991), *Cooperative De-Nuclearization: From Pledges to Deeds* (1993), *Avoiding Nuclear Anarchy: Containing the Threat of Loose Russian Nuclear Weapons and Fissile Material* (1996), *America's Achilles' Heel: Nuclear, Biological, and Chemical Terrorism and Covert Attack* (1998), and *Controlling Nuclear Warheads and Materials: A Report Card and Action Plan* (2003). Leaders of this effort over the decade at the center have included Matthew Bunn, Ash Carter, Richard Falkenrath, John Holdren, Owen Cote, and Steve Miller.

In the final year of the Clinton administration, I had the good fortune to serve as a member of the task force chaired by Howard Baker and Lloyd Cutler. Other members included Andrew Athy, Brian Atwood, David Boren, Lynn Davis, Butler Derrick, Susan Eisenhower, Lee Hamilton, Robert Hanfling, Gary Hart, Daniel Mayers, Jim McClure, Sam Nunn, Alan Simpson, David Skaggs, and John Tuck. That group's *Report Card on Nonproliferation Programs with Russia* and subsequent follow-up by the Nuclear Threat Initiative's U.S.–Russian Nonproliferation Working Group have been a continuing source of ideas and feedback. An extraordinary venture of Ted Turner and Sam Nunn, NTI has become the major catalyst stimulating policy-relevant research and actionable proposals to address this threat. Charles Curtis, Laura Holgate, and Brooke Andersen have been particularly helpful in the work from which this book emerged.

With so many debts recognized, and others who prefer to be anonymous, singling out individuals who have contributed to the current formulation of the argument here inevitably means leaving out many more to whom I am also indebted. Nonetheless, for specific ideas reflected in this book I want to express thanks to Elisabeth Allison, Robert Blackwill, Matthew Bunn, Richard Darman, John Deutch, Pete Domenici, Martin Feldstein, Bob Graham, David Hamburg, John Holdren, Maxine Isaacs, Jim Johnson, Sergei Karaganov, Andrei Kokoshin, Tom Korologos, Charles Krauthammer, Richard Lugar, Steve Miller, Mike Murphy, Sam Nunn, Joe Nye, Richard Perle, Ed Rogers, James Schlesinger, and Ike Williams.

For thoughtful comments on drafts of this manuscript, I express special thanks to Matthew Bunn, John Holdren, Steve Miller, Brenda Shaffer, and Steve Van Evera, as well as Philipp Bleek, Anders Coors, Matt Kohut, Sean Lynn-Jones, Blake Mobley, Eric Rosenbach, Phil Sewell, Jim Walsh, and Richard Weitz.

This product could never have been completed on an accelerated timetable without the extraordinary assistance of a team of research associates and assistants at BCSIA led by Arnold Bogis and Grant Mainland, including Lucy Aitkens, Scott Canty, Sarah Dorland, Danielle Lussier, and Micah Zenko. Steven Brzozowski served not only as chief typist but also as a reality check for nonexpert readers.

Finally, heartfelt thanks to my editor Paul Golob at Times Books, who has served as intellectual gadfly, constructive critic, creative translator from policy wonk to public debate, resilient enthusiast, and straw boss in a process that has been simultaneously exhausting and exhilarating.

INDEX

Graham Allison, founding dean of Harvard's modern John F. Kennedy School of Government, is the director of the Belfer Center for Science and International Affairs and the Douglas Dillon Professor of Government. The author of *Essence of Decision: Explaining the Cuban Missile Crisis,* he served as special advisor to the secretary of defense under President Reagan and as assistant secretary of defense under President Clinton.